Communications in Computer and Information Science 1660

More information about this series at https://link.springer.com/bookseries/7899

Philippe Navaux · Carlos J. Barrios H. ·
Carla Osthoff · Ginés Guerrero (Eds.)

High Performance Computing

9th Latin American Conference, CARLA 2022
Porto Alegre, Brazil, September 26–30, 2022
Revised Selected Papers

 Springer

Editors
Philippe Navaux (ID)
Federal University of Rio Grande do Sul
Porto Alegre, Brazil

Carlos J. Barrios H. (ID)
Universidad Industrial de Santander
Bucaramanga, Colombia

Carla Osthoff (ID)
Laboratório Nacional de Computação
Científica
Petrópolis, Brazil

Ginés Guerrero
Laboratorio Nacional de Computación de
Alto Rendimiento
Santiago, Chile

ISSN 1865-0929   ISSN 1865-0937 (electronic)
Communications in Computer and Information Science
ISBN 978-3-031-23820-8   ISBN 978-3-031-23821-5 (eBook)
https://doi.org/10.1007/978-3-031-23821-5

This Springer imprint is published by the registered company Springer Nature Switzerland AG
The registered company address is: Gewerbestrasse 11, 6330 Cham, Switzerland

Preface

CARLA, the Latin American High Performance Computing Conference, is an international academic meeting aimed at providing a forum to foster the growth and strength of the high performance computing (HPC) community in Latin America and the Caribbean through the exchange and dissemination of new ideas, techniques, and research in HPC and its application areas. Starting in 2014, CARLA has become the flagship conference for HPC in the region. One of its principal goals is to spread, together with the international community, the advances in both HPC and HPC&AI (the convergence between HPC and artificial intelligence), as those two key areas are becoming the predominant engine for innovation and development.

In the previous editions, CARLA offered two main tracks: HPC and HPC&AI. The latter highlights the convergence of HPC with modern machine learning methods and their application to multiple areas. CARLA also has become a fundamental forum to disseminate, discuss, and learn about new international trends in advanced computing.

The 2021 edition addressed topics from advanced computer science applications, which generated a new distinctive track, HPC&APP, for the 2022 edition. It has become clear to the HPC Latin American community that after nine editions, CARLA has matured and consolidated its organization, showing the strength of the academic network behind its organization.

The 9th Latin American High Performance Computing Conference (CARLA 2022) was, for the first time, a hybrid event, which meant an opportunity for more inclusive and flexible participation of the community. The conference was held during September 26–30, 2022, and hosted by the Federal University of Rio Grande do Sul (UFRGS).

In addition to the conference days, there were seven workshops and eight tutorials: five fundamental tutorials and three advanced tutorials, all within the framework and scope of the CARLA conference. The website (http:/carla22.org) provides relevant information on these activities.

CARLA 2022 had 138 registered attendees from 21 countries. Out of the total number of attendees, 112 came from 10 Latin American countries and 26 from 11 other countries (in Europe, Asia, Africa, and Oceania). The board committee gathered more than 40 colleagues in 13 committees and seven workshop committees, representing more than 30 institutions in Latin America. The board committee had over 45 meetings during the organizing year. CARLA 2022 had the sponsorship of four important high-technology companies and six academic institutions or societies.

CARLA 2022 had three keynote speakers: Michela Taufer, Daniel S. Katz, and Alba Cervera-Lierta. In addition, each track had one invited speaker: Luigi Carro for the HPC track, Pablo Mininnni for the HPC&AI track, and Nelson Amaral for the HPC&APP track. The HPC track had six accepted author contributions, the HPC&AI track had five accepted author contributions, and the HPC&APP track had five accepted author contributions. Also, there were eight accepted poster contributions. The poster by Carla Cardoso, Hervé Yviquel, Guilherme Valarini, Gustavo Leite, Marcio Pereira, Alan

Souza, and Guido Araujo, "An OpenMP-only Linear Algebra Library for Distributed Architectures," was selected for the Best Poster Award.

Additionally, there were four industrial talks given by various sponsors. The conference had three panels with 13 international panelists on the themes of was "Latin America HPC", "HPC Actions in Africa and Latin American"; and "HPC collaboration between ASIA and Latin America." Furthermore, the seven workshops featured 10 invited speakers and eight tutorials.

This book contains 16 papers selected from 57 submitted manuscripts. All manuscripts were peer-reviewed by at least three members of the Program Committee in a single blind process. The work by Carlos H. S. Barbosa and Alvaro L. G. A. Coutinho, "Multi-GPU 3-D Reverse Time Migration with Minimum I/O", was selected for the Best Paper Award of the main tracks. It is noteworthy that since 2018, the impact of article citations in the CARLA conference volumes has visibly increased.

November 2022   Philippe Navaux
                                                           Carlos J. Barrios H.
                                                              General Chairs
                                                              Carla Osthoff
                                                             Ginés Guerrero
                                                           Publication Chairs
                                                             Alvaro Coutinho
                                                             Esteban Mocskos

Organization

General Chairs

Navaux, Philippe — Federal University of Rio Grande do Sul, Brazil
Barrios H., Carlos J. — Universidad Industrial de Santander, Colombia

Program Committee Chairs

Coutinho, Alvaro — Federal University of Rio de Janeiro, Brazil
Mocskos, Esteban — Universidad de Buenos Aires, Argentina

Steering Committee

Barrios H., Carlos J. — Universidad Industrial de Santander, Colombia
Castro, Harold — Universidad de los Andes, Colombia
Díaz T., Gilberto J. — Industrial University of Santander, Colombia
Gitler, Isidoro — Center for Research and Advanced Studies of the National Polytechnic Institute, Mexico
Navaux, Philippe — Federal University of Rio Grande do Sul, Brazil
Núñez de V. M., Luis A. — Universidad Industrial de Santander, Colombia
Meneses, Esteban — National High Technology Center, Costa Rica
Mocskos, Esteban — Universidad de Buenos Aires, Argentina
Nesmachnow, Sergio — Universidad de la República, Uruguay
Osthoff, Carla — National Laboratory for Scientific Computing, Brazil
Ossa O., Alvaro — University of Costa Rica, Costa Rica
Valero, Mateo — Barcelona Supercomputing Center, Spain
Wolovick, Nicolás — Universidad Nacional de Córdoba, Argentina

Program Committee

Barrios H., Carlos J. — Universidad Industrial de Santander, Colombia
Bendersky, Ariel — Universidad de Buenos Aires, Argentina
Besseron, Xavier — University of Luxembourg, Luxembourg
Cadenas, Luis — RedCLARA, Chile
Camata, Jose — Federal University of Rio Grande do Sul, Brazil
Carastan-Santos, Danilo — Université Grenoble Alpes, CNRS, Inria, Grenoble INP, LIG, Saint-Martin-d'Hères, France

Cardoso, Douglas	Centro Federal de Educação Tecnológica Celso Suckow da Fonseca, Brazil
Carrillo, Oscar	CITI Lab, University of Lyon, CPE Lyon INSA Lyon, Inria, France
Castro, Márcio	Federal University of Santa Catarina, Brazil
Castro, Harold	Universidad de los Andes, Colombia
Catabriga, Lucia	Federal University of Espírito Santo, Brazil
Chacon A., Claudio H.	Corporación Ecuatoriana para el Desarrollo de la Investigación y la Academia, Ecuador
Cordeiro, Daniel	University of São Paulo, Brazil
Coutinho, Alvaro	Federal University of Rio de Janeiro, Brazil
Díaz, Gilberto	Universidad Industrial de Santander, Colombia
Drummond, Lucia	Federal Fluminense University, Brazil
Francesquini, Emilio	Federal University of ABC, Brazil
Garcia Henao, John Anderson	Nucleus AI, Switzerland
Gitler, Isidoro	Center for Research and Advanced Studies of the National Polytechnic Institute, Mexico
Goldman, Alfredo	University of São Paulo, Brazil
Gomes, Antônio Tadeu	Laboratório Nacional de Computação Científica (LNCC), Brazil
Grave, Malú	Federal University of Rio de Janeiro, Brazil
Griebler, Dalvan	Pontifical Catholic University of Rio Grande do Sul, Brazil
Guerrero, Ginés	Universidad de Chile, Chile
Hernandez, Benjamin	Oak Ridge National Laboratory, USA
Hernandez, Esteban	PSL Software, Colombia
Iturriaga, Santiago	Universidad de la República, Uruguay
Jalife, Salma	Centro México Digital, Mexico
Künas, Cristiano Alex	Federal University of Rio Grande do Sul, Brazil
Lanzarotti, Esteban	Universidad de Buenos Aires, Argentina
Le Mouël, Frédéric	University of Lyon, INSA Lyon, Inria, France
Lozoya Arandia, Jorge	Universidad de Guadalajara, Centro Universitario del Sur, Zapotlan el Grande, Mexico
Lujan, Emmanuel	Massachusetts Institute of Technology, USA
Martinez-Perez, Francisco	Universidad Industrial de Santander, Colombia
Mayo-García, Rafael	Centro de Investigaciones Energéticas, Medioambientales y Tecnológicas, Spain
Melesse Vergara, Verónica	Oak Ridge National Laboratory, USA
Mello Schnorr, Lucas	Federal University of Rio Grande do Sul, Brazil
Meneses, Esteban	Centro Nacional de Alta Tecnología, Costa Rica
Mocskos, Esteban	Universidad de Buenos Aires, Argentina
Monsalve Diaz, Jose M.	Argonne National Laboratory, USA
Montoya, Javier	Universidad de Cartagena, Colombia

Moya, Ulises	Gobierno de Jalisco, México
Nakahara Jr, Jorge	École Polytechnique Fédérale de Lausanne, Switzerland
Navaux, Philippe	Federal University of Rio Grande do Sul, Brazil
Nesmachnow, Sergio	Universidad de la República, Uruguay
Ocaña, Kary	Laboratório Nacional de Computação Científica, Rio de Janeiro, Brazil
Orizaga Trejo, Jose Antonio	Universidad de Guadalajara, Smart Cities Research Center, Mexico
Osthoff, Carla	National Laboratory for Scientific Computing, Brazil
Otero, Alejandro D.	Universidad Nacional de La Plata, Argentina
Padoin, Edson Luiz	UNIJUI, Brazil
Pantoja, Maria	Cal Poly, USA
Pecero Sanchez, Johnatan	University of Luxembourg, Luxembourg
Perez, Gervasio	Universidad de Buenos Aires, Argentina
Raffin, Bruno	Inria, France
Rivas, Robinson	Universidad Central de Venezuela, Venezuela
Rizzi, Silvio	Argonne National Laboratory, USA
Robles, Lizette	Universidad de Guadalajara, México
Rojas, Elvis	Universidad Nacional, Costa Rica
Romo Bucheli, David Edmundo	Universidad Industrial de Santander, Colombia
Sanabria, John	Universidad del Valle, Colombia
Serpa, Matheus	Federal University of Rio Grande do Sul, Brazil
Soba, Alejandro	Universidad de Buenos Aires, Argentina
Steffenel, Luiz Angelo	Université de Reims Champagne-Ardenne, LICIIS Laboratory, France
Stringhini, Denise	Federal University of São Paulo, Brazil
Vasquez, John	Universidad Técnica de Ambato, Ecuador
Wolovick, Nicolás	Universidad Nacional de Córdoba, Argentina
Clua, Esteban	Universidade Federal Fluminense, Brazil

Additional Reviewers

Amaris, Marcos	Federal University of Pará, Brazil
Baldassin, Alexandro	Universidade Estadual Paulista, Brazil
Bruel, Pedro	Hewlett Packard Enterprise, USA
Chacón Velasco, Jorge Luis	Universidad Industrial de Santander, Colombia
Colavecchia, Flavio	Fundación INTECNUS, Argentina
Dematties, Dario	Universidad de Buenos Aires, Argentina
Lima, Willian	Federal University of Sergipe, Brazil
Manacero, Aleardo	University of São Paulo, Brazil

Peretti Pezzi, Guilherme	The Swiss National Supercomputing Centre, Switzerland
Ruiz, John	Tul, Colombia
Santos, Ricardo	Universidade Federal de Mato Grosso do Sul, Brazil
Silva, Romulo	Federal University of Rio de Janeiro, Brazil
Sánchez, Jorge Adrián	Universidad Nacional de Córdoba, Argentina
Clua, Esteban	Universidade Federal Fluminense, Brazil

Contents

A Comparative Evaluation of Parallel Programming Python Tools for Particle-in-Cell on Symmetric Multiprocessors

Oscar Blandino H.[1(✉)] and Esteban Meneses[1,2]

[1] School of Computing, Costa Rican Institute of Technology, Cartago, Costa Rica
oscar.blandino.hernandez@intel.com, emeneses@cenat.ac.cr
[2] Advanced Computing Laboratory, National High Technology Center,
San Jose, Costa Rica

Abstract. The Python programming language has established itself as a popular alternative for implementing scientific computing workflows. Its massive adoption across a wide spectrum of disciplines has created a strong community that develops tools for solving complex problems in science and engineering. In particular, there are several parallel programming libraries for Python codes that target multicore processors. We aim at comparing the performance and scalability of a subset of three popular libraries (Multiprocessing, PyMP, and Torcpy). We use the Particle-in-cell (PIC) method as a benchmark. This method is an attractive option for understanding physical phenomena, specially in plasma physics. A pre-existing PIC code implementation was modified to integrate Multiprocessing, PyMP, and Torcpy. The three tools were tested on a manycore and on a multicore processor by running different problem sizes. The results obtained consistently indicate that PyMP has the best performance, Multiprocessing showed a similar behavior but with longer execution times, and Torcpy did not properly scale when increasing the number of workers. Finally, a just-in-time (JIT) alternative was studied by using Numba, showing execution time reductions of up to 43%.

Keywords: Parallel programming · Python · Particle-in-cell

1 Introduction

Particle-in-cell (PIC) is one of the most important computational methods in physics to study problems in solid, fluid mechanics, but specially in plasma. It solves a set of partial differential equations with a combination of individual particles on a Lagrangian frame and moments computed on Eulerian mesh points. The first PIC simulations were performed in late 1950s using between 100 and 1,000 particles to simulate the motion and interaction between them. Nowadays, this kind of simulations are performed using between 10^5 and 10^{10} particles,

P. Navaux et al. (Eds.): CARLA 2022, CCIS 1660, pp. 1–15, 2022.
https://doi.org/10.1007/978-3-031-23821-5_1

representing a challenge for computer systems. Large PIC simulations require the use of supercomputers and code optimizations to reduce execution time [5].

Traditional programming languages in HPC, such as FORTRAN and C/C++, were used to implement PIC and other well-established numerical methods. However, the community working on computational science adopted Python as a popular option for running simulations. A fundamental reason for that change is the evolution of problem-solving approaches [15]. Python is easier to learn and use than FORTRAN and C/C++. But, it still has great tools for scientific computing (SciPy, NumPy, Matplotlib, PyTorch). The first scientific computing research projects were based on mathematical models simpler than the complex models used by scientists today. The knowledge the scientific community gained over the previous decades led to the development of more complex models to understand bigger or more difficult problems at a higher precision. In fact, it is now common to include machine learning methods within the workflow of scientific applications. The high popularity of Python across scientific disciplines, the broad availability of tools, and a huge user base, has made Python an attractive option for implementing complex mathematical models and simulations.

Chips with multiple cores dominate the processor market these days. The architecture trend is to increase the number of cores per processor. As Moore's Law still holds true, we can only expect this course of action to persist for a few more years. The latest release of the Top500 list [17] shows that nearly 70% of the systems solely rely on symmetric multiprocessors (SMP) for their computing power (no accelerators). It is therefore crucial to address the performance characteristics of parallel programming Python tools for SMP architectures when implementing PIC methods.

This paper sets out to explore three popular parallel programming Python tools for SMP architectures. We use the PIC method as a guiding example. To the best of our knowledge, this is the first study on that topic. Our contribution is twofold. First, we provide a picture of the features these tools provide when implementing a PIC method. Second, we present a comparative analysis of those tools backed up with experimental results on two different SMP architectures.

2   Background

2.1   Particle-in-Cell

Mathematical Base. Particle-in-cell (PIC) is a method used to model physical systems whose behavior varies at macro and micro levels. At the macro level, the electromagnetic fields are calculated using Maxwell's equations. At the micro level, the position, velocity, charge, and current density properties are calculated for a set of particles [5,13]. The main objective of the PIC method is to simulate the motion of plasma particles based on the interaction of position and velocity of the particles, with self induced and external electromagnetic fields. To simulate this dynamic, the PIC model uses a grid, as presented in Fig. 1a. In that grid, the position of each particle is shown. The grid is used to calculate and determine the interaction of the particle with electromagnetic fields, and subsequently the particle's new position and velocity. These particles, depending on the application, could have more assigned properties, such as mass, charge, and material. The particles are the ones responsible of transporting mass and energy through the grid [13].

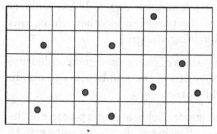

(a) Particle-in-cell Grid.

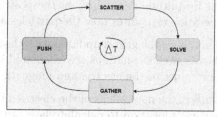

(b) Particle-in-cell Phases.

Fig. 1. Particle-in-cell (PIC) method.

Particle-in-cell simulations normally solve the equations of motion of N particles with the Newton-Lorentz's force [5,9], considering the non-relativistic case, and also solve Maxwell's equations to calculate electromagnetic fields, charge and current density. Considering N particles, with $i = 1, \cdots, N$, the motion equations are presented in Eqs. 1 and 4 of Fig. 2. Variables X_i and V_i correspond to the position and velocity of particle i. Also, e_i and m_i correspond to the electric charge and mass of particle i. Finally, E and B correspond to the electric and magnetic fields. On the other hand, Maxwell's equations are presented in Eqs. 2, 3, 5, and 6. Variable ε corresponds to the permittivity of the medium, H is the magnetic field, J corresponds to the current density, and ρ to the charge density.

$$\frac{dX_i}{dt} = V_i \quad (1) \qquad \frac{\partial B}{\partial t} = -\nabla \times E \quad (2) \qquad \nabla \cdot B = 0 \quad (3)$$

$$\frac{dV_i}{dt} = \frac{e_i}{m_i}(E(X_i) + V_i \times B(X_i)) \quad (4) \qquad \frac{\partial E}{\partial t} = \frac{1}{\varepsilon}(\nabla \times H - J) \quad (5) \qquad \nabla \cdot E = \frac{\rho}{\varepsilon} \quad (6)$$

Fig. 2. Particle-in-cell governing equations.

Computer Simulations. The grid in Fig. 1a is used to locate the particles and to project the effect of electromagnetic fields, charge density, and current density on the particles. Each block of the grid is known as a *cell*. That is where the name *particle-in-cell* comes from. Each cell has four vertex from which it is possible to perform several operations: interpolate the particle's position to project charge and current density into the grid, solve Maxwell's equations to obtain new values of electromagnetic fields, evaluate the changes on electromagnetic fields and its influence onto the particles, push the particles to a new position with velocity changes, and affect the electromagnetic fields. This procedure is executed repeatedly and it is know as the *particle-in-cell loop*, represented in Fig. 1b. The PIC method is based on the aforementioned four operations known as [13]:

Scatter: the particle's position is calculated by using interpolation. The charge and current density is affected from each particle to each vertex. It has a different magnitude depending on the position of the particles; in other words, this operation calculates how the particles are affecting the grid.

Solve: once the grid is updated with the new values of charge and current density, the Maxwell's equations are calculated in every cell of the grid in order to obtain new values of the electric and magnetic fields forces.

Gather: the new values of the electric and magnetic fields are interpolated in the particle's location to calculate how are these affecting it. In an opposite way to Scatter, this phase reflects how the grid is influencing the particles.

Push: the changes on electromagnetic forces and its magnitude modify the speed of the particle pushing it to a new position. The Push phase is in charge of calculating the new speed and position of the particle.

The initialization phase of the Particle-in-cell algorithm consists in declaring a random position for all the particles with an initial speed of zero. Also, all the vertex of the grid should be initialized with a zero value for the electromagnetic fields. The finalization phase consists in reporting to the user the particles and grid information regarding positions, velocities, and values of electromagnetic fields. Using that information, scientists are able to obtain conclusions about the simulation done [13]. Based on the phases previously described, it is possible to create a pseudo code of the Particle-in-cell algorithm as presented by Algorithm 1.

Algorithm 1. Particle-in-cell High Level Algorithm

---

for each particle $p \in N$ do $\qquad\qquad\qquad\qquad\qquad$ ▷ Initialization of particles
$\quad X_p \leftarrow random$
$\quad V_p \leftarrow 0$
for each vertex $v \in Grid$ do $\qquad\qquad\qquad\qquad\qquad$ ▷ Initialization of fields
$\quad E(v) \leftarrow 0$
$\quad B(v) \leftarrow 0$
$\quad J(v) \leftarrow 0$
$\quad \rho(v) \leftarrow 0$
while $t < t_{max}$ do
$\quad \rho(v) \leftarrow \rho(v_{x,y}) + q_p \cdot w(p, v_{x,y})$ $\qquad\qquad$ ▷ Scatter: Particle interaction with the grid
$\quad E(v_{x,y}) \leftarrow E'(v_{x,y})$ $\qquad\qquad\qquad\qquad$ ▷ Solve: Calculate electromagnetic fields
$\quad B(v_{x,y}) \leftarrow B'(v_{x,y})$
$\quad E(p) \leftarrow E(v_{x,y}) \cdot w(p, v_{x,y})$ $\qquad\qquad$ ▷ Gather: Reflect grid's influence to the particle
$\quad X_p \leftarrow X'_p$ $\qquad\qquad\qquad\qquad\qquad\qquad$ ▷ Push: Change particle position
$\quad V_p \leftarrow V'_p$
Print X_p and V_p $\qquad\qquad\qquad\qquad\qquad\qquad$ ▷ Finalization of particle data
Print E, B, J, ρ $\qquad\qquad\qquad\qquad\qquad\qquad$ ▷ Finalization of grid data

---

PythonPIC. A Python implementation of the PIC method was made by Dominik Stańczak [16]. Called PythonPIC, the code models the interaction between a hydrogen plasma target and a laser impulse. The implementation of the Python code used Numba to improve performance, but the parallel programming functions of Numba were not used. In this paper, we use this code to extend it with parallel programming constructs and evaluate their impact on performance.

The code works in the following way. A configuration script describes the simulation that will be executed, along with all its parameters. This script uses a class named `Initial` from a configuration file, which interprets all the parameters and sets up the simulation. The `Initial` class inherits from `Simulation` in the `Classes` directory and uses functions described in the `Algorithms` and `Helpers` directories. The following is a detailed description of how the interaction of a laser with a hydrogen shield plasma is being implemented:

Configuration Scripts: The script `fulllaser.py` imports from `Configs` a file named `run_laser.py`. Several variables and the `initial` function are being imported. The configuration script uses this information to define the input parameters for `initial` function and execute.

Configs: The `run_laser.py` file imports file `BoundaryCondition.py` from Algorithms. From Classes imports `Simulation` and `Species` classes. From Helpers imports different functions and variables. This file describes the class `initial` which is inherited from `Simulation` and it is the one in charge of setting up everything to run the specific case of simulation that wants to be performed by using variables and functions from the files and classes previously mentioned.

Classes: This directory contains the three most important files of PythonPIC: `simulation.py`, `species.py`, and `grid.py`. These three files are used by all the Config files and are the ones in charge of handling and executing the simulation. The `Simulation` class takes all the information from the `Config` file and executes the desired simulation, creating the needed directories, initializing the Particle-in-cell grid, performing all the iterations, doing the post processing, and storing all the information. The `Species` class handles a set of particles and stores the information regarding position, velocity, and other variables. Finally, the `Grid` class handles the information regrading Particle-in-cell grid, like charges, currents, and fields for the particles in the simulation.

Algorithms: This directory contains files for the different algorithms used depending on the simulation case involved. File `BoundaryCondition.py` is being used to represent a boundary condition for the fields in the simulation. These files are in charge of mathematical calculations, and this could be a point to implement parallelization and even code optimization for specific simulation cases.

Helpers: This directory includes two files with different functions. File `helpers.py` has functions mainly for simulation progress configurations, while file `physics.py` includes common functions used in the simulation regarding mathematical calculations for the simulation.

2.2 Python Parallel Programming

Along with C and FORTRAN, Python is one of the most important programming languages in high performance computing. It comes at no surprise that the community has developed many Python tools for parallel programming. According to a recent study [11], there are more than 40 different Python parallel programming tools, each one with their particular combination of type of parallelism, execution mode and programming interface. Three of those tools that stand out for their simplicity and convenience at programming parallel code in Python are Multiprocessing [14], PyMP [10], and Torcpy [6].

Multiprocessing. It is a library that supports spawning processes with an API similar to any classic threading module, supporting local and remote concurrency. Originally, the Global Interpreter Lock (GIL) used by Python is in charge of scheduling the execution of threads, such that only one runs at a time. The Multiprocessing library avoids the limitations of GIL and uses sub-processes instead of threads. Therefore, it allows the use of multiple processors [14,18]. There are two basic ways to exploit parallelism using the multiprocessing library: *Pools* and the *Process class*. The usage of Pool is intended for the execution of one function for multiple input values, distributing the input data across different processes. On the other hand, by using the Process Class, the processes are spawned by creating an object and then calling a start and join methods. These two methods, specially the Process class, are the base to start making parallel code using the multiprocessing library. Below, you will find a code sample for a parallel sum of two arrays.

```
1    from multiprocessing import Pool, Array
2    def sum(i):
3         c[i] = a[i] + b[i]
4    if __name__ == '__main__':
5         global a, b, c
6         N = 5
7         a = [1,2,3,4,5]
8         b = [2,4,6,8,10]
9         c = Array('f', range(N))
10        with Pool(4) as p:
11             p.map(sum, range(N))
12        print(c)
```

PyMP. Build on top of Multiprocessing library, PyMP is a Python library that offers parallel programming functionalities in the style of OpenMP. It takes the small code changes and high efficiency of directive-based programming and combines it with Python usage easiness [10]. Since pragmas are not present in Python, PyMP leverages some language constructs to provide parallel programming features. The **with** statement provides parallel contexts for several threads. The **range** instruction divides loop iterations among active threads. Other configuration options (number of threads, loop scheduling policies, thread-specific identifiers, variable scope) are passed as parameters to functions. Only a portion of the OpenMP standard can be mapped to PyMP language constructs. However, the available functionalities are powerful to represent a modest range of parallel algorithms. Below is the PyMP version of the parallel sum of two arrays.

```
1  import pymp
2  if __name__ == '__main__':
3      N = 5
4      a = [1,2,3,4,5]
5      b = [2,4,6,8,10]
6      c = pymp.shared.array(N, dtype='float64')
7      with pymp.Parallel(4) as p:
8          for i in p.range(N):
9              c[i] = a[i] + b[i]
10     print(c)
```

Torcpy. It is an open source library supported by IBM that provides a parallel computing framework with a unified approach for expressing and executing task and data parallelism on both shared and distributed memory architectures [6]. Although it uses MPI internally in a transparent way to the user, Torcpy also allows the use of explicit MPI code at the application level. It provides support for parallel nested loops, map functions, and task stealing at several levels of parallelism. The **submit** and **wait** functions provide the necessary task parallelism operations, while **map** function implements data parallelism. Below is the Torcpy version of the parallel sum of two arrays.

```
1  import torcpy as torc
2  def sum(i, a, b):
3      return a + b
4  def main():
5      N = 5
6      a = [1,2,3,4,5]
7      b = [2,4,6,8,10]
8      iterations = range(N)
9      c = torc.map(sum, iterations, a, b)
10     print(c)
11 if __name__ == '__main__':
12     torc.start(main)
```

2.3   Related Work

Python implementations of the Particle-in-cell method are easy to find in the available literature. Blandón et al [2] presents a one-dimensional PIC implementation using Anaconda packages. They use their sequential code to study plasma phenomena, such as oscillations, waves, instabilities and damping. Fink et al [3] used a PIC code to compare two parallel programming tools in Python (Charm4Py and mpi4Py). They started with an already parallel MPI version of the code and ported it to parallel objects [4]. Their results highlight the scalability of both approaches on distributed-memory systems, with parallel objects providing an advantage in load imbalanced scenarios. Kadochnikov [7] accelerated a PIC implementation in Python on GPUs, using CUDA through CuPy library. The code in that paper used algebraic multigrid solvers in Python to create a code able to understand some instabilities in electron beam ion sources.

There are previous works comparing tools for parallel programming in Python. Adekanmbi et al [1] implemented a solution to the N-body problem using three different HPC Python tools: Taichi, Numba, and NumPy. The former two provide the shortest execution time, since both are based on a just-in-time compiler. Kim et al. [8] surveyed parallel processing tools in Python and provided experimental results showing the advantages of a couple of tools (Pandaral-lel and Ipyparallel). Using those tools on a multi-core chip, they obtained 5.2x and 2.6x speedups, respectively. Miranda and Stephany [12] used a five-point stencil program to compare HPC Python tools (Cython and Numba) against a reference implementation in FORTRAN. Experimental results show the FORTRAN and F2Py versions are marginally faster than their Python counterparts. Therefore, Python provides a competitive alternative to traditional programming languages for HPC.

3   Implementation

3.1   Profiling

Prior to start any code modification, it is necessary to understand how the code is behaving from the time consumption perspective. The code profiling indicates which are the most time consuming functions in the execution. By understanding these functions, it is possible to prioritize them for parallelism purposes, a reduction of the execution time of these functions is more significant for the global execution time.

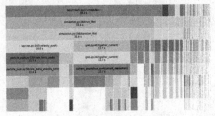
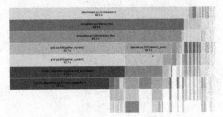

(a) Original Code Profiling.   (b) For Loops Profiling.

Fig. 3. Profiling of PythonPIC code.

Two profiles were created as presented in Fig. 3. In Fig. 3a the original code was profiled. It was possible to notice two main functions consuming the majority of the execution time `rela_boris_velocity_kick` and `current_deposition`, these are part of the Particle-in-cell method. The first function was subdivided into several functions, while `current_deposition` was not subdivided, meaning this is the most time consuming function. There, multiple vectorized operations were observed. These were converted to for loops and a second profile was done presented in Fig. 3b. The `current_deposition` function now takes longer to execute, but the conversion from vectorized functions to for loops is necessary to implement code parallelism. The converted function is a multiplication of arrays, each array has the size of the amount of particles in the simulation.

3.2   Code Transformation

The code is freely available through the following Git repository:
https://github.com/oblandino/PythonPIC/

Multiprocessing. The implementation's structure was developed as presented in the Background section, for a multiplication of arrays. Multiprocessing is part of Python standard libraries, no extra packages were required to be installed in order to use it. The map function only admits two arguments, the function and the iterable, so the arrays were required to be declared as global variables in order to be used by the external function performing the array multiplication. The array that stores the information had to be declared as a multiprocessing Array, in order to be shared by the workers and store information in parallel. The map function allows a third argument, the chunksize, its function is to split the iterable into chunks specified by the number of chunksize, the default value is 1. This is used to improve efficiency, as well as the imap function, which was used in the code due to the large number of iterations.

PyMP. Based on the for loops code, PyMP was very easy to implement because the required changes are minimal, as presented in the background. In PyMP, it was also required to declare the array as a PyMP shared array in order to be shared by the workers. PyMP does require external package installation, but overall this was the easiest implementation.

Torcpy. This implementation was done using a map function similar to Multiprocessing. The main difference is that Torcpy does not handle global variables, instead it allows all the required arguments in the map function. For this reason, the arrays were not declared as global, instead these were given as arguments to the map function, and the external function performing the array multiplication had them as inputs. Torcpy requires a one time initialization by using a start(f) function were f is the function that includes the Torcpy instructions. For PythonPIC, due to the code implementation and amount of iterations, the start() function was required to be integrated in the simulation.py file, initializing the parallel environment sooner than Multiprocessing and PyMP, potentially causing overhead. Torcpy allows the chunksize argument as presented in Multiprocessing.

4   Experimental Results

4.1   Setup

All experiments in this paper were run on *Kabré* supercomputer at the National High Technology Center (CeNAT) of Costa Rica. Kabré is a hybrid compute cluster comprising a total of 52 computing nodes of 4 different architectures. Two of those architectures are relevant for the experiments below. First, the *manycore*

Table 1. Software configuration.

Program	Version
Operating system	CentOS
OS distribution	7.9.2009
OS kernel	3.10.0-1160.62.1.el7.x86_64
Python	3.9.7
Multiprocesing library	Python 3.9.7
PyMP library	0.5.0
Torcpy library	0.1.1
Numba library	0.55.1
cProfile	1.0.7
SnakeViz	2.1.1

Table 2. PythonPIC parameters.

Item	Value
Number of particles	100000, 200000, 400000
Number of iterations	584
Number of trials	10

nodes have each an Intel Xeon Phi KNL 7230 processor, running at 1.30GHz. Each node has 96 GB of main memory. Second, the *multicore* nodes contain an Intel Xeon Gold 6354 processor, running at 3.00GHz. Each node has 512 GB of main memory. Kabré is interconnected with an Ethernet 10Gb network and runs Linux CentOS operating system. Table 1 summarizes the configuration of the software stack used for the experiments. The execution time parameters for PythonPIC are presented in Table 2. Only average results with a coefficient of variation lower than 3% are plotted in the experiments below.

4.2   Experiments

Manycore Processor. After the code was transformed, there was still a missing piece for Multiprocessing and Torcpy, the chunksize. In the documentation of both tools, there is no specification on how to define this parameter. The developers suggest to use a *large* value, but also mention that a *very large* value can actually cause overhead and memory inefficiencies. Figure 4 shows the results obtained in a 100,000 particle simulation. Figure 4a shows that the changes in chunksize did not affect the overall behavior of Multiprocessing. For Torcpy, Fig. 4b shows a difference of around 20x between using the default value against other selected chunksize values. Figure 4c is named Torcpy Reduced, because the default value was removed to provide a better scale, the best execution time was obtained with a chunksize value of 500. In any of the cases a time reduction was observed, meaning that Torcpy does not scale properly in the manycore processor.

The default chunksize value was used for Multiprocessing, and a chunksize value of 500 for Torcpy. Figure 5 presents the results obtained for a strong-scale experiment. The best results were obtained with PyMP, then Multiprocessing, and lastly Torcpy. In Figs. 5a and 5b, for Multiprocessing and PyMP respectively, the best results were obtained by using 16 workers, a greater value introduced overhead and the results started to slowly increase. The best execution times were presented by PyMP. On the other hand, as it was expected for Torcpy, a time reduction was not observed in Fig. 5c. On the contrary, execution times increased as the number of workers increased.

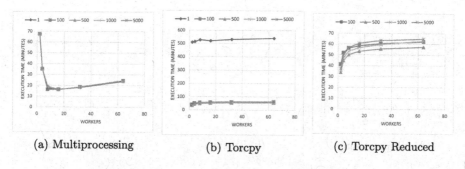

(a) Multiprocessing   (b) Torcpy   (c) Torcpy Reduced

Fig. 4. Manycore processor chunksize comparison.

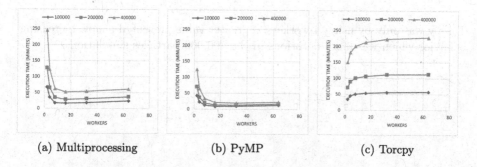

(a) Multiprocessing   (b) PyMP   (c) Torcpy

Fig. 5. Manycore processor strong-scaling results.

Multicore Processor. A similar approach was performed for the multicore processor, the chunksize selection was the first step to follow using the same variables and values presented before. The results presented in Fig. 6 were obtained in a 100000 particles simulation. Figure 6a shows that changes in chunksize value did not affect the overall behavior of Multiprocessing implementation. Figure 6b presents differences around 20x between using the default value of chunksize, against other selected values for Torcpy. To provide a better scale, the default chunksize value was removed as presented in Fig. 6c also named Torcpy Reduced, the best reduction of execution time was obtained with a chunksize value of 500, greater values were causing overhead.

Using the default chunksize value for Multiprocessing, and a chunksize value of 500 for Torcpy, the results presented in Fig. 7 were obtained. Similar execution times were observed, but the best results were presented by PyMP, then Multiprocessing, and lastly Torcpy. Not only the execution times were lower using PyMP, but also the scalability of workers was better. The behavior for Multiprocessing presented in Fig. 7a was similar to the one presented by PyMP in Fig. 7b. The main difference, besides execution time, was that by using 16 workers Multiprocessing showed an increase of execution time, while PyMP presented the expected reduction. Figure 7c shows that the reduction of execution time for

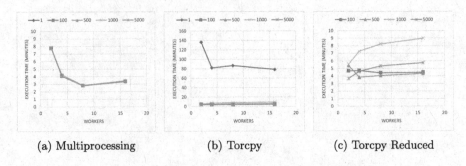

(a) Multiprocessing   (b) Torcpy   (c) Torcpy Reduced

Fig. 6. Multicore processor chunksize comparison.

Torcpy was only by using 4 workers, a greater value presented a slow increasing behavior which was more notorious in the 400,000 particles simulation.

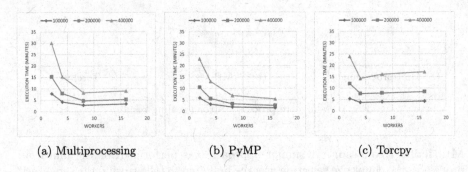

(a) Multiprocessing   (b) PyMP   (c) Torcpy

Fig. 7. Multicore processor strong-scaling results.

Weak-Scaling results are presented in Fig. 8 for the multicore processor, these present the number of particles per worker for the simulation. The expected case is to obtain a line with slope equals to zero, this would mean that as the particles and number of workers increase, the execution time remains the same, indicating perfect scalability. The best results were presented by PyMP in Fig. 8b, the slope does not increase as fast as in Multiprocessing in Fig. 8a or Torcpy in Fig. 8c. The execution times were also shorter. It is important to highlight that the slope was almost zero for Multiprocessing when using 8 workers or less, in contrast to PyMP which had more variation, even when it got better overall results.

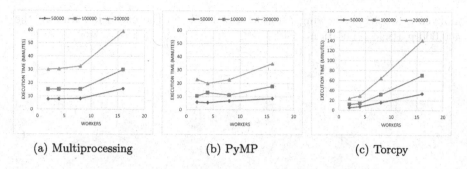

(a) Multiprocessing   (b) PyMP   (c) Torcpy

Fig. 8. Multicore processor weak-scaling results.

5   Discussion

Several parallel programming tools for Python have appeared in the last decade. Presumably, that is a consequence of the original language specification of Python not including native constructs for parallelism. A survey about Python tools for HPC found more than 40 libraries [11]. Those libraries come in all flavors, some mirroring parallel computing paradigms in other languages, some offering supposedly Pythonic alternatives. Also, the set of libraries contain efforts already deprecated, while others are still active. This plethora of options offer an interesting environment for exploring the advantages and downsides of each alternative.

This paper compared three libraries for parallel programming in Python and targeting symmetric multiprocessors. The first option, Multiprocessing, offers generality as it provides features of both task and data parallelism. Performance is competitive and maintenance of the library is active. The second option, PyMP, gives good performance and ease of programming. It truly resembles the basic features of the OpenMP standard in other programming languages. That characteristic facilitates the adoption of this library in a community exposed to traditional shared-memory programming paradigms. The third option, Torcpy, provides a very neat interface for doing both data and task parallelism. Its performance is still lacking, but it has the backup of a legendary company in the world of HPC.

A natural question after examining a group of parallel programming libraries in Python relates to their relative performance compared to a just-in-time (JIT) compiled alternative. To complement the results of this paper, we added an experiment with a PythonPIC implementation that includes Numba instructions. Numba is an open-source JIT compiler that uses LLVM to translate a subset of Python into machine code. Figure 9 shows the result of running and reporting average execution time of 10 repetitions. The plots in 9a and 9b offer the performance results in the multicore and manycore processor, respectively. In both nodes, the execution time is reduced when using Numba, the delta increases as the number of particles also increase. The best performance is observed in the manycore processor showing a reduction of 43% in the execution time of the 400,000 particle simulation.

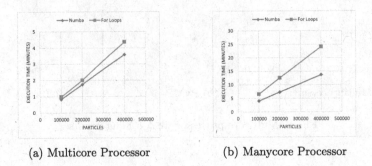

(a) Multicore Processor   (b) Manycore Processor

Fig. 9. Numba experimental results.

6   Final Remarks

The particle-in-cell method has established itself as one of the cornerstones for understanding physical phenomena in a variety of domains, particularly in plasma physics. As scientists extend this method and increase the granularity of the simulation, the computational requirements dramatically grow. Inevitably, high performance computing resources are needed to execute the simulations and push the envelope in scientific research.

Along with FORTRAN and C/C++, Python is a popular programming language for scientific computing and HPC. The broad adoption of Python in scientific communities, makes it an appropriate alternative for scaling applications. There are several Python tools for parallel programming, with some of them focused on symmetric multiprocessor architectures. Hence, it is important to compare those tools according to the programming features they provide and the performance they show.

PyMP obtained better performance results compared to Multiprocessing and Torcpy, its execution time was shorter, its scalability to increasing workers was better, and its implementation was easier. Multiprocessing presented a similar behavior than PyMP, but the execution times were longer. In both architectures analyzed the best results were obtained by using 16 workers. In the multicore processor, Torcpy presented better execution times than Multiprocessing when using 2 and 4 workers, a greater value did not scale properly. In the manycore processor, Torcpy never presented a time reduction. Multiprocessing and Torcpy require a characterization of the chunksize value depending on the problem involved when the map function is used. The behavior of the multicore processor changed depending on the value used. Numba is an excellent option to use depending on how the code is implemented.

Acknowledgments. This research was partially supported by a machine allocation on Kabré supercomputer at the Costa Rica National High Technology Center.

References

1. Adekanmbi, O.G.: Performance comparisons for Python libraries in parallel computing and physical simulation. In: 2022 ASEE Gulf Southwest Annual Conference. ASEE Conferences, Prairie View, Texas, March 2022. https://peer.asee.org/39194
2. Blandón, J.S., Grisales, J.P., Riascos, H.: Electrostatic plasma simulation by particle-in-cell method using ANACONDA package. J. Phys. Conf. Ser. **850**, 012007 (2017)
3. Fink, Z., Liu, S., Choi, J., Diener, M., Kale, L.V.: Performance evaluation of Python parallel programming models: charm4Py and mpi4py (2021). https://doi.org/10.48550/ARXIV.2111.04872, https://arxiv.org/abs/2111.04872
4. Galvez, J.J., Senthil, K., Kale, L.: CharmPy: a Python parallel programming model. In: 2018 IEEE International Conference on Cluster Computing (CLUSTER), pp. 423–433 (2018). https://doi.org/10.1109/CLUSTER.2018.00059
5. Fehske, H., Schneider, R., Weiße, A.: Computational Many-Particle Physics. Springer, Cham (2008)
6. (IBM) Integrated Baseboard Management Controller (iBMC) : torcpy: supporting task-based parallelism in Python (2019). https://github.com/IBM/torcpy
7. Kadochnikov, I.: Accelerating the particle-in-cell method of plasma and particle beam simulation using CUDA tools. In: 27th International Symposium on Nuclear Electronics and Computing (NEC 2019) (2019)
8. Kim, T., Cha, Y., Shin, B., Cha, B.: Survey and performance test of python-based libraries for parallel processing. In: The 9th International Conference on Smart Media and Applications, SMA 2020, pp. 154–157. Association for Computing Machinery, New York (2020). https://doi.org/10.1145/3426020.3426057
9. Lapenta, G.: Kinetic plasma simulation: particle in cell method
10. Lassner, C.: PyMP (2016). https://github.com/classner/pymp
11. Meneses, G.C.S.E.: Parallel programming tools in Python
12. Miranda, E., Stephany, S.: Comparison of high-performance computing approaches in the python environment for a five-point stencil test problem. In: Anais do XV Brazilian e-Science Workshop, pp. 33–40. SBC, Porto Alegre, RS, Brasil (2021). https://doi.org/10.5753/bresci.2021.15786, https://sol.sbc.org.br/index.php/bresci/article/view/15786
13. Pous, X.S.: Particle-in-cell algorithms for plasma simulations on heterogeneous architectures
14. Python: multiprocessing - process-based parallelism. https://docs.python.org/3/library/multiprocessing.html
15. Rao, V.R.: Here's why you should use Python for scientific research (2018). https://developer.ibm.com/blogs/use-python-for-scientific-research/
16. Stańczak, D.: Implementation and performance analysis of particle-in-cell simulation software in Python (2017)
17. Top500: Top500 list. Top500 (2022). https://www.top500.org/
18. Zetcode: Zetcode. https://zetcode.com/python/multiprocessing/

Accelerating GNN Training on CPU+Multi-FPGA Heterogeneous Platform

Yi-Chien Lin$^{(\boxtimes)}$ iD, Bingyi Zhang, and Viktor Prasanna iD

University of Southern California, Los Angeles, USA
{yichienl,bingyizh,prasanna}@usc.edu

Abstract. Training Graph Neural Networks (GNNs) has become time consuming as the graphs grow larger. Thus, many works have been proposed to accelerate GNN training on multi-GPU platforms. Though GPUs feature high computation power, training GNNs on GPU suffers from low resource utilization. We propose to accelerate GNN training on a CPU+Multi-FPGA heterogeneous platform. By utilizing the customizable hardware resources on the FPGAs, we instantiate multiple hardware kernels with optimized data access pattern and memory organization. The optimized hardware kernels can efficiently access graph-structured data and thus achieve high training performance. However, training GNN with multiple FPGAs also leads to high FPGA-to-FPGA communication overhead and workload imbalance. We develop optimized graph partitioning techniques to minimize FPGA-to-FPGA data communication, and develop a task scheduler to balance the workload among the FPGAs. Compared with the state-of-the-art GNN training implementation on a multi-GPU platform, our work achieves up to 24.7× bandwidth efficiency; this superior efficiency enables our work to achieve up to 3.88× speedup and 7.18× energy efficiency using much less compute power and memory bandwidth than GPUs.

Keywords: Graph neural networks · CPU+Multi-FPGA

1 Introduction

Graph Neural Networks (GNNs) have facilitated many applications such as social recommendation system [21], molecular property prediction [9], and traffic prediction [12], etc. Despite the usefulness of GNNs, training a GNN model on a large-scale graph using a single GPU is time-consuming. Thus, there has been an increasing interest in using multi-GPU platforms [7,18] to accelerate GNN training. Although these works accelerate GNN training using multiple GPUs, some challenges remain: (1) inefficiency: GNN training underutilizes the available resources because traditional cache policies fail to capture the data access pattern in GNN training, resulting in high cache miss rate [11,20]. In addition, each data element goes through multi-level caches before being computed, which incurs high latency. Due to the aforementioned reasons, most of the training time

P. Navaux et al. (Eds.): CARLA 2022, CCIS 1660, pp. 16–30, 2022.
https://doi.org/10.1007/978-3-031-23821-5_2

is spent on reading and writing data from/to the GPU global memory, instead of the actual computation; (2) power consumption: though GPU features superior peak performance, it also comes with high power consumption. Power consumption is an essential consideration for cloud service providers like Amazon Web Service (AWS) and Microsoft Azure since it directly relates to the operating cost of the data centers.

Recently, Field Programmable Gate Array (FPGA) has emerged as a popular platform to accelerate GNN inference [16,25] and training [17,22]. This is because FPGAs are highly customizable; this allows developers to customize their hardware kernels, datapath, and memory hierarchy. In contrast, in CPUs and GPUs, the datapath, memory controller and memory hierarchy are all fixed. Utilizing the customized hardware designs, previous works [16,17,22,25] achieve high performance and energy-efficient GNN computations on a single FPGA platform. Cloud platforms like AWS F1 [1], Azure NP-series [2], and Intel DevCloud [3] are all equipped with FPGAs, making FPGAs easily accessible to researchers and developers.

Motivated by the challenges of training GNN on GPU platforms and the emergence of FPGAs, we propose to accelerate GNN training on a CPU+Multi-FPGA heterogeneous platform; such a platform consists of a multi-core CPU processor, connected to multiple FPGAs. We utilize the flexibility of CPU to perform control-intensive tasks such as graph preprocessing, mini-batch sampling and task scheduling. We exploit customizable hardware resources of FPGAs to develop kernels with optimized memory organization and data access pattern to reduce the communication overhead during GNN training. In addition to efficient data access, training GNNs with application-specific architecture on FPGAs allows us to achieve superior energy efficiency. Though a CPU+Multi-FPGA heterogeneous platform provides more hardware resources and memory bandwidth than a single FPGA platform, it is challenging to achieve a scalable speedup due to the complex data dependency of graph-structured data. In particular, during GNN training, the input graph is partitioned and distributed to each FPGA and trained in parallel. However, a straightforward graph partitioning would lead to significant FPGA-to-FPGA communication overhead [7] since each FPGA may need to read significant amount of data from other FPGA local DDR memory. To overcome this issue, we use METIS [13] to partition the input graph; METIS graph partitioning can minimize edge-cut between graph partitions and thus minimize data communication among the FPGAs. However, since each graph partition contains different number of vertices and edges, the workload of each partition is different. Thus, we develop a task scheduler to handle the workload imbalance among the FPGAs. Though we exploit multi-level parallelism and various optimization techniques, none of them alter the GNN training algorithm; thus, we achieve the same training accuracy and convergence rate as in training on a multi-GPU platform. We summarize our contributions as follows:

– We accelerate GNN training on a CPU+Multi-FPGA heterogeneous platform. We demonstrate the acceleration of GNN training using two well-known GNN models on three widely-used datasets.

- We develop hardware kernels with optimized memory organization and data access pattern, which reduce the data access overhead in GNN training.
- We develop several optimizations, including: (1) graph partitioning, and (2) workload balancing to improve the training performance on our target platform.
- Compared with a state-of-the-art GNN training framework on a multi-GPU platform, our implementation on a CPU+multi-FPGA platform achieves up to 24.7× bandwidth efficiency, 3.88× speedup, and 7.18× energy efficiency.

2   Background

2.1   GNN Models

Given an input graph $\mathcal{G}(\mathcal{V}, \mathcal{E}, \boldsymbol{X})$, where $\mathcal{V}$, $\mathcal{E}$, and $\boldsymbol{X}$ is the vertices, edges, and vertex features of the graph, a GNN model is specified by:

- L: number of layers.
- $\mathcal{V}^t$: a set of target vertices to be inferred.
- f^l: hidden dimension in layer l $(1 \leqslant l \leqslant L)$.
- A mechanism of constructing mini-batches, including:
  - The mechanism to construct $\mathcal{V}^l$: the set of vertices in layer l $(0 \leqslant l \leqslant L)$. $|\mathcal{V}^l|$ denotes the number of vertices in layer l. Moreover, $\mathcal{V}^L = \mathcal{V}^t$.
  - The mechanism to construct $\boldsymbol{A}^l \in \mathbb{R}^{|\mathcal{V}^{l-1}| \times |\mathcal{V}^l|}$: adjacency matrix for feature aggregation in layer l $(1 \leqslant l \leqslant L)$. $\boldsymbol{A}^l$ defines the inter-layer connectivity between $\mathcal{V}^{l-1}$ and $\mathcal{V}^l$.
- **Aggregate()** function that is used by each vertex to aggregate information from its neighbors.
- **Update()** function including an one-layer multi-layer perceptron (MLP) and an activation function $\sigma()$ that is used to perform feature update.
- $\boldsymbol{W}^l \in \mathbb{R}^{f^{l-1} \times f^l}$: weight matrix of layer l $(1 \leqslant l \leqslant L)$ that is used in update function to perform linear transformation of vertex features.
- $\boldsymbol{X} \in \mathbb{R}^{|\mathcal{V}| \times f^l}$: input feature matrix.
- $\boldsymbol{h}^l \in \mathbb{R}^{|\mathcal{V}^l| \times f^l}$: the vertex matrix in layer l $(0 \leqslant l \leqslant L)$. Moreover, $\boldsymbol{h}^0 = \boldsymbol{X}$.

GNNs learn to generate low-dimensional vector representation (i.e., node embedding) for a set of target vertices $\mathcal{V}^t$. We illustrate the above process in Fig. 1 with an example of a L-layer GNN model. Starting from layer 1, the GNN model computes the feature vector of each vertex in $\mathcal{V}^1$ by aggregating and updating the feature vectors of its neighbor vertices in $\mathcal{V}^0$; this process is repeated L times until the node embedding of the target vertices $\mathcal{V}^t$ (which is $\mathcal{V}^L$) is derived. The derived node embedding capture the structural information $\boldsymbol{A}$ and vertex features $\boldsymbol{X}$ of the input graph and can be used to facilitate many downstream applications as mentioned in Sect. 1.

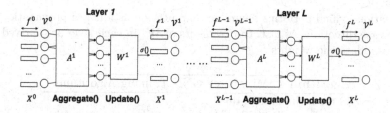

Fig. 1. GNN computation abstraction

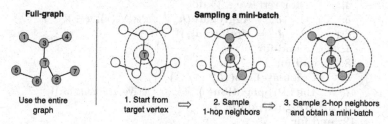

Fig. 2. Full-graph vs. Mini-batch

2.2   Mini-Batch GNN Training

GNNs can be trained in full-graph [15], or in a mini-batch fashion [9,23]. The former approach uses the entire graph to compute the node embeddings of all the vertices; the latter approach first samples a set of vertices and edges and only utilizes the sampled vertices and edges to compute the node embeddings of the target vertices. Mini-batch GNN training demonstrate advantages compared with full-graph training in terms of accuracy, and scalability for large-scale graphs [9,23]; thus, this work focuses on accelerating mini-batch GNN training. We illustrate the difference between the two approaches in Fig. 2, the blue-colored vertices are selected to compute the node embedding of the target vertex (labeled with the letter "T"). Note that there are various mini-batch sampling algorithms [19], Fig. 2 only depicts the Neighbor Sampling algorithm [9] for simplicity. It is also worth noticing that the numbers labeled on the vertices in Fig. 2 are in random order since graph-structured data is non-Euclidean. Since accessing the vertices in random order incurs random memory access, GNN training suffers from high communication overhead. The mini-batch training process consists of five stages [9,23]: sampling, forward propagation, loss calculation, back propagation, and weight update. In the sampling stage, a set of vertices and adjacency matrices are sampled from the input graph topology $\mathcal{G}(\mathcal{V}, \mathcal{E})$. We use $\mathcal{V}^l$ to denote the vertices sampled from $\mathcal{V}$ in layer l. $\boldsymbol{A}^l$ denotes the sampled adjacency matrix, which describes inter-layer connections (edges) between $\mathcal{V}^{l-1}$ and $\mathcal{V}^l$ within the mini-batch. A mini-batch consists of target vertices $\mathcal{V}^t$, sampled vertices for each layer $\{\mathcal{V}^l : 0 \leqslant l \leqslant L-1\}$, and sampled adjacency matrices $\{\boldsymbol{A}^l : 1 \leqslant l \leqslant L-1\}$. In the forward propagation stage, the mini-batch is processed layer by layer as in Fig. 1. The node embeddings in the last layer $\{\boldsymbol{h}_i^L : v_i \in \mathcal{V}^L\}$ are compared with the ground truth for loss calculation. The calculated loss is used for backpropagation, which performs a similar computation as forward propagation but in a reverse direction. At last, the gradients of $\boldsymbol{W}^l$ in each layer are derived and used to update the weights.

Algorithm 1. Mini-batch GNN Training Algorithm

1: **for** each iteration **do**
2:     **Sampling**$(\mathcal{G}(\mathcal{V}, \mathcal{E}))$ ▷ Derive mini-batches
3:     **for** $l = 1...L$ **do**   ▷ Forward Propagation
4:         **for** vertex $v \in \mathcal{V}^l$ **do**
5:             $a_v^l = $ **Aggregate**$(h_u^{l-1} : u \in \mathcal{N}_s(v), u \in \mathcal{V}^{l-1})$
6:             $h_v^l = $ **Update**$(a_i^l, \boldsymbol{W}^l, \sigma())$
7:         **end for**
8:     **end for**
9:     **CalculateLoss**$(\{h_i^L : v_i \in \mathcal{V}^L\})$
10:     **BackPropagation**( )   ▷ Derive gradient of W^l
11:     **WeightUpdate**( )
12: **end for**

We show the steps of GNN training in Algorithm 1, $\mathcal{N}_s(v)$ denotes neighbors of v in $\mathcal{V}^{l-1}$ that are specified in $\boldsymbol{A}^l$.

2.3   Related Work

Hardware Acceleration for GNN Training. GraphACT [22] accelerates GNN training on a CPU-FPGA heterogeneous platform by exploiting both task-level parallelism and data parallelism. It adopts a redundancy reduction technique to reduce the number of memory access; however, the technique can only be applied to graphs with binary edge weight. Thus, GraphACT cannot support certain GNN models such as Graph Convolutional Network (GCN) [15] with non-binary edge weight. HP-GNN [17] proposes a general framework that is able to accelerate various GNN models. Given a sampling algorithm, GNN model, and platform metadata, the framework automatically generates a GNN training implementation that runs on a CPU-FPGA heterogeneous platform. Though HP-GNN is able to accelerate various GNN models on a CPU-FPGA platform, it does not support CPU+Multi-FPGA heterogeneous platform which needs to address the high FPGA-to-FPGA communication overhead and tackle the workload imbalance issue.

GNN Training Using Multiple CPUs or GPUs. DistDGL [26] accelerates GNN training on a cloud platform with multiple CPU instances. It shows that GNN training on multiple instances with synchronous stochastic gradient descent (SGD) quickly converges to almost the same accuracy as training on a single machine. In addition, DistDGL proposes to use graph partitioning to reduce the communication overhead among different nodes and achieve high training performance. PaGraph accelerates GNN training on a multi-GPU platform. PaGraph partitions the input graph using a greedy algorithm that

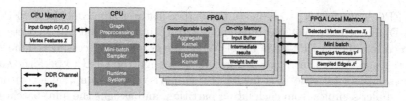

Fig. 3. CPU+Multi-FPGA heterogeneous Platform

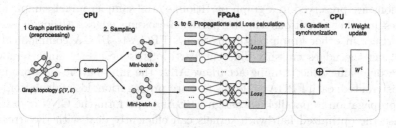

Fig. 4. GNN training on a CPU+Multi-FPGA heterogeneous platform

balances the workload among partitions. In addition, it caches vertex feature of high out-degree vertices since these vertices are expected to be frequently accessed. Utilizing multiple CPUs or GPUs, these works improve GNN training performance compared with a single CPU or GPU. However, as mentioned in Sect. 1, training GNNs using general-purpose processors with fixed data access patterns and complex memory hierarchy suffers from inefficiency; this motivates us to accelerate GNN training on a CPU+Multi-FPGA heterogeneous platform, which is not yet explored by any previous work.

3 GNN Training on CPU+Multi-FPGA Platform

We illustrate a CPU+Multi-FPGA Heterogeneous Platform in Fig. 3. The platform consists of a multi-core CPU connected to the CPU memory via DDR memory channel. The CPU is connected to multiple FPGAs via PCIe. Each FPGA has a local DDR memory.

We depict the workflow of GNN training on a CPU+Multi-FPGA heterogeneous platform in Fig. 4. The training algorithm on a CPU+Multi-FPGA heterogeneous platform is similar to Algorithm 1, but with two additional stages: graph preprocessing and gradient synchronization. We assign the CPU to perform graph preprocessing since the preprocessing is well-supported by existing library[1]. Thus, we store the input graph $\mathcal{G}(\mathcal{V}, \mathcal{E}, \boldsymbol{X})$ in the CPU memory for the CPU to perform graph preprocessing. Note that the preprocessing overhead can be amortized since the graph partitioning is a one-time cost. During the graph processing phase, the input graph $\mathcal{G}(\mathcal{V}, \mathcal{E}, \boldsymbol{X})$ is partitioned and distributed to

---

[1] https://github.com/KarypisLab/METIS.

each FPGA, we use X_i to indicate the vertex features stored in the ith FPGA local DDR memory. We use different colors to indicate that the vertices are assigned to different FPGAs in Fig. 4. When the graph preprocessing is done, the five stages in Algorithm 1 are performed. We assign the CPU to perform mini-batch sampling because it is flexible to support various sampling algorithms. The sampler samples from each graph partition, and assigns the mini-batches to each FPGA. Note that it is possible to sample vertices from different graph partitions as shown in the mini-batches of Fig. 4; because the edges crossing graph partitions are preserved in a graph partition, so the sampler might sample some vertices in other partitions via the partition-crossing edges. Although accessing vertices in other graph partitions incurs FPGA-to-FPGA communication, preserving the edges crossing different partitions is necessary since removing them would affect the training accuracy. After the mini-batches are produced and distributed, each FPGA performs forward propagation, loss calculation, and back propagation in parallel; we assign FPGAs to perform the GNN operations because the optimized hardware kernels can efficiently deal with the irregular data access patterns in GNNs. Thus, we store the mini-batch topology $\mathcal{V}^l$, A^l, and selected vertex features X_i in the FPGA local DDR memory to perform GNN operations. Finally, we assign the CPU to perform gradient synchronization and weight update since it's easier to synchronize using the CPU.

We perform GNN training using synchronous stochastic gradient descent (SGD) [8], which is widely used in related works that accelerate GNN training on a multi-GPU platform. We accelerate the GNN computations but do not alter the training algorithm; thus, the convergence rate and the accuracy are the same as training on a multi-GPU platform using synchronous SGD.

4   Optimizations

4.1   Graph Partitioning and Workload Balancing

Assume there are p FPGAs on the target platform, we partition the input graph into p partitions, and store each partition in one FPGA local DDR memory. During feature aggregation (Algorithm 1), the vertex features of the neighbor vertices are fetched and aggregated. If the vertex required resides in the same graph partition, the vertex feature can be fetched directly from the local DDR memory; otherwise, the vertex feature needs to be fetched from another DDR memory, which incurs high overhead FPGA-to-FPGA communication.

To minimize the FPGA-to-FPGA communication overhead, we utilize METIS [13] algorithm to perform graph partitioning. METIS can minimize cross-partition edge connection and thus reduce FPGA-to-FPGA communication overhead. However, each graph partition consists of a different number of vertices and edges; thus, the workload of training on each graph partition is also different. We develop a task scheduler to balance the workload among FPGAs. Figure 5 illustrates the idea with an example of 4 FPGAs. First, a Mini-batch

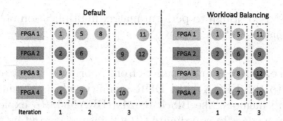

Fig. 5. Workload balancing scheduler

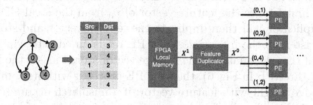

Fig. 6. Data structure

Sampler samples a mini-batch from each graph partition in a round-robin fashion. Each circle in the figure represents a mini-batch, the labeled number indicates the order that each mini-batch is produced, and the color indicates from which graph partition it is sampled. 4 mini-batches is executed in each training iteration, and then a synchronized SGD is performed to update the model weights. In iteration 2, all the mini-batches in partition 3 have been executed. Thus, the sampler continues to sample another mini-batch to produce 4 mini-batches. By default, mini-batch 8 should be computed by FPGA 1 according to the graph partitioning, which causes workload imbalance. Our task scheduler addresses the workload imbalance by assigning the additional mini-batches to idle FPGAs. For example, on the right side of Fig. 5, mini-batch 8 is assigned to FPGA 3. Similarly, in iteration 3, an additional mini-batch is sampled from partition 2 and is then assigned to FPGA 3. Note that this workload balancing technique does not alter the algorithm. As we can see in Fig. 5, the mini-batches being computed in each iteration are the same in both scheduling strategies.

4.2   Optimized GNN Kernels

As mentioned in Sect. 2.2, each GNN layer performs two major steps: feature aggregation and feature update. The aggregation kernel fetches the feature vectors of source vertices, performs an aggregation function which depends on the GNN model, and then writes the result to the destination vertices; the update kernel performs a multi-layer perceptron, which can be implemented using matrix multiplication, to update the feature vectors of the destination vertices. In this subsection, we focus on the optimizations done in the aggregate kernel since it is the bottleneck of GNN training; for the update kernel, we adopt a systolic-array-based design to perform matrix multiplication of feature matrix h^l and weight matrix $\boldsymbol{W}^l$.

Data Structure. GNN training suffers from poor data reuse, resulting in frequent accesses to the FPGA local DDR memory, which is much slower than accessing on-chip memory like Block RAMs (BRAMs). To exploit data reuse, we store the graph edges in coordinate (COO) format, sorted by the source vertices; this allows our kernels to maximize the opportunity for data reuse. We illustrate the idea in Fig. 6 with a toy example. During GNN training, the aggregation kernel first fetches the feature vector of v_0 from the local DDR memory, a Feature Duplicator will then duplicate the feature vector and store it inside each PE's register. In the meantime, each PE reads an edge to compute. If the source value of the edge matches the feature vector stored inside the PE register (e.g., the first three PE in Fig. 6), then the PE proceeds with its computation of multiplying edge weight with feature vector; if a mismatch occurs (e.g., the 4th PE), the PE stalls and waits for the next feature vector (e.g., feature vector of vertex 1) to compute. Using the proposed data structure and hardware design, the feature vector of each source vertex only needs to be fetched once from the DDR memory, which reduces the communication cost from $O(|\boldsymbol{A}^1|)$ to $O(|\mathcal{V}^0|)$.

Memory Organization and Datapath. Sorting the graph edges by source vertices allows us to exploit data reuse, but also incurs random memory write since the destination vertices are in random order. To mitigate the overhead of random memory write, the aggregate kernel buffers the intermediate results on-chip instead of writing them back to the DDR memory; this allows the intermediate results to be stored in one cycle. After the aggregation is done, the aggregated results are directly transferred to the update kernel. Similarly, after the update is done, the updated results are directly transferred to the aggregate kernel for the computation of next layer. After all L layers are executed, the final results are written back to the local DDR memory sequentially. Utilizing the FPGA on-chip memory to buffer the intermediate results, we reduce the overhead of the random memory access; the datapath design allows the kernels to directly read input data in one cycle since the data do not need to travel through a complex memory hierarchy. In addition, the datapath avoids frequent access to the local DDR memory because it does not need to write back the intermediate results.

5   Experiments

5.1   Experimental Setup

Environments. We run our experiments on a dual-socket server. For the multi-GPU platform, we equip the server with 4 GPUs; and for the CPU-Multi-FPGA heterogeneous platform, we equip the server with 4 FPGAs. The GPUs or FPGAs are connected to the host CPU via PCIe. We list the information of

Table 1. Specifications of the platforms

Platforms	CPU AMD EPYC 7763	GPU Nvidia RTX A5000	FPGA Xilinx Alveo U250
Technology	TSMC 7 nm+	Samsung 8 nm	TSMC 16 nm
Frequency	2.45 GHz	2000 MHz MHz	300 MHz
Peak performance	3.6 TFLOPS	27.8 TFLOPS	0.6 TFLOPS
TDP power	280 W	230 W	225 W
On-chip memory	256 MB L3 cache	6 MB L2 Cache	54 MB
Memory bandwidth	205 GB/s	768 GB/s	77 GB/s

Table 2. Statistics of the datasets and GNN-layer dimensions

Dataset	#Vertices	#Edges	f_0	f_1	f_2
Reddit (RD)	232,965	23,213,838	602	128	41
Amazon (AM)	1,569,960	264,339,468	200	128	107
ogbn-products (PR)	2,449,029	61,859,140	100	128	47

the host CPU, GPUs, and FPGAs in Table 1. Note that the peak performance and memory bandwidth of FPGA is significantly lower than GPU; thus, the speedup of our work highly relies on our optimizations. We develop our hardware kernels using Xilinx Vitis HLS v2021.2, and implement the host program using C++14 with the openCL library. We implement the multi-GPU baseline using Python v3.6, PyTorch v1.11, CUDA v11.3, and PyTorch-Geometric v2.0.3.

Measurements. We use the built-in $time^2$ library to measure the GNN training time on the multi-GPU platform. We build a cycle-accurate simulator to measure the GNN training time on the CPU-multi-FPGA heterogeneous platform. To verify the simulator, we implement the host program and GNN kernels, measure the program execution time on the CPU and post-synthesis execution time on the FPGA using the *time* library, and then tune our simulator according to the data we collected from the actual hardware. We use the Vitis Analyzer [14] to obtain the power consumption of the FPGAs. Vitis Analyzer creates a power trace report, and the power consumption can be calculated using the report. We use Nvidia System Management Interface (SMI) [5] and PowerTop tool [6] to monitor the power consumption of GPUs and CPUs, respectively; these two tools only monitor the power usage instead of providing a power trace report. Thus, we create a script to trace the power consumption to manually obtain the power trace report. Since the sample period of Nvidia SMI is between 1/6 to 1 s, we set our script to read the power consumption from SMI every 0.1 s. In all of our experiments, we measure the data by training 10 epochs and taking the average of the measured value. In our experiments, the observed variation for each epoch is approximately the same (relative standard deviation less than

---

[2] https://docs.python.org/3/library/time.html

5%), so measuring the values from 10 epochs is similar as measuring the values from all the epochs that it takes for the model to converge.

GNN Models and Datasets. We run our experiments using two well-known GNN models: GraphSAGE (GSG) [9] and GCN [15]. We use a 2-layer model with a hidden feature size of 128 for all the tasks since this is a widely-used setup [9,24]. We choose three datasets with over 10 million edges for evaluation, namely the Reddit dataset (RD), Amazon dataset (AM) [23], and ogbn-products (PR) [10]. We use the Neighbor Sampler [9] to produce mini-batches; we set the size of target vertices $|\mathcal{V}^t|$ as 1024, the neighbor sampling size of each layer is 25 and 10, and the learning rate is 0.01. Note that under the setup of synchronized SGD, training 4 mini-batches of size 1024 in parallel is equivalent to training a mini-batch of size 4096 on a single GPU or FPGA. Details of the datasets and the GNN-layer dimensions are shown in Table 2.

5.2 Hardware Parameter Selection and Resource Utilization

There are two parameters in our kernel design. We use n and m to denote the parallelism of the aggregate kernel and update kernel, respectively. In particular, n indicates the number of processing elements (PEs) in the aggregate kernel. Figure 6 shows an example of n equals 4. m indicates the number of multiply-and-accumulate (MAC) units in the systolic-array-based kernel design.

Given a GNN model, we aim to find a set of parameters that optimizes the throughput. We first assign an initial value for n and m, evaluate its performance on the three datasets (Sect. 5.1), and observe which kernel is the bottleneck. Then we increase the parallelism of the bottleneck kernel and re-evaluate the performance. We repeatedly increase the parallelism of the bottleneck kernel in each iteration until we saturate the available hardware resources. Both the GCN model and the GraphSAGE model lead to the same set of parameters when the hardware resources are saturated. We show the selected parameters and resource utilization in Table 3.

Table 3. Hardware parameters and resource utilization

Parallelism (n, m)	LUTs	DSPs	URAM	BRAM
(8, 2048)	72%	90%	48%	40%

5.3 Performance Metrics

- Epoch time: the time it takes to train one epoch (seconds).
- Throughput: we define the training throughput as the Number of Vertices Traversed Per Second (NVTPS).
- Bandwidth efficiency: throughput divided by available memory bandwidth of the target platform (NVTPS/(GB/s)). Since the bandwidth varies on different platforms, normalizing the throughput with the available bandwidth provides a clear indication of the effectiveness/efficiency of the accelerator.

Table 4. Comparison with multi-GPU platform

			RD	AM	PR	Geo. Mean
GCN [15]	Epoch time	GPU	1.21	4.04	4.61	–
		This work	0.57	1.05	2.81	–
	Throughput	GPU	25.3 M	27.6 M	106 M	42.0 M (1×)
		This work	53.8 M	107 M	175 M	100 M (2.38×)
	BW efficiency	GPU	7.71 K	8.42 K	32.5 K	12.8 K (1×)
		This work	105 K	208 K	340 K	195 K (15.2×)
	Energy efficiency	GPU	0.47	1.58	1.80	1.10 (1×)
		This work	0.12	0.22	0.59	0.25 (4.40×)
GSG [9]	Epoch time	GPU	1.25	4.16	4.89	–
		This work	0.71	1.78	4.27	–
	Throughput	GPU	24.4 M	26.8 M	100 M	40.4 M (1×)
		This work	42.9 M	62.7 M	115 M	67.6 M (1.67×)
	BW efficiency	GPU	7.46 K	8.17 K	30.6 K	12.3 K (1×)
		This work	83.6 K	122 K	224 K	132 K (10.7×)
	Energy efficiency	GPU	0.49	1.63	1.91	1.15 (1×)
		This work	0.15	0.38	0.90	0.37 (3.10×)

– Energy efficiency: the energy consumption of training one epoch on the target
  platform (kJ/epoch).

5.4   Comparison with Multi-GPU Platform

Performance. We compare the performance of our design on a CPU+Multi-
FPGA heterogeneous platform, with a state-of-the-art GNN training
implementation using PyTorch-Geometric on a multi-GPU platform. Both the
multi-GPU baseline and our work adopts the METIS algorithm for graph pre-
processing. In our work, we overlap the sampling stage and GNN operations in
each training iteration since they are performed on CPU and FPGAs, respectively. We use the performance metrics defined in Sect. 5.3 to compare with
the multi-GPU baseline. We list the results in Table 4. As noted in Sect. 5.1,
we obtain the experimental results by training 10 epochs and then average the
measured values. The measured values from each epoch are very close to each
other: the maximum relative standard deviation in our experiments is 3.3%. We
use *GPU* to indicate the multi-GPU baseline, and use *This work* to indicate
our work which runs on the CPU+Multi-FPGA heterogeneous platform. We
achieve 2.38× and 1.67× speedup on the GCN model and GraphSAGE model,
respectively; this is because (1) our task scheduler balances the workload on each
FPGA which reduces the parallel execution time; and (2) our optimized GNN
kernels effectively reduce the memory access overhead.

Note that GPUs have much higher peak performance and memory bandwidth than FPGAs; thus, to illustrate the effectiveness of our optimizations, we
further compare the bandwidth efficiency on both platforms which normalized

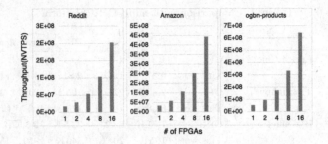

Fig. 7. Throughput scales linearly w.r.t. number of FPGAs on the target platform

the throughput with the available bandwidth on the platform. We achieve up to 24.7× bandwidth efficiency than the multi-GPU baseline; in other words, our design is able to achieve up to 24.7× throughput given the same memory bandwidth. While the workload balancing technique can also be applied to the multi-GPU platform, the GNN kernel optimizations are specific for FPGAs. If we apply the same data structure to the multi-GPU baseline, we are able to exploit some data reuse with the GPU cache since the edges are sorted by the source vertices; however, we can not mitigate the random memory write overhead since we have no control over the datapath and on-chip memory on a GPU platform. On an FPGA platform, we overcome this issue by utilizing the abundant on-chip memory to buffer the intermediate results; we also design a datapath to avoid any unnecessary write to the local DDR memory during GNN training (Sect. 4.2). Thus, even if we speed up the memory read phase on the multi-GPU platform, the memory write bottlenecks the performance.

In addition, unlike our kernels which can access the data in one cycle (3.3 ns), GPUs require multiple cycles to access the data in multi-level caches. Taking Nvidia RTX 3090 as an example, the L2 cache latency is over 130 ns [4]. Note that we use Nvidia RTX A5000 for our experiments, which uses the same GPU architecture (GA102) as Nvidia RTX 3090, so we expect similar cache latency on both GPUs. Finally, our work achieves up to 7.18× energy efficiency than the multi-GPU baseline. This is because our dedicated hardware designs can efficiently perform GNN training, while GPUs launch massive amount of CUDA cores with low utilization.

Convergence. As mentioned in Sect. 3, our work does not alter the original training algorithm; thus, the convergence rate of our work is the same as the serial training algorithm.

5.5   Scalability

We evaluate the scalability of our work using the three datasets on a two-layer GCN model. As shown in Fig. 7, our work achieves a scalable speedup as we increase the number of FPGAs. We do not consider cases with more than 16 FPGAs since it exceeds the number of PCIe channels on our target platform.

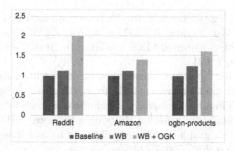

Fig. 8. Throughput improvement due to optimizations

5.6   Impact of Optimizations

We evaluate the two optimizations of workload balancing (WB) and optimized GNN kernels (OGK) described in Sect. 4 on a two-layer GCN model. We first measure the throughput of the baseline implementation with no optimizations, and then incrementally apply the two optimizations. The throughput in Fig. 8 is normalized with the baseline design. Both optimizations increase the GNN training throughput and can deliver up to 2× improvement in total.

6   Conclusion

In this work, we accelerated GNN training using a CPU+Multi-FPGA heterogeneous platform. We developed several techniques to efficiently accelerate GNN training on our target platform. Using much less compute power and memory bandwidth than GPUs, our work achieved up to 2.38× speedup and 4.40× energy efficiency compared with the multi-GPU baseline due to the 24.7× bandwidth efficiency. In the future, we plan to extend our work to a general framework that can automatically map GNN training on any given CPU+Multi-FPGA platform.

Acknowledgement. This work has been supported by the U.S. National Science Foundation under grant number OAC-2209563.

References

1. Amazon ec2 f1. https://aws.amazon.com/tw/ec2/instance-types/f1/. Accessed 23 June 2022
2. Azure np-series. https://docs.microsoft.com/en-us/azure/virtual-machines/np-series. Accessed 23 June 2022
3. Intel devcloud. https://www.intel.com/content/www/us/en/developer/tools/devcloud/overview.html. Accessed 23 June 2022
4. Measuring GPU memory latency. https://chipsandcheese.com/2021/04/16/measuring-gpu-memory-latency/. Accessed 20 June 2022
5. Nvidia system management interface. https://developer.nvidia.com/nvidia-system-management-interface. Accessed 21 June 2022

6. PowerTOP. https://github.com/fenrus75/powertop. Accessed 21 June 2022
7. Cai, Z., Yan, X., Wu, Y., Ma, K., Cheng, J., Yu, F.: DGCL: an efficient communication library for distributed GNN training. In: 16th European Conference on Computer Systems (2021)
8. Chen, J., Monga, R., Bengio, S., Jozefowicz, R.: Revisiting distributed synchronous SGD. In: International Conference on Learning Representations Workshop (2016)
9. Hamilton, W.L., Ying, R., Leskovec, J.: Inductive representation learning on large graphs. In: 31st Neural Information Processing Systems (2017)
10. Hu, W., et al.: Open graph benchmark: datasets for machine learning on graphs. arXiv preprint arXiv:2005.00687 (2020)
11. Huang, K., Zhai, J., Zheng, Z., Yi, Y., Shen, X.: Understanding and bridging the gaps in current GNN performance optimizations. In: 26th ACM SIGPLAN Symposium on Principles and Practice of Parallel Programming, PPoPP 2021 (2021)
12. Jiang, W., Luo, J.: Graph neural network for traffic forecasting: a survey. arXiv preprint arXiv:2101.11174 (2021)
13. Karypis, G., Kumar, V.: A fast and high quality multilevel scheme for partitioning irregular graphs. SIAM J. Sci. Comput. **20**, 359–392 (1998)
14. Kathail, V.: Xilinx vitis unified software platform. In: ACM/SIGDA International Symposium on Field-Programmable Gate Arrays (2020)
15. Kipf, T.N., Welling, M.: Semi-supervised classification with graph convolutional networks. In: International Conference on Learning Representations (2017)
16. Lin, Y.C., Zhang, B., Prasanna, V.: GCN inference acceleration using high-level synthesis. In: IEEE High Performance Extreme Computing Conference (2021)
17. Lin, Y.C., Zhang, B., Prasanna, V.: HP-GNN: generating high throughput GNN training implementation on CPU-FPGA heterogeneous platform. In: ACM/SIGDA International Symposium on Field-Programmable Gate Arrays (2022)
18. Lin, Z., Li, C., Miao, Y., Liu, Y., Xu, Y.: PaGraph: scaling GNN training on large graphs via computation-aware caching. In: ACM Cloud Computing (2020)
19. Liu, X., Yan, M., Deng, L., Li, G., Ye, X., Fan, D.: Sampling methods for efficient training of graph convolutional networks: a survey. IEEE/CAA J. Autom. Sinica **9**, 205–234 (2022)
20. Yan, M., et al.: HYGCN: a GCN accelerator with hybrid architecture. In: International Symposium on High Performance Computer Architecture (HPCA) (2020)
21. Ying, R., He, R., Chen, K., Eksombatchai, P., Hamilton, W.L., Leskovec, J.: Graph convolutional neural networks for web-scale recommender systems. In: 24th ACM SIGKDD Knowledge Discovery & Data Mining (2018)
22. Zeng, H., Prasanna, V.: GraphACT: accelerating GCN training on CPU-FPGA heterogeneous platforms. In: ACM/SIGDA Field-Programmable Gate Arrays (2020)
23. Zeng, H., Zhou, H., Srivastava, A., Kannan, R., Prasanna, V.: GraphSAINT: graph sampling based inductive learning method. In: International Conference on Learning Representations (2020)
24. Zhang, B., Kannan, R., Prasanna, V.: BoostGCN: a framework for optimizing GCN inference on FPGA. In: 29th Annual International Symposium on Field-Programmable Custom Computing Machines (FCCM). IEEE (2021)
25. Zhang, B., Zeng, H., Prasanna, V.: Hardware acceleration of large scale GCN inference. In: 31st International Conference on Application-specific Systems, Architectures and Processors (ASAP). IEEE (2020)
26. Zheng, D., et al.: DistDGL: distributed graph neural network training for billion-scale graphs. CoRR (2020)

Implementing a GPU-Portable Field Line Tracing Application with OpenMP Offload

Diego Jiménez[1]([✉])(iD), Javier Herrera-Mora[1,2](iD), Markus Rampp[3](iD),
Erwin Laure[3](iD), and Esteban Meneses[1,2](iD)

[1] Advanced Computing Laboratory, National High Technology Center,
San José, Costa Rica
{djimenez,jherrera,emeneses}@cenat.ac.cr
[2] School of Computing, Costa Rica Institute of Technology,
Cartago, Costa Rica
[3] Max Planck Computing and Data Facility, Garching, Germany
{markus.rampp,erwin.laure}@mpcdf.mpg.de

Abstract. Accelerated computing is becoming more diverse as new vendors and architectures come into play. Although platform-specific programming models promise ease of development and better control over performance, they still restrict the portability of scientific applications. As the OpenMP offloading specification becomes adopted by more compilers, this programming model stands out as a vendor-neutral portable approach to heterogeneous programming. In this study, we port a plasma physics oriented field line tracing code from a CPU-based MPI+OpenMP approach to a GPU accelerated version, using OpenMP's offloading capabilities. We analyze GPU performance across different vendors with respect to the original CPU version and test both *prescriptive* and *descriptive* approaches to accelerator programming. A maximum 6× acceleration over the CPU implementation was achieved using OpenMP's high-level offloading directives. In addition, we demonstrate portability across three different vendor GPUs with no code modifications.

Keywords: High performance computing · Computational plasma physics · OpenMP GPU offload

1 Introduction

Plasma physicists rely on computer simulations to understand the trade-offs of new designs for nuclear fusion confinement devices, before building them. These simulations require ever-increasingly complex mathematical models to recreate a variety of physical variables of interest. Fortunately, High Performance Computing (HPC) technology is also evolving rapidly, with the integration of massive multi-core processors and the addition of hardware accelerators. The latest edition of the Top500 list [15] shows that 7 systems in the top 10 use Graphical

© The Author(s), under exclusive license to Springer Nature Switzerland AG 2022
P. Navaux et al. (Eds.): CARLA 2022, CCIS 1660, pp. 31–46, 2022.
https://doi.org/10.1007/978-3-031-23821-5_3

Processing Units (GPU) to quicken computation. Not only are GPUs success-ful at speeding up simulations, but also at accelerating data science and artifi-cial intelligence workflows. Hence, exploiting the massive parallelism of GPUs is imperative.

Effectively programming for GPUs is still a demanding task, mainly due to the need of matching the program structure with the hardware features of the accelerator. The Open Multi-processing (OpenMP) standard has established itself as one of the most important programming tools for multi-core processors. OpenMP is based on directives, code annotations that hint the compiler which program pieces can be parallelized. Directives are added as comments to the main code, providing a flexible mechanism to incrementally add parallelism to an already existing sequential code. These high-level language constructs still provide several control variables for the programmer to express where and how the parallelism shall be performed. OpenMP also offers directives allowing pieces of the code to be offloaded on a GPU. Although other directive-based models exist, namely OpenACC, OpenMP is supported across all three GPU platforms that are relevant in HPC: NVIDIA, AMD and Intel. As such, it can be regarded as a vendor-neutral approach to GPU programming.

We embarked on the task of migrating an already existing MPI+OpenMP plasma physics field line tracing code from multi-core nodes to GPU-enabled nodes by using OpenMP directives for accelerators. This paper describes the insights we gained in the process. Section 2 discusses OpenMP's offloading exe-cution and memory details. Section 3 describes our implementations of the Biot-Savart Solver for Computing and Tracing Magnetic Field Lines (BS-SOLCTRA) code using OpenMP on GPUs. Section 4 analyzes the resulting performance of this new approach and discusses scaling, portability and performance-costs putting into context the benefit of GPU acceleration. Finally, Sect. 5 presents the key takeaways from this study.

2 Background

2.1 Directive-Based Programming for Accelerators with OpenMP

Responding to the trend of accelerators in HPC, the OpenMP API incorporated *device constructs* starting from standard 4.0 and updating it subsequently [13]. Through these high-level directives, developers can use OpenMP to create single-source parallel software that is able to execute on either traditional multi-core processors or accelerators, like GPUs. This approach to accelerator programming is conceptually portable and avoids the troublesome maintenance problem of having multiple versions of a code module that arises when working with vendor-specific programming models.

Heterogeneous Execution. Pertaining to the execution workflow in OpenMP offloading, the *host device* is where program execution starts and this is where code sections and data are offloaded to the *target device*, i.e. accelerator. In general, OpenMP makes no distinction about the underlying *target*, so CPUs, GPUs, FPGAs or other specialized processors could be used. The `#pragma omp target` directive is used to define a *target* region. These are usually computationally intensive sections of an application like work-sharing loops or regions of code that can be executed as kernels.

As the *host* runs into the *target* directive, a new thread potentially running on the accelerator is created to handle said region, whilst the *host* thread awaits its completion. GPUs provide massive parallelism capabilities and utilizing just one thread on such a device would not be sufficient. The `teams` construct along with the `target` directive, initializes a league of concurrent thread teams on the device. The initial thread inside each team executes the bounded region without distributing any of the work across the individual master threads of each team.

OpenMP developers can choose one of two possible design decisions: *prescriptive* or *descriptive* parallelism. Under a *prescriptive* approach, the programmer indicates to the compiler and runtime where and how parallelization should occur. Using a *descriptive* approach, the programmer just hints what code segments should be parallelized but not how [14].

Under the *prescriptive* approach, worksharing is achieved through the conjunction of both the `teams` and `distribute` constructs in a single directive. By doing so, the iterations of one or multiple loops are distributed across all active thread teams and executed by the master thread of each team. The traditional `parallel for` construct can then be used to further distribute iterations across the different threads of each thread team.

The *descriptive* model, on the other hand, seeks to provide better performance portability while offering higher productivity. Under this approach, parallelism is hinted through the `#pragma omp target teams loop` directive but the compiler is given the responsibility of figuring out how to map it to the accelerator. This reduces the number of directives and clauses needed to accelerate program execution and frees the programmer from dealing with the specifics of how parallelism is mapped to the different accelerators.

Memory Management. As previously stated, data management is another crucial aspect of the offloading model. Minimizing the amount of data transfers between the *host* and *target* devices is key to achieving good performance on current GPU architectures. In OpenMP, variables needed on the different offloaded code regions should be *mapped* on to the accelerator. The device has its own *data environment* that contains all the variables allocated in its memory. The `map` clause is used along with the `target` directive to specify a list of variables, array sections or structures that should be created or copied to and from the *target* device. This construct applies to the subsequent code block after which the data may be deleted or moved back to the CPU.

However, when a variable is needed across multiple *target* regions, avoiding constant data movement can be achieved by using the `target enter data` and `target exit data` constructs. These directives are not associated with a specific *target* region but rather move data to and from the device when specified. When needed, data can be copied back to the *host* or updated on the device by using the `target update` directive.

Whether or not an application is successful under the offloading model heavily depends on the decisions that the programmer takes in relation to mapping parallelism to the accelerator and how data is moved back and forth from *host* to *device*.

2.2   Simulating Plasma Confinement in Stellarator Devices

The Biot-Savart Solver for Computing and Tracing Magnetic Field Lines (BS-SOLCTRA) is our target application in this study [8]. This is a C++ code developed for the Stellarator of Costa Rica 1 (SCR1). This nuclear fusion reactor was designed and constructed by the Plasma Laboratory for Fusion Energy and Applications of the Costa Rica Institute of Technology in 2016 [4]. BS-SOLCTRA uses the field line tracing technique to provide information about the 3D-vacuum magnetic field, computed through Biot-Savart's Law, that is generated by a specific design of modular coils for the reactor. Currently, this application is used in production as part of an experimental campaign where plasma diagnostics are being designed and implemented to characterize the real conditions of plasma inside the fusion device.

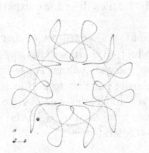
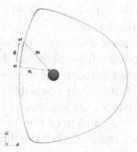

(a) Top view of modular coils present in the SCR-1 and particle trajectory over time

(b) Filamentary segment modeling for Biot-Savart's Law

Fig. 1. BS-SOLCTRA modeling of modular coils and filamentary segment representation

Figure 1a shows a top level view of the simplified modular coils used by BS-SOLCTRA and the trajectory of one input particle. The simulator traces a group of input particles over time, following their trajectory to track down the magnetic field lines that are generated by the set of coils. Output files of the simulation are then post-processed to provide physicists with a map of magnetic flux surfaces, helping them understand how confinement is affected by coil designs and input electric currents.

Particle trajectories in BS-SOLCTRA are computed by using a fourth-order Runge-Kutta method (RK4) where in each iteration, and for each input particle, the magnetic field is computed by applying Biot-Savart's Law to take into account the influence of each filamentary segment that makes up a coil (shown in Fig. 1b) and integrating over all twelve existing coils. As particle dynamics is not the purpose of this simulator, particle interactions are not relevant in BS-SOLCTRA. Particle trajectories are computed until the number of iteration steps is completed or a divergence criterion is met. In particular, device dimensions are used to verify if a particle has gone out of bounds, in which case its time integration is stopped.

The existing version of BS-SOLCTRA is based on a typical MPI+OpenMP parallelization strategy and relies on guided auto-vectorization by the compiler, using OpenMP SIMD directives. This application has been used to generate scientific and communicative visualizations [3] and has been ported to other parallel programming paradigms [9] to tackle some specific imbalance scenarios. Given that there is only very little communication involved and particle trajectory computations are mututally independent, this application is a promising target for acceleration with GPU devices.

2.3 Related Work

An early study by Lopez et al. [11] compared the performance portability of directive-based programming for accelerators. Their paper uses a handful of kernels, and both OpenMP and OpenACC standards, to show how to remain performance-competitive when programming with directives compared to the native version of the kernels. However, they noted the programmer must be aware of the architectural characteristics of the specific accelerator and rely on a decent compiler to be effective. Newer versions of the OpenMP standard, particularly OpenMP 4.5, brought a set of capabilities for simplifying code portability between CPU and GPU. Karlin et al. [10] reported good results in porting three mini-applications to GPUs using OpenMP. They pointed out existing challenges when OpenMP interacts with C++ language, including virtual functions. Gayatri et al. [7] used OpenMP 4.5 to port a material science application to several CPU and GPU architectures. Their results show that OpenMP performance on a V100 matches an OpenACC implementation.

Recent studies highlight the progress high-level performance-portable tools have had in the last 5 years. Marowka [12] surveyed hundreds of case studies of these tools, and defined a new performance-portability metric that takes into account a number of platforms and the relative performance on each platform. Using that metric, the author reported that OpenMP, OpenACC, Kokkos and RAJA all achieve more than 80% portability across CPU and GPU architectures without significantly losing performance between different combinations of architectures and compilers. Ozen and Wolfe [14] argued that the OpenMP pragma loop avoids using different directives depending on the architecture, and thus offers a productive programming method. Such pragma relies on a proper compiler implementation.

Parallelization of a field-line tracing tool with OpenMP pragmas was reported by Bogdanović et al. [2]. They presented the tool L2G, written in C++ with a Python interface. L2G computes field-line tracing and heat loads mapping within the SMITER framework, a software specific for the ITER fusion reactor. Their performance tests show a speedup higher than 2x when running with 16 threads on a CPU, compared to the sequential version.

3   Directive-Based GPU Offloading Implementation

3.1   Breakdown of the Execution Flow

The first step towards a GPU implementation with OpenMP required figuring out at what granularity level should parallelism be exploited in the accelerator. Figure 2 shows a sketch of the execution flow of the simulation. Given a set of input particles, specified by their (x, y, z) coordinates, and initialized according to some prescribed or random distribution, the simulation consists of N iteration steps. In each iteration, all particle positions are updated in lockstep.

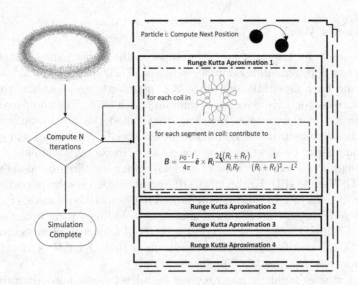

Fig. 2. Basic execution flow of the BS-SOLCTRA simulation

Calculating the new particle position is a compute intensive task. A fourth-order Runge Kutta method is used requiring four calls to the magnetic field computation procedure. In this function, a nested loop structure computes the magnetic field force components over the particle. Device coils are modeled as filamentary segments and thus, the resulting magnetic field on a given position is computed as the contribution of each infinitesimal segment, calculated through Biot-Savart's Law.

Our starting point for the port to GPU offloading was an already parallelized implementation that relies on MPI+OpenMP and SIMD vectorization. MPI is used to distribute the input set of particles among multiple processes and OpenMP handles the time integration of the corresponding subset of particles per MPI process. Usually, a single MPI process is allocated per compute node. The computationally intensive portion of the code, the magnetic field procedure, takes advantage of `omp simd` directives, e.g. to exploit Intel's AVX-512 instruction set on the latest generation of Xeon CPUs.

Given this execution flow and the existing implementation of BS-SOLCTRA, we had to choose the granularity at which we wanted to parallelize the code using GPUs. There are two possible granularity levels where parallelism can be exploited in this simulation: *i)* at the particle level, *ii)* at the magnetic field computation level.

Parallelism at the magnetic field computation level is limited by the amount of coils present in the device (twelve coils) and the amount of points used to model each coil as filamentary segments (360 points). This amount of parallelism is not enough to saturate the GPU and furthermore, when offloading, the particle position would have to be transferred to and from the GPU each time the magnetic field computation is called.

Following a similar approach as in the baseline implementation, we then decided to offload the simulation at the particle level. This is, transferring the set of input particles to the GPU and using OpenMP's teams and threads inside the GPU to simultaneously compute each iteration step for all particles. The following subsections detail the necessary changes to the data structures and how OpenMP directives were used to offload the computations to the GPU.

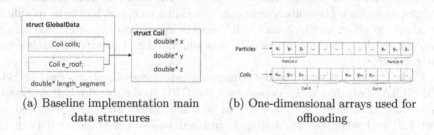

(a) Baseline implementation main
data structures

(b) One-dimensional arrays used for
offloading

Fig. 3. Data structure modifications for offloading

3.2   Data Management for Offloading

The next step was figuring out which data had to be moved to the GPU and at what point during the simulation. Particle coordinates, coil data points and the values for the unit vector along each filamentary segment have to be available in the GPU before the main time looping is reached.

The baseline implementation relies on structures to encapsulate the main data objects. Particles are represented using an array of structures, each one composed of three double values (x, y, z). Coil data points and the unit vector data are encapsulated in a structure of arrays like the one shown in Fig. 3a. In order to facilitate data handling on the GPU, we decided to collapse all these structures into one-dimensional arrays that could be easily transferred to the GPU.

```
1   #pragma omp target enter data map(to:coils[0:size_3D], e_r[0:size_3D],
↪       leng_segment[0:size_2D], particles[0:size_particles])
2
3       //Time looping and particle computation in GPU
4       for(int i=1;i<=steps;i++){
5           for(int p=0; p<particle_count;p++)
6           //computeIteration(...)
7       }
8
9   #pragma omp target exit data map(release:coils[0:size_3D], e_r[0:size_3D],
↪       leng_segment[0:size_2D], particles[0:size_particles])
```

Listing 1: Data offloading with OpenMP in BS-SOLCTRA

Given that the information needed for all these objects are coordinates, we standardized this information by using an array convention of storing contiguous x, y, z values. Figure 3b shows the resulting scheme we used for data transfers. Computations involving the different coils and the values of unit vectors ($\hat{e}$ in Fig. 1b) along each filamentary segment, stored in e_roof, just had to be modified based on the offset at which each coil/e_roof is located on the associated array. In doing so, data transfer to the GPU was simplified and required a single data environment.

Code Listing 1 shows the data mapping associated directives used in BS-SOLCTRA. Data has to be copied into the GPU just once, simulation "snapshots" are transferred to the CPU at a configurable frequency (detailed in Sect. 3.3) and when the simulation is finished no data is transferred back to the CPU.

3.3   Parallelism Implementation

In this subsection we discuss how a *prescriptive* parallelism approach was used to accelerate the simulation on the GPU and then, how we modified the code to allow for a single-source *descriptive* approach for both, GPU-accelerated and CPU-only platforms.

Prescriptive OpenMP Model. The *prescriptive* approach requires that the programmer explicitly specifies how algorithmic parallelism should be mapped

```
1   # Enter Data transfer pragma from Code Listing 1
2   #pragma omp parallel num_threads(2)
3   {
4       #pragma omp single
5       {
6           for (int i = 1; i <= steps; i++){
7               #pragma omp target teams distribute parallel for
8               for(int p=0; p < particle_count ; p++){
9                   int base = p*DIMENSIONS;
10                  if((particles[base] == MINOR_RADIUS) && (particles[base+1] ==
                    ↪   MINOR_RADIUS) && (particles[base+2] == MINOR_RADIUS)){
11                      continue;
12                  }
13                  else{
14                      computeIteration(coils, e_r, leng_segment, &particles[base],
                        ↪   step_size, mode);
15                  }
16              }
17              if(i%100 == 0){
18                  #pragma omp taskwait
19                  #pragma omp target update from(particles[0:size_particles])
20                  {
21                      #pragma omp task shared(particles)
                        ↪   firstprivate(i,output,size_particles)
22                      printIterationFile(particles, i, output,particle_count);
23                  }
24  }}}}
25  #Exit Data transfer pragma from Code Listing 1
```

Listing 2: Prescriptive parallelism with OpenMP in BS-SOLCTRA

to parallelism in the hardware. In our application we decided on parallelizing at the particle level, meaning that the computation of new particle positions could be done concurrently for all particles at each iteration step. As no particle interaction is required, synchronization is not an issue in this simulation.

Particle distribution is done among teams and threads, so that the GPU can be sufficiently utilized, by using the worksharing clauses distribute parallel for. Code Listing 2 shows our *prescriptive* implementation of the time integration loop. Of special interest is line 7, where the computation is actually offloaded to the GPU.

Snapshot files of particle positions are generated, e.g. after every 100 iterations by updating the particle array on the CPU using the target update from directive. The CPU then handles the file writing. In order to achieve an overlap of the I/O with subsequent iterations, we leverage the fact that the target construct generates an explicit task, as specified in the standard and thus, task synchronization features may be used. Initially, two CPU threads are created. When entering the time integration loop, a single pragma is created to avoid computation replication. One of the threads handles the offloading while the other is idle. When a snapshot must be created, the previously idle thread handles the I/O operation as specified in line 22 of Listing 2 while the other single thread continues to service the GPU offloaded computation.

Descriptive OpenMP Model. Under the *prescriptive* approach, we had to explicitly specify to the compiler how to distribute work among execution units on the GPU. Although this approach should work across different GPU models and vendors, it doesn't provide a single-source implementation that could also be executed on a CPU. OpenMP's `loop` construct, by constrast, is a platform-agnostic directive that could be used to create single-source applications. This directive hints at the compiler that a code section should be parallelized but does not specify how to map it to the underlying hardware.

We implemented a *descriptive* version of the application by changing the `#pragma omp target teams distribute parallel for` to a `#pragma omp target teams loop` directive. We added the `bind` clause to hint the compiler on how to distribute work. If no hint was given, the compiler distributed work just among teams and their master threads, affecting performance significantly. Due to current compiler limitations with CPU code generation, our task-based computation-I/O overlap had to be left out for the moment because the multicore CPU code would become nested due to the parallel region enclosing the target block.

All implementations are publicly available in the following repository: https://gitlab.com/CNCA_CeNAT/bs-solctra-gpu.git.

4   Results

This section describes how our *prescriptive* and *descriptive* OpenMP offloading implementations fare against the baseline CPU implementation and how portable they are across multiple vendor GPUs and compilers. All timings reported throughout this section are the result of 10 repetitions. Reported execution times correspond to simulation runs without particle-snapshot I/O.

4.1   Experimental Setup

Experimental Platforms. We have used three different platforms to analyze our implementations. Our main target is the Raven HPC system at the Max Planck Computing and Data Facility where all scalability experiments were performed. The baseline CPU version was also executed on this platform. Single GPU performance was analyzed across these three systems:

- **Max-Planck Society's HPC System "Raven":** the HPC system "Raven" operated by the Max Planck Computing and Data Facility comprises 1592 compute nodes, each with two Intel Xeon IceLake-SP processors (Platinum 8360Y), 72 cores and 256 GB RAM. In addition, Raven has 192 GPU-accelerated nodes, with the same host processors and 4 NVIDIA A100-SXM4 GPUs (40 GB HBM2 and NVLink3), each.
- **AMD MI250 GPU test system:** we had access to an AMD test cluster which provides a single node with two AMD EPYC 7763 processors with a total of 128 cores and 256 GB RAM, and four AMD MI250 GPUs. Note

that the MI250 GPU is composed of two multi-chip modules (MCMs) each of which is exposed by the operating system as an individual (logical) GPU. Hence, our single-GPU benchmarks could utilize only half of the hardware resources provided by an entire MI250 GPU. For a conventional comparison with the A100 GPU our performance numbers for MI250 may be doubled, given the scalability of BS-SOLCTRA over multiple GPUs (see below).

– **Intel Xe GPU test system:** we had access to an Intel test system with some "preview" hardware resembling an upcoming Intel Xe GPU. While we are not allowed to disclose the hardware specifications and obtained performance numbers, our experiments do serve as an early demonstration of the viability of our approach on the new Intel software platform (oneAPI) and upcoming line of GPU hardware.

Compilers and Environment Variables. Table 1 shows information about the compilers, compilation flags and environment variables used. We used Intel-MPI (2021.5) for multi-node runs of both, CPU and GPU implementations. The baseline MPI+OpenMP CPU version was compiled with the "classic" Intel C++ compiler (icpc) on Raven.

Table 1. Compilers, flags and environment variables used on different platforms

Compiler	Flags	Environment Variables
Intel icpc 2021.5.0 20211109 (CPU implementation	-O3 -qopenmp -xICELAKE-SERVER -qopt-zmm-usage=high	OMP_NUM_THREADS=72 OMP_SCHEDULE=dynamic OMP_PLACES=cores
NVIDIA nvc++ 22.5-0 (NVHPCSDK)	-O3 -mp=gpu -gpu=pinned,fastmath -Minfo=mp	OMP_TARGET_- OFFLOAD=MANDATORY
AMD amdclang++ 14.0.0 (rocm 5.1.0)	-Ofast -ffast-math -fopenmp -fopenmp-targets=amdgcn-amd-amdhsa -Xopenmp-target=amdgcn-amd-amdhsa -march=gfx90a	OMP_TARGET_- OFFLOAD=MANDATORY
Intel icpx 2022.0	-O3 -qopenmp -fopenmp-targets=spir64	OMP_TARGET_- OFFLOAD=MANDATORY

4.2 Baseline Comparison: Single CPU Node Versus Single GPU

The main goals of this study were: *i)* understanding whether a GPU implementation based on OpenMP offload could provide better performance than our already CPU-optimized implementation and, *ii)* determining how well OpenMP can deliver on performance portability across different GPUs, with little-to-no code modifications. As there are no particle interactions in BS-SOLCTRA during the simulation, application behavior can be analyzed on the level of single-GPU (or single CPU-node) performance, i.e. all reported GPU speedups are based on a comparison of runtimes obtained on an entire IceLake-based node (72 cores, 1

OpenMP thread per core) versus a single GPU. Table 2 summarizes our experimental results for both these questions. In these set of experiments, we tested three different problem sizes on all target platforms by running 1000 iteration steps: *i)* Small problem size: 102 400 particles; *ii)* Medium problem size: 512 000 particles; *iii)* Large problem size: 1 024 000 particles.

Table 2. Single CPU-node versus Single-GPU performance comparison of the baseline implementation and OpenMP implementations

Test case	Average total execution time [s]			
	Intel Xeon IceLake SP Node (72 cores, 1 thread per core)	NVIDIA A100 Prescriptive	NVIDIA A100 Descriptive	AMD MI250 (1 MCM)
Small	115.34	25.83	24.83	21.99
Medium	576.72	111.44	109.29	96.79
Large	1155.60	216.52	213.30	191.56

In terms of performance acceleration with respect to the baseline CPU implementation, all GPU executions were faster in general across all three problem sizes. The highest speedup was achieved on the large problem size with the AMD MI250 GPU, exhibiting a 6× speedup over the CPU implementation. All GPU executions were at least 4× faster than the CPU version when running on either NVIDIA's A100 or AMD's MI250 GPUs. The relative performance gain on the MI250 GPU falls somewhat short of the A100 GPU, given the significantly larger double-precision (FP64) peak performance of the MI250 GPU (22.6 TFlop/s for a single MCM) as compared to the A100 GPU (9.5 TFlop/s) and the fact that the application is largely compute bound. Identifying the cause for this lower efficiency (compared to peak performance) would require an in-depth performance analysis for the MI250 GPU which is beyond the scope of this work, given the novelty of the hardware and the AMD software ecosystem. We speculate that the OpenMP `clang` compiler is not yet able to generate as efficient GPU code compared to the NVIDIA compiler which is more mature.

Regarding performance portability, given that no architecture-specific optimizations were used, it is worth noting that no code changes were made to execute on the different vendor GPUs, recompilation was enough in this case. Table 1 shows the set of compilation flags needed on each platform.

Prescriptive Versus Descriptive Implementations. Table 2 shows the performance of both approaches on NVIDIA's A100 GPUs. The compiler is of central importance when using high-level programming models like OpenMP, in particular, how well is it able to map an application to the underlying hardware. In this study, the performance of both implementations was essentially the same. Indeed, a performance analysis of both *prescriptive* and *descriptive* code bases with the NVIDIA Nsight tools (Compute and Systems) shows that our application is largely compute bound and achieves 5.6 TFLOP/s FP64 performance when executing the large test case. An in-depth analysis of the performance metrics collected with the Nsight tools confirmed that the NVIDIA compiler produced highly efficient GPU code with little room for additional improvement from the OpenMP standpoint. Further optimizations would require platform-specific code transformations, which is not the point of this study.

Although our application did not require involved OpenMP programming, we wanted to test the OpenMP *descriptive* model as a way to keep a single source code for all platforms, including the multicore CPU. At the time of writing, the `amdclang++` compiler provides no support for the OpenMP `loop` directive, which impedes the single-source approach on the AMD GPU platform. The *descriptive* approach was also successfully executed on the Intel Xe GPUs platform under oneAPI. However, when following this single-source approach, simulation performance on the CPU was severely downgraded with respect to the baseline CPU implementation, in which vectorization hinting pragmas were used in the magnetic field computation to significantly boost performance. Design decisions that we took to facilitate and reduce data movement to/from the GPU resulted in code modifications to the magnetic field computation procedure. This code changes precluded us from using vectorization and, as a result, the single-source implementation is not as efficient when executed on the CPU as the baseline implementation.

4.3   Multi-GPU Scalability

Finally, we added MPI to our *prescriptive* implementation to achieve a scalable application which enables scientists to run much larger problems or substantially shorten the time to solution. MPI is used to distribute particles among the different GPUs, i.e. a single MPI process is allocated per GPU. Table 3 shows the experimental results for both strong and weak scaling. For strong scaling, we used a problem size of 16 384 000 particles and 1000 iteration steps. Weak scaling was performed by fixing an 512 000 particles-per-node ratio and using 1000 iteration steps. As previously mentioned, each scenario timing reported in this section is the result of 10 repetitions.

Table 3. Scaling results for the Prescriptive OpenMP Implementation of BS-SOLCTRA

Scaling	Average execution time per iteration					
	1 GPU	2 GPUs	4 GPUs	8 GPUs	16 GPUs	32 GPUs
Strong	3.36 s/step	1.68 s/step	0.92 s/step	0.43 s/step	0.22 s/step	0.11 s/step
Weak	109.96 ms/step	110.11 ms/step	110.27 ms/step	110.27 ms/step	110.28 ms/step	110.26 ms/step

Strong scaling shows very good speedups for the multi-GPU approach, provided the problem size is enough to saturate each unit. Weak scaling, as expected, was close to perfect. This behavior is expected from an application like ours where there are no particle interactions thus no communication bottlenecks appear as the GPU count increases.

4.4 Economic Analysis

As impressive a substantially reduced time to solution obtained for a specific application may appear, the actual speedups might not warrant the use of more powerful hardware from an economic perspective. It is thus mandatory, in our opinion, to put bare application speedups into the context of the economic costs to solution, i.e. to compare relative speedups obtained on a specific hardware platform with the approximate (additional) costs that apply, e.g. for procuring and operating (electricity, cooling) GPUs in our case. In the absence of published data, some rough estimates can be derived from comparing the pricing for different instance types offered by commercial cloud providers. Amazon EC2, for example, charges [1] an extra factor of about 3 for a "p3.8xlarge" instance with 4 A100 GPUs compared with a "c6i.32xlarge" instance with 64 Xeon IceLake cores. This translates to a required "speedup" of at least 0.75, when comparing a single A100 GPU with an entire Xeon IceLake node on Raven (72 CPU cores), which is the basis for the speedups reported in this work.

In the light of these considerations, the increase of application performance we have achieved by porting BS-SOLCTRA to modern GPUs has not only significantly reduced time to solution (which enables to do more science and hence is a value *per se*), but can also substantially overcompensate the additional cost of such type of hardware and thus makes the new GPU version of BS-SOLCTRA appear economically highly efficient.

Thanks to the adopted high-level and portable programming paradigm using OpenMP, the human effort for the actual porting and future maintenance (the costs of which are hardly ever taken into account in academic HPC) can be considered as very moderate.

5   Conclusions

As the HPC community gains access to exascale computing power, scientific applications must be adapted to effectively utilize these complex and often heterogeneous platforms. Currently, one of the main challenges is developing applications that can be easily ported *and* maintain good performance across different platforms. The OpenMP standard offers high-level software parallelization and offloading capabilities and as more compilers become compliant to its specification, the more it becomes a vendor-neutral option for attaining performance portability [5,6].

In this study, we ported a plasma physics field line tracing production code, BS-SOLCTRA, used to simulate plasma confinement in stellarator devices, from a traditional MPI+OpenMP implementation to an OpenMP offload approach. We tested both *prescriptive* and *descriptive* models to GPU programming and analyzed portability across all three relevant GPU platforms, namely NVIDIA, AMD, and Intel. The new, GPU-accelerated version of the BS-SOLCTRA code achieved a maximum speedup of $6\times$ and on average was at least $4\times$ faster than the original CPU implementation, when comparing the runtimes on an entire CPU node with 72 Intel Xeon IceLake cores vs. a single GPU unit. We also successfully demonstrated portability across all three GPU platforms by being able to compile and execute our application with no code modifications. This now enables physicists working with this application to achieve a much better turn-around to results and the possibility to execute this code on a wider set of target platforms.

The promise of single-source development was part of the allure of the *descriptive* model that motivated this study. However, execution times when offloading was disabled were not acceptable, mainly due to design decision in our code-base that were focused on enhancing GPU execution. Although we applied the correct directives, developing a "single-source" performance-portable application can be a challenge given the considerable differences between CPU and GPU in hardware capabilities and organization. We plan on finding alternative implementations of the code that could potentially unlock performance portability across GPUs and multicore systems. Another key aspect we plan on working is understanding how different compilers deal with offloading directives as a way of unveiling best practices in OpenMP offload programming to achieve efficient GPU-utilization.

Acknowledgments. This research was partially funded by the Max Planck Society of Germany (MPG) - Costa Rica National Council of Rectors (CONARE) joint research projects framework. We also thank: Markus Hrywniak from NVIDIA for consulting on A100 performance; Andre Heidekrueger from AMD for enabling access to MI250 and providing technical support and we acknowledge Intel for giving us early access to the upcoming Xe GPU hardware and Alexander Poeppl for support.

References

1. Amazon: Compute Savings Plans for Amazon EC2, 22 June 2022. https://aws.amazon.com/savingsplans/compute-pricing/
2. Bogdanovic, L., Simič, G., Kos, L.: L2G PFC heat loads and field-line tracing in the SMITER framework. In: 30th International Conference Nuclear Energy for New Europe (NENE2021) (2021)
3. Campos-Duarte, L., et al.: Towards photorealistic visualizations for plasma confinement simulations. Association for Computing Machinery, New York (2021). https://doi.org/10.1145/3437359.3465608
4. Coto-Vílchez, F., et al.: Progress on the small modular stellarator SCR-1: new diagnostics and heating scenarios. J. Plasma Phys. **86**(4), 815860401 (2020). https://doi.org/10.1017/S0022377820000677
5. Diaz, J.M., Pophale, S., Hernandez, O., Bernholdt, D.E., Chandrasekaran, S.: OpenMP 4.5 validation and verification suite for device offload. In: de Supinski, B.R., Valero-Lara, P., Martorell, X., Mateo Bellido, S., Labarta, J. (eds.) IWOMP 2018. LNCS, vol. 11128, pp. 82–95. Springer, Cham (2018). https://doi.org/10.1007/978-3-319-98521-3_6

6. ECP Sollve Project: OpenMP validation and verification test suite, 22 June 2022. https://crpl.cis.udel.edu/ompvvsollve/
7. Gayatri, R., Yang, C., Kurth, T., Deslippe, J.: A case study for performance portability using OpenMP 4.5. In: Chandrasekaran, S., Juckeland, G., Wienke, S. (eds.) WACCPD 2018. LNCS, vol. 11381, pp. 75–95. Springer, Cham (2019). https://doi.org/10.1007/978-3-030-12274-4_4
8. Jiménez, D., Campos-Duarte, L., Solano-Piedra, R., Araya-Solano, L.A., Meneses, E., Vargas, I.: BS-SOLCTRA: towards a parallel magnetic plasma confinement simulation framework for modular stellarator devices. In: Crespo-Mariño, J.L., Meneses-Rojas, E. (eds.) CARLA 2019. CCIS, vol. 1087, pp. 33–48. Springer, Cham (2020). https://doi.org/10.1007/978-3-030-41005-6_3
9. Jiménez, D., Meneses, E., Vargas, V.: Adaptive plasma physics simulations: dealing with load imbalance using Charm++. Association for Computing Machinery, New York (2021). https://doi.org/10.1145/3437359.3465566
10. Karlin, I., et al.: Early experiences porting three applications to OpenMP 4.5. In: Maruyama, N., de Supinski, B.R., Wahib, M. (eds.) IWOMP 2016. LNCS, vol. 9903, pp. 281–292. Springer, Cham (2016). https://doi.org/10.1007/978-3-319-45550-1_20
11. Lopez, M.G., et al.: Towards achieving performance portability using directives for accelerators. In: 2016 Third Workshop on Accelerator Programming Using Directives (WACCPD), pp. 13–24 (2016). https://doi.org/10.1109/WACCPD.2016.006
12. Marowka, A.: On the performance portability of OpenACC, OpenMP, Kokkos and RAJA. In: International Conference on High Performance Computing in Asia-Pacific Region, HPCAsia2022, pp. 103–114. Association for Computing Machinery, New York (2022). https://doi.org/10.1145/3492805.3492806
13. OpenMP Architecture Review Board: OpenMP application programming interface. version 5.2, November 2021. https://www.openmp.org/wp-content/uploads/OpenMP-API-Specification-5-2.pdf
14. Ozen, G., Wolfe, M.: Performant portable OpenMP. In: Proceedings of the 31st ACM SIGPLAN International Conference on Compiler Construction, pp. 156–168 (2022)
15. Top500: Top500 list. Top500, 26 May 2022. https://www.top500.org/

Quantitative Characterization
of Scientific Computing Clusters

Aurelio Vivas[✉][iD] and Harold Castro[iD]

COMIT Reserach Group, Universidad de los Andes, Bogotá, Colombia
{aa.vivas,hcastro}@uniandes.edu.co

Abstract. Several forms of non-HPC clusters named cluster of workstations and cluster of virtual machines have become available in universities
and research institutions as cost effective solutions for scientific computing. With the need to characterize the cluster computing systems that
are traditionally used to run high-performance computing applications
and those that are not, the terms tightly- and loosely- coupled clusters
were adopted. However this qualitative characterization of clusters does
not provide further characterization of non-HPC systems, and does not
reveal real insights into their capacity to tackle many scientific applications. As a consequence, researchers who use these computing systems do
not have the tools to make informed decisions about what type of applications better fits the capacity and capabilities of every kind of non-HPC
cluster. In this work, we propose the cluster performance profile. This
profile enables the quantitative characterization, initially, on non-HPC
clusters in order to support decisions in the use and development of these
clusters.

Keywords: Cluster computing · High-performance computing ·
Cluster overhead · Cluster coupling · Cluster benchmarking

1 Introduction

Although supercomputers have been considered as the de facto computer architectures for the execution of high-performance computing (HPC) applications,
their operation and maintenance costs have increased at higher rates [9] when
compared to other forms of cluster architectures. These increasing rates have
led the scientific community into the development of emerging and low-cost
non-HPC clusters such as cluster of workstations (COW), cluster of desktops
(COD), and cluster of virtual machines (COV), which are commonly found in
research laboratories and institutions.

In non-HPC clusters, researchers have sought to give answers to the following questions. First, *what kind of cluster better fits the needs of a given scientific application (HPC and non-HPC)*. Second, which is a common and recur-
ring question made among scientists when considering the execution of scientific
applications on these clusters, *what configuration (nodes, and processors) of these*

P. Navaux et al. (Eds.): CARLA 2022, CCIS 1660, pp. 47–62, 2022.
https://doi.org/10.1007/978-3-031-23821-5_4

clusters render the best performance for a given scientific application. In order to give answers to the above-mentioned research questions, we propose the **cluster performance profile**, this profile summarizes the performance obtained for a variety of scientific applications in strong scaling benchmarking experiments. From these performances, we derive further cluster specific metrics named cluster overhead and cluster coupling, based on a previously proposed methodology [14]. The cluster performance profile that includes the applications performance metrics, the cluster overhead, and cluster coupling enables the characterization of not only non-HPC, but also HPC clusters by quantifying their strengths and weaknesses when executing well-known scientific computing kernels such as the seven dwarfs of scientific computing. The seven dwarfs of scientific computing exhibit a variety of communication and computation patterns common to many scientific applications, they enable further characterization of the capacity of clusters under different kinds of workloads.

Research questions are addressed as follows in this research paper. Section 2 presents related work on characterizing scientific computing clusters and evaluating their capacity for the execution of scientific applications. Section 3 presents a background on cluster overhead, cluster coupling and the proposed cluster performance profile. Section 4 presents the performance evaluation of four clusters and the calculation of their cluster performance profiles. Section 5 discusses our findings on these cluster profiles and provides answers to the proposed research questions. Conclusions on the use of the cluster performance profile and future directions are drawn in Sect. 6.

2   Related Work

The quantification of the capacity of scientific computing clusters for the execution of high-performance computing applications is a common and ongoing research problem, named performance evaluation and benchmarking. These evaluations provide to some extent an estimate of the performance that computers can deliver for specific applications. On non-HPC clusters, related works have been conducted in virtual clusters built on top of containers or virtual machines over cloud [1,6,8,10,12], IoT [3,11], workstations [2], and desktops [4] infrastructures. Bare-metal cluster deployments on top of workstations [7] and desktops [13] have also been considered. Furthermore, those related works usually estimate the capacity in terms of the metrics delivered by the traditional compute-intensive benchmarks such as high-performance Linpack (HPL), NAS Parallel Benchmarks (NPB), or HPC Challenge Benchmark (HCB).

Most related works that estimate the capacity of virtual and containerized clusters concentrate their efforts in the determination of the computation and communication overhead these technologies pose on the performance of HPC applications. These works usually compare the capacity (given in FLOPS, latency, bandwidth, and related metrics) of the bare-metal host system with the same system when hosting containers or virtual machines. On the other hand, related works that estimate the capacity of bare-metal deployments, such as clusters of workstations and desktops use the capacity estimated in supercomputers as base line to determine if the system under study has a satisfactory capacity.

In this work we extend the state of the art in performance evaluation and benchmarking of scientific clusters in the following directions: (i) we extend the performance analysis commonly conducted in strong scaling analyses by including the cluster performance profile that comprises the traditional performance metric, and our previously proposed metrics (cluster overhead and cluster coupling [14]), finally (ii) we provide a quantitative characterization of four small size scientific computing clusters and demonstrate the validity of this characterization, the characterization being summarized in a cluster performance profile per cluster.

3   Background

Here we define the concepts that are relevant for the quantitative characterization of scientific computing clusters; namely, cluster overhead, cluster coupling, and the cluster performance profile.

3.1   Cluster Overhead and Coupling

Cluster distributed systems have been categorized as loosely- or tightly-coupled according to the storage, interconnection, processing technology and the components packing strategy employed in their development. In addition, the speed and reliability of the interconnection channel have been considered as the criteria for this classification [5]. Nevertheless, the loosely- and tightly-coupled classification does not provide quantitative information about how coupled these different computing systems are. Accordingly, in [14] we proposed a methodology to quantitatively estimate the coupling of clusters using a metric we called cluster overhead.

The **cluster overhead** is estimated by determining how similar a given cluster is to its tightly-coupled counterpart, assumed to be a single node. Figure 1 depicts the performance for a single node of a cluster ($P_h(1)$) and the performance for the same cluster with n computing nodes ($P_h(n)$), for the high-performance computing application building block h. This figure also depicts $P_h'(1)$ and $P_h'(n)$ serving as linear approximations of $P_h(1)$ and $P_h(n)$ respectively. Then, the cluster overhead with respect to h is given by the following formula.

$$\alpha = \angle \overline{P_h'(1)} \; \overline{P_h'(n)} \tag{1}$$

Although computers' performance does not have linear behavior, linear approximations led us to derive properties of lines that allow further understanding of cluster's performance. For instance, in the formula, the angle (α) between the segments $\overline{P_h'(1)}$ and $\overline{P_h'(n)}$ stand as the performance loss also known as the cluster overhead, this measured in degrees. Note that there is an inverse relationship between the cluster overhead and coupling, as shown in Fig. 2. In Fig. 2, large values for α stand for large overhead, resulting in a poor similarity between a node and the whole cluster, this being rendered in a loose cluster coupleness.

On the other hand, small values for α stand for small overhead, resulting in a higher similarity between a node and the whole cluster, this being rendered in a tightly cluster coupleness. Then, the **cluster coupling** is defined by the following formula, where α stands for the cluster overhead.

$$c = \frac{1}{\alpha} \tag{2}$$

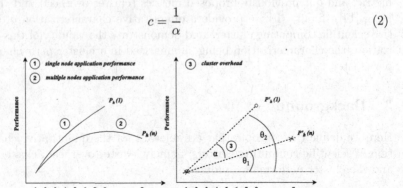

Fig. 1. Cluster overhead

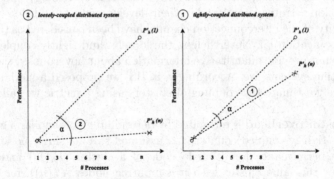

Fig. 2. Cluster coupleness

Note that the performance measure used for the calculation of coupling and overhead metrics variates according to the specific application being used for the measurement; for instance, NAS Parallel benchmarks use the MOP/s (millions of operations per second) as the standard to deliver benchmark performance, the type of operation OP variates according to the specific benchmark. Benchmarks such as FT, MG and CG use as an operation unit the Float Point whilst EP use Random Numbers Generated.

3.2 Cluster Performance Profile

Table 1 presents the cluster performance profile for an hypothetical cluster. This profile summarizes the properties of segments such as $\overline{P'_h(1)}$ and $\overline{P'_h(n)}$ that are of interest for clusters characterization. These properties are: the slope (m), the angle between a segment and the x-axis (θ), the cluster overhead (α) that is calculated with respect to another segment, and the coupling (c) which is derived from the cluster overhead. In the cluster performance profile, m and θ bring information about how fast the performance increases when considering a segment established between points $(p, P'_h(p))$ and $(p + 1, P'_h(p + 1))$, where $\overset{\bullet}{p}$ is the number of processors considered and $P'_h(p)$ is the performance of h when considering p processors of the cluster. If we think in terms of a line segment, m is the segment's slope and θ the angle formed between the x-axis and the segment, both m and θ are directly proportional. In a similar way, α describes how close the performance of a cluster being represented by a segment is to a tightly-coupled instance being represented by another segment.

The baseline for the cluster performance profile is a single node. Since this is supposed to be a tightly-coupled instance, when compared to itself, the cluster overhead is defined to equal zero, $\alpha = 0$. As the number of computational resources (processors, nodes) used in computing h increases, performance will tend to drop due to the parallel overhead. This also may affect the performance growth rate being estimated by m and θ, increases the cluster overhead α, and decreases the system coupling. However, although the above is the expected behavior, different computation and communication patterns might differ from this behavior for different settings of nodes and processors. These differences are intended to be caught in the cluster performance profile.

Table 1. Cluster performance profile

Application	Nodes	$(p, P_h(p))$		m	θ	α	c
h	1	$(1, P_h(1))$	$(4, P_h(4))$	m_1	θ_1	0	c_1
	2	$(1, P_h(1))$	$(8, P_h(8))$	m_2	θ_2	> 0	$< c_2$
	4	$(1, P'_h(1))$	$(16, P_h(16))$	m_3	θ_3	$>> 0$	$<< c_3$

4   Performance Evaluation

Five scientific computing dwarves (spectral methods, sparse linear algebra, unstructured meshes, structured meshes and monte carlo) represented in four NAS parallel benchmarks (FT, CG, MG and EP) are used to evaluate the performance of three non-HPC clusters C_{w_1}, C_{w_2}, C_{cov} and one HPC cluster C_{hpc} which is used for validation purpose. The resulting performance delivered by the applications in a strong scaling evaluation is then used to the elaboration of a cluster performance profile per cluster, according to the methodology proposed in Sect. 3.2. The findings on these profiles are further discussed in Sect. 5.

4.1   Experimental Setup

The experiment comprises a strong scaling performance evaluation on dedicated clusters C_{w_1}, C_{w_2}, C_{cov} and C_{hpc} whose technical details are shown in Table 2. C_{hpc} is the university high-performance computing system; C_{cov} is a Microsoft Hyper-V-based cluster of virtual machines whose cluster computing nodes were deployed on different servers at the university datacenter, although virtual machines are dedicated, the datacenter is not; C_{w_1} and C_{w_2} are clusters of workstations differing in their network bandwidth and latency capabilities. The FT, CG, MG, and EP benchmarks are executed over the only-MPI execution scheme. Here, we increased the number of MPI processes and the number of nodes. The Class C of NAS parallel benchmark problem sizes is considered and remains fixed through experiments. The MPI processes mappings considered for the experiment are described in Table 3. In Table 3, *ppn* stands for MPI processes per node and *tp* for the total number of processes in the cluster.

Table 2. Clusters specifications

Specs	C_{hpc}	C_{cov}	C_{w_1}	C_{w_2}
# of nodes	4	4	4	4
CPU(s)	28	4	4	4
CPU model	Intel(R) Xeon(R) CPU E5-2690 v4	Intel(R) Xeon(R) CPU E5-2680 v4	Intel(R) Core(TM) i7-4790	Intel(R) Core(TM) i7-4790
CPU clock speed	2.60 GHz	2.40 GHz	3.60 GHz	3.60 GHz
Thread(s) per core	2	1	2	2
Core(s) per socket	14	1	4	4
Socket(s)	2	4	1	1
NUMA node(s)	2	1	1	1
Network bandwidth	40 Gb/s 4x QDR	10 Gb/s	100 Mb/s	1 Gb/s
Network latency	1.3 us	~77 us	~380 us	~81 us

Table 3. Processes mappings

# of nodes	1	1	1	1	1	1	2	2	2	2	2	4	4	4	4	4
ppn	1	2	4	8	16	32	1	2	4	8	16	1	2	4	8	16
tp	1	2	4	8	16	32	2	4	8	16	32	4	8	16	32	64

4.2   Threats to Validity

The performance exhibited by a cluster is susceptible to a countless number of software parameters. To name a few: the problem size, the parallelization scheme, the supporting numerical libraries and the algorithms. Given the actual difficulty in providing an accurate measure of overall computers performance, our estimation considers a simplified version of the problem. Here, we consider small-scale clusters, and well-known scientific computing kernels with fixed problem sizes and execution schemes; these in order to validate our methodology. Regarding the execution scheme, in the HPC cluster we do not use all the physical cores in order to be able to use only powers of 2 number of processors, then this must be considered when performing comparisons between clusters. Also although experiments were executed three times, we observe no significant variations that lead to errors in our estimations of performance. In this regard, results are well supported by theory.

Finally, note the performance is a compound metric that measures the application and computing system performance, not the computing system in isolation, the former is what we mean when referring to the performance of the cluster.

4.3   Results

Figures 3, 4, 5 and 6 describe the performance achieved for clusters C_{hpc}, C_{cov}, C_{w_1} and C_{w_2} in the FT, CG, MG and EP benchmarks, respectively. These figures compare the performance achieved in the clusters for the different settings of nodes and processors considered for the computations.

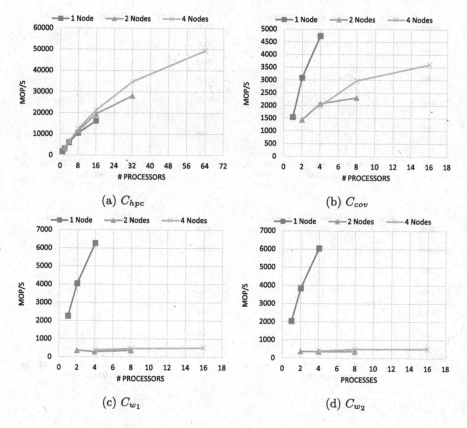

(a) C_{hpc}

(b) C_{cov}

(c) C_{w_1}

(d) C_{w_2}

Fig. 3. FT - fast Fourier Transform - spectral methods

In FT, Fig. 3, C_{hpc} achieves strong scalability when compared to the other clusters, as expected. However, this cluster exhibits a particular performance behavior which is the divergence in the performance seen on different settings of nodes from 16 processors. This divergence is explained by the NUMA memory architecture commonly present in high-performance computing cluster nodes. Here the performance attained for one, two, and four nodes is similar until the number of processors used per node cross the processors' capacity of a single socket or NUMA domain. This suggests intra-node communication issues being rendered in the node performance degradation. Note that these issues are solved when we distributed 16 processes in two or four nodes, that is, by considering $2n * 8p$ and $4n * 4p$ settings, respectively. Regarding the non-HPC computing systems, although C_{cov}, C_{w_1} and C_{w_2} achieve strong single node scaling, C_{cov} outperform the multi-node performance of C_{w_1} and C_{w_2}. Finally, even though C_{cov} exhibits better inter-node communication capabilities, better overall performance is achieved for a single node in either C_{w_1} or C_{w_2} clusters.

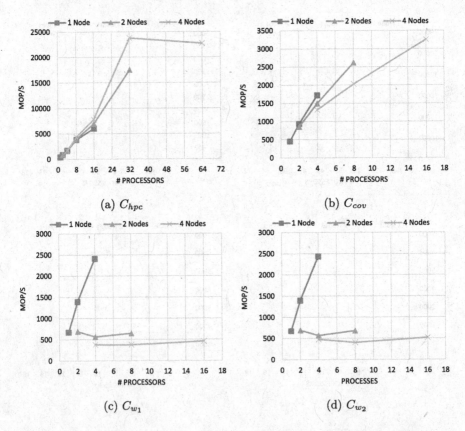

(a) C_{hpc}

(b) C_{cov}

(c) C_{w_1}

(d) C_{w_2}

Fig. 4. CG - Conjugate Gradient - sparse linear algebra and unstructured meshes

In CG, Fig. 4, C_{hpc} also demonstrates an upward trend in performance when increasing the number of nodes and processors; however, the effect of the NUMA memory architecture substantially hurts the performance of this computing kernel. For example, for 32 processors, the $4n * 8p$ nodes-processors setting outperforms the $2n * 16$ setting, since in the former setting, the eight processors per node do not cross the boundaries of a single node socket. The above-mentioned NUMA effect is also seen for 64 processors, but here the increasing performance tendency dramatically drops. Concerning the non-HPC computing systems, all sustain scalable performance for a single node; however, C_{cov} exceeds the multinode performance of its counterparts. In addition, C_{cov} achieves the best overall performance in four nodes. If we compare the maximum performance achieved in the whole C_{cov} cluster and the maximum performance achieved in a single C_{hpc} node, C_{cov} just reaches 54.29% of the C_{hpc} single node capacity. Moreover, if we compare the maximum performance achieved in C_{w_2} against the one achieved in C_{cov}, a single C_{w_2} node reaches 74.79% of the whole C_{cov} cluster capacity.

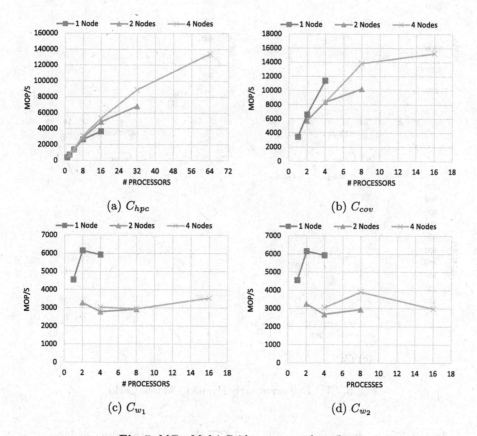

(a) C_{hpc}

(b) C_{cov}

(c) C_{w_1}

(d) C_{w_2}

Fig. 5. MG - Multi Grid - structured meshes

In MG, Fig. 5, C_{hpc} demonstrates the same upward scaling pattern seen in the FT computing kernel. This similarity suggests the same communication and computation pattern. Both kernels solve the Poisson equation and employ short- and long-distance communication operations, but MG, unlike FT, is a memory-intensive kernel [14]. In the non-HPC computing systems, this computing kernel reports poor scalability in C_{cov}, and no scalability is seen in the C_{w_1} and C_{w_2} clusters. In particular, the lack of scalability in C_{w_1} and C_{w_2} might be attributed to the memory-intensive nature of MG, suggesting a memory bandwidth issue. Conclusively, for the MG computing kernel, C_{cov} outperform clusters C_{w_1} and C_{w_2} in all node settings, namely one, two and four nodes. Finally, when compared to C_{hpc}, the whole C_{cov} cluster reaches only 41.75% of a single C_{hpc} node capacity.

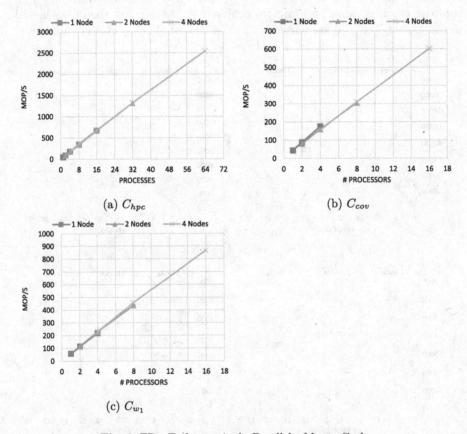

(a) C_{hpc}

(b) C_{cov}

(c) C_{w_1}

Fig. 6. EP - Embarrassingly Parallel - Monte Carlo

In EP, Fig. 6, clusters C_{hpc}, C_{cov}, and C_{w_1} demonstrate strong scalability as expected. Note that C_{w_2} was not considered since it will achieve roughly the same performance of C_{w_1} as computing nodes are the same, but variate in the inter-nodes interconnection. When considering the non-HPC computing systems, the overall performance achieved in cluster C_{w_1} outperforms the performance achieved in C_{cov}. Here, C_{cov} just reaches 69.40% of the overall performance of C_{w1}.

4.4   Clusters Performance Profiles

Tables 4, 5, 6 and 7 provide four performance-derived metrics for the clusters under study; namely *slope*, θ, α, and *coupling*. These metrics characterize the clusters under study with respect to the four fundamental computing kernels: FT, MG, CG, and EP. Note that unlike the previous section where application performance was analyzed per node and per processing unit, here the performance is described for the clusters as whole entities.

Table 4 depicts the characterization computed for the C_{hpc} cluster. The *slope*, as mentioned in Sect. 3, describes the rate of growth in the performance delivered by an application for a given processors and computing nodes setting. A downward trend is expected in this rate as the number of computing nodes and processors climb due to the parallel overhead. This pattern is being exhibited by FT, MG, and EP. CG, on the contrary, describes a particular behavior. Here the rate attained when considering a two-nodes C_{hpc} cluster is higher than the one achieved for one and four nodes C_{hpc} clusters. This is explained by the increasing performance tendency seen in two nodes, Fig. 4a, that is contrary to that observed for one and four nodes. Note that the *slope* also tells us the performance cost of increasing the number of computational resources (processors and nodes). In the case of C_{hpc}, the increase in cost tends to be linear in all applications except for CG.

C_{hpc} proof consistency in the cluster overhead and coupling when considering the expectation that the overhead might tend to increase as more computing resources are added for the computation; as a consequence, the resulting coupling might decrease at the same extent. Note that this expectation is consistent in all applications except for CG which proof a negative -0.0501 cluster overhead. This means that instead of having overhead, the application is exhibiting a performance rate (*slope*) that surpasses the single node rate. Since the trend seen in two nodes C_{hpc} cluster surpass the one exhibited by a single node that was considered as the tightly coupled instance of the cluster for the computation of coupling, -19.9600 can't represent the coupling of the two nodes C_{hpc} cluster; because a single node is not any more a tightly coupled instance of the cluster. Another particular behavior seen in C_{hpc} is the one exhibited for FT. Here the performance rate in FT decreases significantly from two to four nodes; this suggests scalability issues of FT for many computing nodes. Lastly, in general, C_{hpc} exhibits a cluster overhead close to zero and higher degree of coupling, being this a characteristic of high-performance computing systems. However, cluster overhead and coupling will really make sense when we are able to compare these values with the ones obtained from other clusters.

Table 5 depicts the characterization computed for the C_{cov} cluster. Here, the *slope* decreases significantly describing a polynomial behavior, except for CG

Table 4. Cluster performance profile C_{hpc}

Kernel	Nodes	$(p, P'(p))$	$(p+1, P'(p+1))$	slope	θ	α	coupling
FT	1	(1,1762.41)	(16,16184.33)	961.4613	89.9404	0.0000	–
	2	(1,1762.41)	(32,28131.62)	850.6197	89.9326	0.0078	128.7781
	4	(1,1762.41)	(64,19124.67)	275.5914	89.7921	0.1483	6.7427
MG	1	(1,3810.23)	(16,36541.11)	2182.0587	89.9737	0.0000	–
	2	(1,3810.23)	(32,68435.4)	2084.6829	89.9725	0.0012	815.3292
	4	(1,3810.23)	(64,134120.4)	2068.4154	89.9723	0.0014	693.1671
CG	1	(1,406.55)	(16,5991.34)	372.3193	89.8461	0.0000	–
	2	(1,406.55)	(32,17519.91)	552.0439	89.8962	−0.0501	−19.9600
	4	(1,406.55)	(64,22721.68)	354.2084	89.8382	0.0079	127.0909
EP	1	(1,46.94)	(16,666.79)	41.3233	88.6137	0.0000	–
	2	(1,46.94)	(32,1318.02)	41.0026	88.6029	0.0108	92.2507
	4	(1,46.94)	(64,2540.23)	39.5760	88.5526	0.0612	16.3457

where there is a linear decrease in *slope*. Regarding cluster overhead, this cluster keeps consistency in the expectation that the overhead might tend to increase as more computing resources are added for the computation; as a consequence, there is also a consistency in the resulting coupling. Note that the values for cluster overhead and coupling on this cluster can be compared to the ones achieved in C_{hpc}; however, when doing this comparison, we need to consider that C_{hpc} was evaluated up to 16 processors while C_{cov} only considered four. If we consider C_{hpc} as a base line, we can conclude that C_{cov} exhibits the characteristics of a loosely coupled computing system; these are higher cluster overhead and lower coupleness.

Table 5. Cluster performance profile C_{cov}

Kernel	Nodes	$(p, P'(p))$	$(p+1, P'(p+1))$	slope	θ	α	coupling
FT	1	(1,1535.95)	(4,4731.63)	1065.2267	89.9462	0.0000	–
	2	(1,1535.95)	(8,2307.81)	110.2657	89.4804	0.4658	2.1468
	4	(1,1535.95)	(16,3611.28)	138.3553	89.5859	0.3603	2.7753
MG	1	(1,3428.22)	(4,11388.69)	2653.4900	89.9784	0.0000	–
	2	(1,3428.22)	(8,10229.9)	971.6686	89.9410	0.0374	26.7567
	4	(1,3428.22)	(16,15256.62)	788.5600	89.9273	0.0511	19.5825
CG	1	(1,449.58)	(4,1718.61)	423.0100	89.8646	0.0000	–
	2	(1,449.58)	(8,2611.97)	308.9129	89.8145	0.0500	19.9891
	4	(1,449.58)	(16,3252.4)	186.8547	89.6934	0.1712	5.8417
EP	1	(1,44.35)	(4,175.16)	43.6033	88.6862	0.0000	–
	2	(1,44.35)	(8,304.24)	37.1271	88.4571	0.2291	4.3656
	4	(1,44.35)	(16,600.7)	37.0900	88.4556	0.2306	4.3363

Table 6 show the performance derived metrics computed for the C_{w_1} cluster. Although we expected a downward trend in *slope* as we increased the number of computing nodes and processors, C_{w_1} depicts an unexpected trend. We observe negative *slopes* for the communication intensive computing kernels, this being the rates of performance degradation. We also observe that for the FT and MG computing kernels the performance degradation rate is greater in the two nodes setting than in the four nodes setting, whereas in GC the major degradation rate takes place, as expected, in the four nodes setting. We attributed the higher degradation in the two nodes setting to the poor network capacity of this cluster, this degradation seems to be compensated by the amount of computing processors used in the four nodes cluster setting. The equivalent behavior seen in FT and MG obeys the similarity these computing kernels have in terms of computation and communication. Finally, the negative *slope* renders higher cluster overheads, thus poor cluster coupling.

Table 6. Cluster performance profile C_{w_1}

Kernel	Nodes	$(p, P'(p))$	$(p+1, P'(p+1))$	slope	θ	α	coupling
FT	1	(1,2261.71)	(4,6264.74)	1334.3433	89.9571	0.0000	–
	2	(1,2261.71)	(8,363.13)	−271.2257	−89.7888	179.7458	0.0056
	4	(1,2261.71)	(16,500.53)	−117.4120	−89.5120	179.4691	0.0056
MG	1	(1,4544.48)	(4,5920.05)	458.5233	89.8750	0.0000	–
	2	(1,4544.48)	(8,2924.32)	−231.4514	−89.7525	179.6275	0.0056
	4	(1,4544.48)	(16,3539.47)	−67.0007	−89.1449	179.0200	0.0056
CG	1	(1,670.57)	(4,2408.03)	579.1533	89.9011	0.0000	–
	2	(1,670.57)	(8,644.73)	−3.6914	−74.8425	164.7436	0.0061
	4	(1,670.57)	(16,458.49)	−14.1387	−85.9543	175.8554	0.0057
EP	1	(1,57.69)	(4,217.92)	53.4100	88.9274	0.0000	–
	2	(1,57.69)	(8,436.51)	54.1171	88.9414	−0.0140	−71.3638
	4	(1,57.69)	(16,865.55)	53.8573	88.9363	−0.0089	−112.2702

Table 7 contains the performance derived metrics computed for the C_{w_2} cluster. This cluster demonstrates the same performance degradation rate pattern

Table 7. Cluster performance profile C_{w_2}

Kernel	Nodes	$(p, P'(p))$	$(p+1, P'(p+1))$	slope	θ	α	coupling
FT	1	(1,2023.55)	(4,6031.51)	1335.9867	89.9571	0.0000	–
	2	(1,2023.55)	(8,368.31)	−236.4629	−89.7577	179.7148	0.0056
	4	(1,2023.55)	(16,508.38)	−101.0113	−89.4328	179.3899	0.0056
MG	1	(1,4550.05)	(4,5934.79)	461.5800	89.8759	0.0000	–
	2	(1,4550.05)	(8,2940.89)	−229.8800	−89.7508	179.6266	0.0056
	4	(1,4550.05)	(16,2982.86)	−104.4793	−89.4516	179.3275	0.0056
CG	1	(1,671.32)	(4,2432.56)	587.0800	89.9024	0.0000	–
	2	(1,671.32)	(8,679.92)	1.2286	50.8560	39.0464	0.0256
	4	(1,671.32)	(16,515.7)	−10.3747	−84.4943	174.3968	0.0057

seen in C_{w_1}, since clusters computing nodes are the same except for the nodes interconnection. Although the negative *slopes*, cluster overhead and cluster coupling metrics are similar on C_{w_1} and C_{w_2} for FT and MG, there are subtle improvements in these metrics due to the improvement in the interconnection network in the C_{w_2} cluster. In addition, the network enhancement improved the coupling of the cluster in terms of the CG computing kernel.

5   Discussion

A scalability analysis and the one focused on cluster overhead and coupling metrics, were conducted on four scientific computing clusters in order to quantitatively characterize their capacity to execute scientific applications. The scalability analysis suggests memory bandwidth issues in C_{w_1} and C_{w_2} that might prevent the scalability of memory intensive computing kernels such as MG. In addition, the analysis demonstrates the negative effect of the NUMA memory architecture, established in C_{hpc} cluster nodes, that can slightly affect the scalability of scientific applications exhibiting computing patterns similar to FT and MG; being these spectral methods and structured meshes. But the NUMA architecture substantially hurts the scalability of sparse linear algebra and unstructured meshes computations such as the ones exhibited in CG for the C_{hpc} cluster. Finally, when considering the non-HPC clusters, C_{w_1} and C_{w_2} demonstrate best overall performance for FT in one node and EP in four nodes whilst C_{cov} demonstrate best overall performance in CG and MG in the four nodes setting.

The cluster performance profile reveals numerous cluster specific behaviors that might be considered, first, for the selection of clusters for specific scientific applications, and, second, to guide architectural design decisions on the development of these clusters. In the first matter, when considering the non-HPC clusters, under the experimental conditions, the workstations based clusters C_{w_1} and C_{w_2} best fits the needs of FT and EP workloads, for the given problem size and the only-MPI parallelization scheme. On the other hand, the virtual machines based cluster C_{cov} best fits the need of CG and MG workloads.

In the second matter, for instance, the performance rate of most computing kernels executed in C_{hpc} decreases linearly when increasing the number of computing resources. In contrast, C_{cov} exhibits polynomial decrease in this rate and C_{w_1} and C_{w_2} exhibit negative performance rates. Note that these performance rates can be improved by cluster designers by considering enhancements, for example, in the nodes interconnection as demonstrated when improving the interconnection of C_{w_1} in C_{w_2}.

6   Conclusion

In this work we proposed the cluster performance profile, this profile comprises performance related metrics for specific computing kernels and cluster specific metrics derived from the performance exhibited on these computing kernels. This profile was introduced to support both researchers running scientific applications on HPC and non-HPC clusters and cluster designers mainly developing low cost scientific computing clusters.

In this regard, the profile delivers two main benefits for researchers; first, serve as a guide for non HPC experts to determine what kind of scientific applications would strong scale, in a given cluster, when increasing the number of computing resources and which might not; second, as this profile is based on well-known building blocks seen in many scientific applications, it can be considered as a first glance when determining the appropriate cluster for the execution of applications developed by the combination of these building blocks. In addition, the cluster performance profile also serves as a guideline for cluster designers that will be able to perform improvements led by metrics such as the cluster overhead and coupling on scientific computing clusters.

Future work may involve the use of the cluster performance profile in large scale scientific computing clusters to fulfill two main objectives; first, determine the validity of the proposed quantitative characterization in this type of clusters; then, determine how this profile constructed on well-known building blocks executed on large scale clusters can anticipate the performance that could be achieved from applications made by the combination of well-known scientific computing building blocks.

References

1. Aljamal, R., El-Mousa, A., Jubair, F.: Benchmarking Microsoft Azure virtual machines for the use of HPC applications. In: 2020 11th International Conference on Information and Communication Systems (ICICS), pp. 382–387. IEEE (2020)
2. Beserra, D., et al.: Performance evaluation of hypervisors for HPC applications. In: 2015 IEEE International Conference on Systems, Man, and Cybernetics, pp. 846–851. IEEE (2015)
3. Beserra, D., Pinheiro, M.K., Souveyet, C., Steffenel, L.A., Moreno, E.D.: Performance evaluation of OS-level virtualization solutions for HPC purposes on SoC-based systems. In: 2017 IEEE 31st International Conference on Advanced Information Networking and Applications (AINA), pp. 363–370. IEEE (2017)
4. Chavarriaga, J., Gómez, C.E., Bonilla, D.C., Castro, H.E.: Capacity of desktop clouds for running HPC applications: a revisited analysis. In: Florez, H., Leon, M., Diaz-Nafria, J.M., Belli, S. (eds.) ICAI 2019. CCIS, vol. 1051, pp. 257–268. Springer, Cham (2019). https://doi.org/10.1007/978-3-030-32475-9_19
5. Ebbers, M., Hastings, C., Nuttal, M., Reichenberg, M.: Introduction to the new mainframe: networking. Copyright IBM Corp (2006)
6. He, Q., Zhou, S., Kobler, B., Duffy, D., McGlynn, T.: Case study for running HPC applications in public clouds. In: Proceedings of the 19th ACM International Symposium on High Performance Distributed Computing, pp. 395–401 (2010)
7. Huse, L.P., Bugge, H.: High-end computing on SHV workstations connected with high performance network. In: Sørevik, T., Manne, F., Gebremedhin, A.H., Moe, R. (eds.) PARA 2000. LNCS, vol. 1947, pp. 324–332. Springer, Heidelberg (2001). https://doi.org/10.1007/3-540-70734-4_38
8. Mehrotra, P., et al.: Performance evaluation of amazon elastic compute cloud for NASA high-performance computing applications. Concurr. Comput. Pract. Exp. **28**(4), 1041–1055 (2016)

9. Muraña, J., Nesmachnow, S.: Simulation and evaluation of multicriteria planning heuristics for demand response in datacenters. Simulation 00375497211020083 (2021)
10. Ostermann, S., Iosup, A., Yigitbasi, N., Prodan, R., Fahringer, T., Epema, D.: A performance analysis of EC2 cloud computing services for scientific computing. In: Avresky, D.R., Diaz, M., Bode, A., Ciciani, B., Dekel, E. (eds.) CloudComp 2009. LNICSSTE, vol. 34, pp. 115–131. Springer, Heidelberg (2010). https://doi.org/10.1007/978-3-642-12636-9_9
11. Rajovic, N., Carpenter, P.M., Gelado, I., Puzovic, N., Ramirez, A., Valero, M.: Supercomputing with commodity CPUs: are mobile SoCs ready for HPC? In: Proceedings of the International Conference on High Performance Computing, Networking, Storage and Analysis, pp. 1–12 (2013)
12. Saini, S., et al.: An application-based performance evaluation of NASA's nebula cloud computing platform. In: 2012 IEEE 14th International Conference on High Performance Computing and Communication & 2012 IEEE 9th International Conference on Embedded Software and Systems, pp. 336–343. IEEE (2012)
13. Setiawan, I., Murdyantoro, E.: Commodity cluster using single system image based on Linux/Kerrighed for high-performance computing. In: 2016 3rd International Conference on Information Technology, Computer, and Electrical Engineering (ICITACEE), pp. 367–372. IEEE (2016)
14. Vivas, A., Castro, H.: Estimating the overhead and coupling of scientific computing clusters. Simulation 00375497211064198 (2021)

Towards Parameter-Based Profiling for MARE2DEM Performance Modeling

Bruno da Silva Alves[✉], Luciano Paschoal Gaspary, and Lucas Mello Schnorr

Graduate Program in Computer Science (PPGC/UFRGS), Porto Alegre, Brazil
{bsalves,paschoal,schnorr}@inf.ufrgs.br

Abstract. The Controlled Source Electromagnetic (CSEM) combined with seismic surveys has been used to explore new oil and gas reservoirs. The MARE2DEM application generates as mesh that represents a resistivity model of the seafloor underground. From a set of electromagnetic readings, the application runs a data inversion (using Maxwell's equations) along many steps to converge to a resistivity model that more closely matches the measured data. This data inversion procedure is very compute-bound because of the large amount of arithmetic operations involved. As consequence, the MARE2DEM application divides the workload into smaller work grains, called refinement groups due to the usage of Adaptive Mesh Refinement (AMR). These groups are processed independently in a parallel fashion by a set of workers. It is known that parallel processing suffers from delays and resource underutilization if the load remains imbalanced. In this article, we propose an analysis of the performance and imbalance of the MARE2DEM through source code inspection and trace analysis. The novelty of our investigation consists in the usage of runtime parameters to more profoundly understand and characterize the refinement groups' execution time and variability. Our results show that the execution time of the refinement groups is strongly impacted by both the number of processed nodes present on the input mesh and the measured data associated to each refinement group.

1 Introduction

The oil and gas exploration industry has been using marine Controlled Source Electromagnetic (CSEM) methods for the past years. CSEM data provides complementary information to seismic surveys. Besides, CSEM data acquisition is a better cost-effective alternative to new seismic surveys in areas where legacy seismic data is already present [2]. Figure 1 depicts the CSEM data acquisition. Firstly, stationary receivers are positioned on the seafloor above the region of interest. Then, a particular boat towing an electromagnetic wave transmitter (tx) navigates over the area. The receivers (rx) capture the electromagnetic fields influenced by the materials under the seabed. The boat navigates by following a vertical (from south to north, crossline) or horizontal (from west to east, inline) path that drives the data acquisition. In Fig. 1.A, we depict a crossline (Line-01) and an inline (Line-07) captured from the receivers at different times.

© The Author(s), under exclusive license to Springer Nature Switzerland AG 2022
P. Navaux et al. (Eds.): CARLA 2022, CCIS 1660, pp. 63–77, 2022.
https://doi.org/10.1007/978-3-031-23821-5_5

The set of measurement lines completes the final dataset that represents the region of interest. In Fig. 1.B, we represent the Line-01 with a 2D representation as a slice from the 3D space. Obtaining the data is only the first step in the marine CSEM workflow. The key step relies on data inversion, where one can obtain a resistivity model by calculating the data inversion through Maxwell's equations [12]. Those equations describe how an electromagnetic field diffuses through a material depending on its resistivity [12]. And the output model identifies potential reservoirs in the areas where resistivity values are similar to the known oil and gas resistivity values. However, the electromagnetic fields' inversion involves iterative and expensive math operations. In this context, the MARE2DEM [7] application emerged as an open-source project for CSEM data inversion. MARE2DEM is an iterative program that searches for 2.5D resistivity models using adaptive refinement meshes.

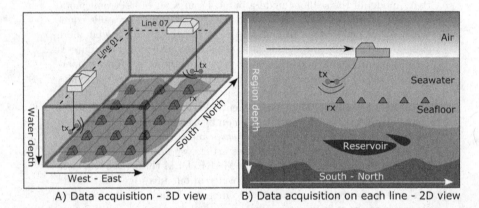

Fig. 1. CSEM data acquisition in 3D and 2D spaces. A boat tows the electric dipole transmitter (antenna in green). Receivers (in red) positioned on the seafloor capture the electromagnetic fields influenced by the materials under the seafloor. Distances and sizes were simplified for visualization. (Color figure online)

MARE2DEM receives as input a) the CSEM data described above, b) the region's geometry, and c) an initial resistivity model. The region's geometry is basically a polygon mesh that identifies the air, seawater, and seafloor areas where the mesh granularity can vary depending on the investigation interests. The initial resistivity model stores a resistivity value for each mesh section. A specialist can help define the initial resistivity values by evaluating the region. However, when resistivities are unknown, one can simply assign the same value for all mesh sections. The application does the CSEM data inversion on each iteration and searches for a better resistivity model than the current one. On this search, MAREDEM calculates an error for each mesh section representing a difference between the calculated electromagnetic fields and the measured data. Then, it identifies the areas with the highest errors, refines them using the adaptive refinement strategy, and calculates new resistivity values for each refined region and surroundings. Furthermore, the application uses parallelization to speed up the processing time. In this way, the code splits the domain problem into small sections called refinement groups, and those are assigned to workers through the coordinator-worker scheme. Each refinement group contains a copy of the whole mesh, and the data collected by the transmitters and receivers present in the group. However, the processing time for each refinement group varies depending on its configuration. The significant difference in processing time among the refinement groups leads to performance issues that make load balancing a challenging task.

Identifying the factors leading to a load imbalance is very challenging since MARE2DEM is a complex parallel application that relies on the Adaptive Mesh Refinement (AMR) technique. Performance visualization has proven its value for load imbalance characterization on the CSEM data inversion context [5] and also in other scenarios [1,6,11]. As consequence, we apply the same performance visualization methodology and tools to characterize the performance of the MARE2DEM application. As far as we are aware, there are no other reported investigation that tackles a performance analysis of the MARE2DEM application that considers the internal operations and their runtime parameters. Thus, an analysis of the MARE2DEM performance is proposed through the evaluation of the execution traces and the source code of the MARE2DEM application. The results show that the processing times of the refinement groups are guided by the number of mesh nodes processed in the refinement mesh and by the amount of input data mapped to each refinement group.

The article is organized as follows. Section 2 presents the dataset and application background. Section 3 details our experimental methodology and context. Section 4 presents our results, including the performance characterization of MARE2DEM's microkernels and of the refinement groups. Finally, Sect. 5 brings a summary of our observations and draw future work.

2   Dataset and Application Background

We present an overview of the MARE2DEM execution workflow, including its CSEM input dataset, the application's steps for data inversion, and the refinement groups used in the domain division.

2.1   CSEM Data

We use the CSEM data from the open-source MR3D (Marlim R3D) dataset available on [3]. The MR3D contains the geoelectric model of the Marlim field present in the Campos Basin, it occupies an area of $257.6 \, Km^2$ in a region off the northern Rio de Janeiro coast in Brazil [10]. This model emerged as a standard for CSEM studies of the particular turbiditic reservoirs on the Brazilian coast [4]. The dataset contains the electromagnetic components of 25 inlines (Weast-East) and 20 crosslines (North-South) captured at six different frequencies that range from 0.125 Hz to 1.25 Hz. We selected one arbitrary line for the following evaluations since the application process one line at a time and we expect the lines to have similar characteristics. Figure 2 depicts the chosen inline referenced as Line 04Tx013a. We show the model height and length on the Y and X axis. Figure 2.A shows the initial mesh refinement with a heavily refined rectangular area with 64 Km of length and 6 Km of depth. Each inline has a length of 42 Km from the first transmitter to the last one and an additional 11 Km area to the left and right of the first and last transmitters. Figure 2.B shows a smaller area closer to the transmitters and receivers. The blue points identify the 206 transmitters and the red triangles identify the 20 receivers placed in the irregular seafloor. Each transmitter is within 100 m of the next.

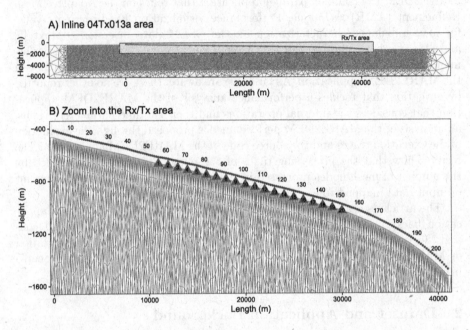

Fig. 2. Line 04Tx013a of the MR3D dataset: the initial refinement mesh (A), where the polygon sizes reflects the refinement degree; and the rectangular Rx/Tx area (B), where the numbered red triangles represents the 20 receivers, and the blue points represents the 206 transmitters. (Color figure online)

One might expect the data to have a measured electromagnetic field for each transmitter-receiver pairs at each of the used frequencies. However, the selected inline contains less data than the possible combinations of 206 tx, 20 rx, and the 6 frequencies due to the usage of a filter that eliminates non-relevant information. The transmitted fields can reach receivers in three ways: guided fields, reflected fields, and noisy fields. Figure 3 shows the field types captured by the receiver number 10 before applying the filter. We can see that the field classification depends on the distance between the transmitter and the receiver. When the elements are closer, the field directly reaches the receiver without capturing

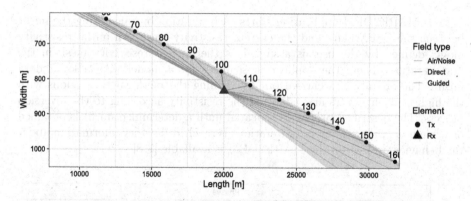

Fig. 3. The CSEM field classification using the data registered by the received number 10 of the MarlimR3D dataset: we depict that the field type (color) depends on the geographical distance between the transmitter and receiver (a Rx-Tx pair, the lines). (Color figure online)

the underground material signature (the green lines on Fig. 3). On the other hand, when the elements are far apart, the reaching field may capture undesired signatures like the ones present in the air (the red lines). The field that we are interested in are the ones influenced by the materials under the seabed (the blue lines). Those are considered guided fields. This last field type occurs when the transmitter and receiver are at a safe distance, not too close or far away. The MarlimR3D dataset contains only guided fields.

2.2   MARE2DEM

The MARE2DEM application is an open-source project[1] for 2D modeling in the context of electromagnetic geophysics. The application generate as output resistivity models for both CSEM (Controlled Source Electromagnetics) and MT (Magnetotelluric) data, but we focus our analysis on the CSEM inversion. The code is mainly written in Fortran, with some features written in MATLAB and C. The MATLAB's source code allows the users to create input models and visualize the results through routines that display a MATLAB graphical interface. The Fortran source code handles the bulk of compute-intensive operations, which mainly include the data inversion operations and the parallel job distribution policy. The use of Adaptive Mesh Refinement (AMR) is MARE2DEM's main feature. This feature removes the responsibility from the user of creating numerically accurate meshes, since it can refine an arbitrary input model's mesh on the regions with the highest possible errors, such as the ones closer to receivers and transmitters. We can also highlight that MARE2DEM can be run in parallel for large CSEM datasets. In what follows, we describe how the application calculates the resistivity models from the input data.

---

[1] MARE2DEM repository: https://mare2dem.bitbucket.io/.

The MARE2DEM application starts each iteration by calculating the misfit between the CSEM data and the current resistivity mesh. An initial resistivity model defined by the user is assumed as the current resistivity mesh in the first iteration. Then, the application searches for a model with a lower data misfit. The operation is carried out by refining the mesh on the regions with the highest misfit errors and adapting the resistivity according to the inversion process. The described process is repeated until a determined misfit is obtained or when a maximum number of iterations is reached. Further information about the behavior present on the MARE2DEM is available [7,8].

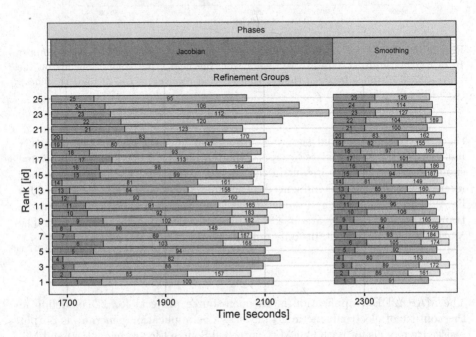

Fig. 4. The two MARE2DEM phases as gathered on its third iteration. The refinement groups processing is also shown for the first 25 workers (rank id) of a total of 80. The X-axis shows the elapsed time since application's start.

We can also explain how MARE2DEM works from the source code perspective by evaluating its function call stack. Figure 4 shows the main regions present on the application. MARE2DEM runs the Jacobian and Smoothing phases for each iteration (we show here the third iteration). The Jacobian phase (in red, left) calculates the model misfit and searches for a μ value that produces a model with a lower data misfit. Then, the Smoothing phase (in blue) seeks for the model with the smallest roughness given the calculated μ. This step stabilizes the inversion and prevents unexpected structures from appearing in the model. The application process the filtered CSEM data on each phase by grouping it into refinement groups. Each refinement group contains the data from a set of transmitters, receivers and frequencies. We show the refinement group's processing on the bottom facet. The Y axis shows parallel worker ranks, the X axis shows the time in seconds, and the labels on the orange rectangles identify each refinement group. Each phase processes all available refinement groups (from a total of 190 in this example), however, we only show the first 25 workers to facilitate the visualization reasons. The slowest rank determines the phase's processing time. The next section describes how the MARE2DEM creates the refinement groups.

2.3   Refinement Groups

The refinement groups composition is an essential step in the application's workflow, as it determines the size of the working grain that will be processed in parallel. The user defines a triplet, prior to execution, with the maximum number of transmitters, receivers, and frequencies that should have each refinement group. We set the application to use refinement groups with a maximum of 6 transmitters, 20 receivers, and 1 frequency. This means that each refinement group has a maximum of 120 transmitter-receiver pairs. However, the groups end up having fewer pairs due to the guided waves filtering of the CSEM data. A previous analysis showed that by setting the receivers and frequencies at 20 and 1, the chosen configuration (with 6 receivers) had the shortest execution time among the possible values for the receivers. Figure 5 shows the amount of Rx-Tx pairs (on the Y axis) for each refinement group (on the X axis). The colors identify the distinct frequencies used. We can see that all central refinement groups (identification ranging from 50 to 150) have a higher number of Rx-Tx pairs, and the peak appears around the refinement group 100. This behavior happens because the number of receivers is more significant around the central transmitters, leading to higher number of pairs in this central area. Another observation is that refinement groups with a higher frequency (1.250 Hz) have less data when compared to a lower frequency (0.125 Hz). The reason is that lower frequencies are capable to penetrate further in the medium, resulting in

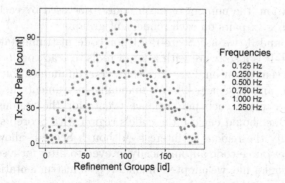

Fig. 5. Number of Rx-Tx pairs present on each of the refinement groups. The colors depict the CSEM frequency associated to each refinement group. (Color figure online)

more number of pairs in the dataset. While this example has been created with a MARE2DEM configuration setup that limits each refinement group to have only one frequency, one can change that parameter so one refinement group can have more frequencies. Such configurations would imply in a more elaborated mapping from data to refinement groups.

3   Methodology and Experimental Context

We adopted a five-step methodology to characterize the MARE2DEM application's behavior. 1) Code inspection to select the code's relevant regions and parameters. 2) Code instrumentation via manual region instrumentation and parameter-based profiling. 3) Parallel MARE2DEM execution for traces acquisition with the MR3D dataset. 4) Conversion from the OTF2 (Open Trace Format Version 2) traces to CSV (Comma-Separated Values) files with the inspected parameters. 5) Trace analysis and behavior characterization. These steps represent a cyclic process where step 1 may follow step 5 in a new analysis cycle. We repeat the cycle until a sufficient number of regions and parameters allow us to explain application behavior. In the following, we detail the software and hardware

In the first step, we started our search for the code's crucial regions by first looking at the wider regions and then refining it by inspecting the functions inside those regions. From the manager's code, we select three relevant regions: the application's main function, the iteration processing and phases processing. The other regions comes from the worker's code inspection: the refinement group processing, the subset-group processing, and the microkernels. The microkernels are the most elementary functions during the refinement group processing, we detail the worker's stack call in the next section. Then, we fully characterize each region by selecting a set of parameters to be collected. The parameters are the values of the variables present at the scope of each region. We select the following parameters for each worker's region: the iteration number, the phase name, the worker identification, the refinement group identification, the subset-group identification, the number of mesh nodes processed by each microkernel, the number of Rx-Tx pairs on each refinement group.

For steps 2 and 3, we use Score-P 7.0 for code instrumentation and trace gathering. Score-P is a software with a set of tools to track performance-related events such as event duration, hardware counters, communication metrics, function stack level, among others [9]. We manually instrument the MARE2DEM source code to capture such performance events for the regions identified in the first step. One should enclose the code's region with Scorep special flags to manually identify the regions of interest. Although Score-P allows to track all functions on the source code automatically or even to filter for a set of functions listed on a particular file, we adopted manual region instrumentation since it can increase control over the region's coverage and reduce instrumentation overhead significantly. This strategy allows one to group functions together or to even select a part of a function to be instrumented. Also, the control over the output trace file size increases. We also set the Score-P to collect the regions' start and end timestamp and the previously mentioned parameters.

In the third step, we use four computing nodes from our local cluster[2] . Each of the nodes is equipped with 2 Intel Xeon E5-2650v3 processors (20 cores, 40 threads) running at 2.3 GHz with 128 GB DDR4 RAM memory. The nodes run the Debian 10 (buster) operating system with the Linux kernel 4.19.0-20-amd64, and they are interconnected with a 1 Gbit/s local network. We configure the MPI (OpenMPI 3.1.4) to use all the available cores on each node, leading to 20 processes per node that were mapped into 79 MARE2DEM workers and 1 manager. For step 4, we use the otf2csv[3] tool to convert the OTF2 format to CSV and improve it to associate the parameters values with each tracked region. For the last step, we build a mean trace as a result of four executions of the application. Our mean trace represents the mean duration for each captured region by using an unique key created from the captured parameters. At least 99% of the regions have a relative standard error less than 5%, therefore our mean trace is considered representative. Furthermore, we conducted the traces analysis using reproducible notebooks filled with experiments annotations and R codes blocks with the Tidyverse package. We made available a reproducible companion[4] of the analysis phase associated with this article.

4   Results

We present the performance characterization by evaluating the MARE2DEM's elementary functions, called microkernels, and then by extending our analysis to wider regions such as iterations and refinement groups.

4.1   Performance Characterization of the Microkernels

The refinement groups represent the workload that each worker receives to compute independently. To compute each refinement group, the application needs to calculate 30 Fourier transformations. Those transformations are grouped in subset-groups of size 5. Figure 6 depicts the processing of the 7th refinement group (red rectangle) for the Jacobian and Smoothing phases. We show the elapsed time since the application's start in the X-axis, the colored rectangles represent the operations, and the rectangle position on the Y-axis represents the operation's stack level (operations on the top call the ones on the bottom). In what follows, we identify the worker's mesh copy as base-mesh. On each subset-group (orange rectangles), the worker refines its base-mesh on the first subset (blue rectangle, `local_refinement`). The following subsets at the same subset-group reuse the mesh previously refined. When moving to the next subset-group, the worker starts again by using the base-mesh. For example, in the first subset-group that contains the subsets from 1 to 5, the worker refines the base-mesh

---

[2] UFRGS-PCAD cluster: http://gppd-hpc.inf.ufrgs.br/.

[3] otf2csv: https://github.com/schnorr/otf2utils.

[4] Companion: https://github.com/Alves-Bruno/CARLA2022-companion.

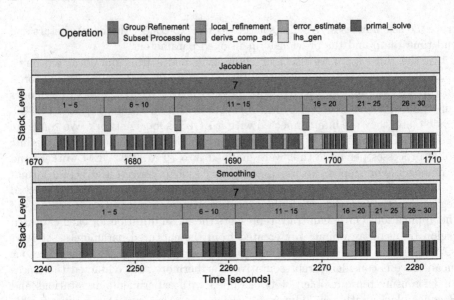

Fig. 6. Stack state of the refinement group processing (number 7) for both Jacobian and Smoothing phases: the orange rectangle shows the subset-group processing; the pink, green, brown, and yellow rectangles represent the microkernels. (Color figure online)

when processing subset 1 and then reuses the resulting refined mesh in the subsets 2 to 5. The operations at the bottom of each facet represent the microkernels (pink, green, yellow, and brown rectangles). They are the most basic operations carried out by MARE2DEM during the refinement group processing. The main functional difference between the phases is that the `derivs_comp_adj` operation is only present at the Jacobian phase.

We compare the relative time of each operation in order to determine the impact of the operations when compared to the total execution time taken by the application. The Table 1 resumes the operations' impact by showing the number of calls (instances), the relative time, and the variability (minimum, mean, and maximum durations) for each basic operation. The application spend more than 48% of its execution time in the `primal_solve`, and this operation has the highest number of instances. Thus the `primal_solve` is the most expensive operation. The `error_estimate` operation follows the `primal_solve` as the second most expensive operation by occupying a significant relative time and by having the higher mean duration. The `derivs_comp_adj` is a particular microkernel, since it is only present at the Jacobian phase. Thus, it leads to a low number of instances that consume a significant amount of (relative) time. Despite its number of instances, the `derivs_comp_adj` is considered expensive as the duration mean is the second highest when compared to the other microkernels. The `lhs_gen` and `local_refinement` represent less than 7% of the execution time, and we exclude the `local_refinement` operation from the following evaluations since this operation has the lowest instance number and its impact on the execution is low.

Table 1. Microkernel's impact on the MARE2DEM performance: the relative time, operation's variability (minimum, mean, and maximum durations), and number of instances called during execution for each microkernel.

Operation	Instances	Relative time	D. min	D. mean	D. max
local_refinement	43.3 K	3.14%	0.26 s	0.81 s	1.77 s
lhs_gen	304.1 K	3.86%	0.03 s	0.14 s	0.66 s
derivs_comp_adj	45.6 K	11.11%	0.03 s	2.72 s	19.01 s
error_estimate	105.3 K	33.72%	0.19 s	3.57 s	14.42 s
primal_solve	304.1 K	48.16%	0.20 s	1.77 s	8.41 s
Total →	802.4 K	100.00%	–	–	–

Figure 7 shows the duration (Y-axis) for each instance of the microkernels (facets) as a function of the number of processed nodes (X-axis). We can observe that error_estimate, lhs_gen, and primal_solve duration is strongly impacted by the number of processed mesh nodes in both phases. However, the derivs_comp_adj differs from the others microkernels because the number of processed mesh nodes cannot fully explain the duration. There are many instances with the same number of processed nodes, but with different durations. To fully understand this particular microkernel, we need to also consider the number of Rx-Tx pairs as an impacting factor. The derivs_comp_adj rightmost facet shows the number of Rx-Tx pairs with a binned color scale. Thus, we can conclude that the derivs_comp_adj duration is impacted by both the number of processed nodes and Rx-Tx pairs.

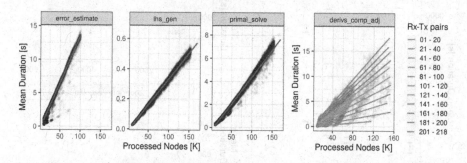

Fig. 7. Microkernels' duration of the Jacobian (all facets) and Smoothing (only the three facets from left-to-right) MARE2DEM phases as a function of the number of processed mesh nodes and Rx-Tx pairs (note the different Y scales).

4.2 Iterations and Refinement Groups

We now consider the previous parameters in evaluating the processing of the iterations and refinement groups. We start by taking a closer look into the iterations durations that is guided by the slowest parallel worker. Figure 8 shows (at the left) the mean duration (Y-axis) of each MARE2DEM's iteration (X-axis). Previous evaluations have revealed that the iterations' duration for both phases increases as the application progresses, and we confirm this for the present configuration. Besides that, we can observe that the Smoothing phase becomes more expensive than the Jacobian when considering the final iterations (iterations 5 to 8). The higher execution times observed at the Smoothing phase happens because the application may repeat the processing of all refinement groups due to convergence conditions controlling the search of the smallest roughness value. We show the number of repetitions needed for the Smoothing phase on each of the iterations (numeric labels on top of each point). Still in Fig. 8 (at the right), we show the duration as a function of the number of processed nodes. The number of processed nodes is a sum of the number of nodes present on the mesh at each microkernel function call on a given iteration. The iteration duration during Smoothing is completely explained by the number of processed nodes. However, this explanation remains insufficient when considering the Jacobian phase. For example, the iterations 3 and 5 (during Jacobian) decrease the duration from the previous iteration despite the increase of processed nodes.

Figuring out the size of the workloads is an important step towards distributing workloads efficiently among parallel workers. In this sense, we consider the duration of each refinement group as the size of the parallel tasks. The Fig. 9 shows the refinement groups' duration pattern (top-row) for the last four iterations, as they are the most expensive ones. We also show the processed

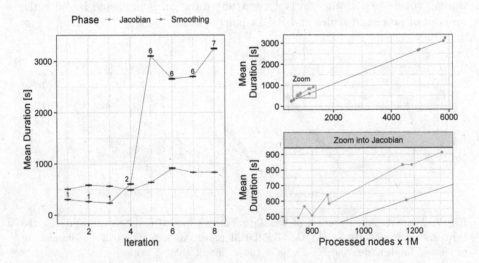

Fig. 8. The duration and number of processed nodes for each iteration and phase.

nodes pattern (bottom-row). The colors represents the 6 CSEM frequencies that reflects the Rx-Tx pairs showed on Fig. 5. The pairs count remains equal on all iterations as they represents the collected data. Despite the differences in scale, the pattern of processed nodes is similar for the two phases, where the central (near to 100) and central-right groups (100 to 160) have higher values than the side groups (0 to 25 and 175 to 206). However, the duration pattern is slightly different in the two phases. During Smoothing, the pattern of the groups follows the same pattern as in the bottom row. During the Jacobian, the pattern of refinement groups reflects a mix between what is shown in the bottom-row and the number of pairs on Fig. 5. Although the duration is strongly driven by the amount of processed nodes, there are differences between the two phases due to the presence of the `derivs_comp_adj` microkernel during the Jacobian.

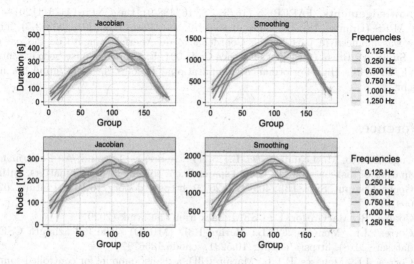

Fig. 9. The signature of each refinement group's duration and processed nodes at the last four iterations. The colours indicate the CSEM frequency of each group. Center and center-right groups are the ones that take longer to process. (Color figure online)

5   Conclusion

MARE2DEM is an open-source application for 2D resistivity modeling on the context of oil and gas exploration using CSEM data. In this work, we evaluated the performance of the MARE2DEM application when running with the Brazilian MR3D dataset. The code inspection, trace evaluation and performance visualization lead us to the following conclusions. The application spends more than 92% of the execution time on the `primal_solve`, `error_estimate` and `derivs_comp_adj` microkernels, hence those functions deserve some optimization efforts in a eventual code review. The imbalance on the parallel tasks, identified as refinement groups in the MARE2DEM terminology, is a consequence of the Adaptive Mesh Refinement algorithm that refines the groups differently depending on the configuration of the refinement group (number and placement of receivers, transmitters, and frequencies). The variability on the refinement groups' duration is mainly explained by the number of processed mesh nodes for both Jacobian and Smoothing phases. We show that the central and central-right refinement groups have longer execution times, while side groups need shorter execution times. In building a more efficient load distribution, one must consider the presented duration patterns for each of the CSEM frequencies used. As future work, we intend to conduct a wider performance analysis considering all possible configurations for the refinement groups definition during the MARE2DEM initialization phase. Our goal would be to estimate the best MARE2DEM's configuration for a given set of compute resources.

Acknowledgements. FAPERGS (16/354-8, 16/488-9), the CNPq (447311/2014-0), the CAPES (Brafitec 182/15, Cofecub 899/18), and Petrobras (2018/00263-5). This study was financed in part by the Coordenacao de Aperfeicoamento de Pessoal de Nivel Superior - Brasil (CAPES) - Finance Code 001. Experiments have been executed in INF/UFRGS's High-Performance Computational Resources, http://gppd-hpc.inf.ufrgs.br.

References

1. Cogo Miletto, M., Leandro Nesi, L., Mello Schnorr, L., Legrand, A.: Performance analysis of task-based multi-frontal sparse linear solvers: structure matters. Future Gener. Comput. Syst. **135**, 409–425 (2022). https://doi.org/10.1016/j.future.2022.05.013
2. Cooper, R., MacGregor, L.: CSEM: back from the brink (2020)
3. Correa, J.L., Menezes, P.T.L.: Marlim R3D (MR3D) - the full azimuth CSEM dataset (2018). https://doi.org/10.5281/zenodo.1256787
4. Correa, J.L., Menezes, P.T.L.: Marlim R3D: a realistic model for controlled-source electromagnetic simulations phase 2: the controlled-source electromagnetic data set. Geophysics **84**(5), E293–E299 (2019). https://doi.org/10.1190/geo2018-0452.1
5. Dagostini, J.I., da Silva, H.C.P., Pinto, V.G., Velho, R.M., Gastal, E.S.L., Schnorr, L.M.: Improving workload balance of a marine CSEM inversion application. In: 2021 IEEE International Parallel and Distributed Processing Symposium Workshops (IPDPSW), pp. 704–713 (2021). https://doi.org/10.1109/IPDPSW52791.2021.00107
6. Isaacs, K.E., et al.: State of the art of performance visualization. In: Borgo, R., Maciejewski, R., Viola, I. (eds.) EuroVis - STARs. The Eurographics Association (2014). https://doi.org/10.2312/eurovisstar.20141177
7. Key, K.: MARE2DEM: a 2-D inversion code for controlled-source electromagnetic and magnetotelluric data. Geophys. J. Int. **207**(1), 571–588 (2016). https://doi.org/10.1093/gji/ggw290
8. Key, K., Ovall, J.: A parallel goal-oriented adaptive finite element method for 2.5-d electromagnetic modelling. Geophys. J. Int. **186**(1), 137–154 (2011). https://doi.org/10.1111/j.1365-246X.2011.05025.x

9. Knüpfer, A., et al.: Score-P: a joint performance measurement run-time infrastructure for periscope, scalasca, tau, and vampir. In: Brunst, H., Müller, M.S., Nagel, W.E., Resch, M.M. (eds.) Tools for High Performance Computing 2011, pp. 79–91. Springer, Heidelberg (2012). https://doi.org/10.1007/978-3-642-31476-6_7

10. Nascimento, T.M., Menezes, P.T.L., Braga, I.L.: High-resolution acoustic impedance inversion to characterize turbidites at Marlim field, Campos basin, Brazil. Interpretation **2**(3), T143–T153 (2014). https://doi.org/10.1190/INT-2013-0137.1

11. Veroneze Solórzano, A.L., Leandro Nesi, L., Mello Schnorr, L.: Using visualization of performance data to investigate load imbalance of a geophysics parallel application. In: Practice and Experience in Advanced Research Computing, pp. 518–521. Association for Computing Machinery, New York (2020). https://doi.org/10.1145/3311790.3400844

12. Zhdanov, M.S.: Geophysical Electromagnetic Theory and Methods. Elsevier, Oxford (2009)

Time-Power-Energy Balance of BLAS Kernels in Modern FPGAs

Federico Favaro[1]([⊠]), Ernesto Dufrechou[2], Juan P. Oliver[1], and Pablo Ezzatti[2]

[1] Instituto de Ingeniería Eléctrica,
Facultad de Ingeniería, Universidad de la República, Montevideo, Uruguay
{ffavaro,jpo}@fing.edu.uy
[2] Instituto de Computación, Facultad de Ingeniería, Universidad de la República,
Montevideo, Uruguay
{edufrechou,pezzatti}@fing.edu.uy

Abstract. Numerical Linear Algebra (NLA) is a research field that in the last decades has been characterized by the use of kernel libraries that are de facto standards. One of the most remarkable examples, in particular in the HPC field, is the Basic Linear Algebra Subroutines (BLAS). Most BLAS operations are fundamental in multiple scientific algorithms because they generally constitute the most computationally expensive stage. For this reason, numerous efforts have been made to optimize such operations on various hardware platforms. There is a growing concern in the high-performance computing world about power consumption, making energy efficiency an extremely important quality when evaluating hardware platforms. Due to their greater energy efficiency, Field-Programmable Gate Arrays (FPGAs) are available today as an interesting alternative to other hardware platforms for the acceleration of this type of operation. Our study focuses on the evaluation of FPGAs to address dense NLA operations. Specifically, in this work we explore and evaluate the available options for two of the most representative kernels of BLAS, i.e. GEMV and GEMM. The experimental evaluation is carried out in an Alveo U50 accelerator card from Xilinx and an Intel Xeon Silver multicore CPU. Our findings show that even in kernels where the CPU reaches better runtimes, the FPGA counterpart is more energy efficient.

Keywords: Dense numerical linear algebra · Energy-efficiency · HPC · Matrix-matrix multiplication

1 Introduction

The Numerical Linear Algebra (NLA) is one of the most important fields in scientific computing. A support for this claim is the existence of several computational kernels involved in the most widespread benchmarks. One of the most notorious is the Linpack benchmark [12] that is employed to define the Top500 list [2]. This benchmark is based on the LU-factorization operation to compute

P. Navaux et al. (Eds.): CARLA 2022, CCIS 1660, pp. 78–89, 2022.
https://doi.org/10.1007/978-3-031-23821-5_6

the peak performance reached by a specific combination of a hardware platform and software implementations.

The LU-factorization is part of the LAPACK specification [3] and typically these kinds of methods are built over BLAS kernels. This philosophy of developing several layers of kernels specifications, has guided the dense NLA landscape since the 70s. Firstly, with the BLAS-1 specification [17], later with BLAS-2 [11] and BLAS-3 [10], and subsequently LAPACK and ScaLAPACK [7], this field offers a the facto standard for the definition and interoperativity of its basic kernels.

In recent years, another constraint that emerged in the HPC field, and in particular in NLA, is the energy consumption required to compute the different kernels [5,13,14]. This situation motivated, among other things, the development of the Green 500 list [1]. This effort reorders the Top500 hardware platform considering, instead of the attainable peak performance, the ratio between performance and energy consumption (e.g. GFLOPs per watts). Thus, in the last decade the energy consumption of both, algorithm and hardware platforms, has been a matter of utmost importance.

Field-Programmable Gate Arrays (FPGAs) technology is gaining attention in the HPC community. As a reconfigurable device, FPGAs are very efficient for implementing parallel algorithms. Even though they offer lower memory bandwidth and clock frequencies, FPGAs are becoming more powerful, narrowing the gap with other heterogeneous platforms like GPUs. They are still behind in raw computing power with GPUs, but given their considerably lower power consumption, there is an active topic of research for energy efficiency on FPGAs. In addition to the hardware upgrades, High-Level Synthesis (HLS) tools are becoming more and more refined which enables higher productivity and (may provide) more access to non-hardware experts.

In the previously described context we advance in the study of the potential of FPGAs to address NLA operations. More in detail, in this work we explore and evaluate the available options for two of the most representative kernels of BLAS, i.e. GEMV and GEMM. The experimental evaluation was carried out in an Alveo U50 accelerator card from Xilinx and an Intel Xeon Silver multi-core CPU. It shows that even in kernels where the CPU reaches better runtimes, the FPGA counterpart requires less energy consumption.

The rest of the paper is structured as follows. In Sect. 2 we summarize the main concepts of BLAS and the use of FPGAs platforms for HPC. Later, in Sect. 3, we present the different versions of both studied kernels. This is followed by the experimental evaluation in Sect. 4. Finally, in Sect. 5 we close with the main concluding remarks and some lines of future work.

2   FPGAs and NLA

In this section we briefly introduce the BLAS specifications and the main concepts related with the use of FPGAs for HPC.

2.1 BLAS

Numerical Linear Algebra (NLA) is a research field that in the last decades has been characterized by the use of kernel-libraries that are de facto standards. One of the most remarkable examples, in particular in the HPC field, is the Basic Linear Algebra Subroutines (BLAS) [8]. This library has become essential for HPC due to its efficiency, portability and availability. BLAS is composed of routines for computing common linear algebra operations. It is organized into levels according to the degree of complexity. The level 1 involves scalar, vector and vector-vector operations, the level 2 includes matrix-vector operations, and the level 3 performs matrix-matrix operations. BLAS libraries have become one of the main building blocks in linear algebra applications, such as solving linear system of equations, linear least square problems or eigenvalue problems. Two of the most important operations are GEMM and GEMV from levels 3 and 2 respectively. We describe these operations next.

GEMM This operation belongs to Level 3 of the BLAS specification [10] and is defined as follows:

$$C = \alpha A * B + \beta C \tag{1}$$

where A, B and C are matrices and α and β are scalars. This kernel is considered the main building block in dense linear algebra because many other operations can be expressed in terms of several GEMM invocations [6].

GEMV This operation is defined as follows:

$$y = \alpha A * x + \beta y \tag{2}$$

where A is a matrix, x and y are vectors and α and β are scalars. GEMV belongs to Level 2 of the BLAS specification.

2.2 FPGAs

FPGAs are composed of a matrix of configurable logic blocks (or logic elements) and hard coded blocks such as memories, hardware adder/multipliers (DSPs) and clock managers. On top of that, a programmable routing structure enables the interconnection of the different blocks. They also feature several programmable input/output pins that allow interfacing with the outside world.

To *program* an FPGA means that an actual electrical circuit is synthesized inside the device through the programmable logic's interconnection-elements and hard-coded blocks. This allows very low latency (as there is little to none control overhead), great flexibility (as they can be reprogrammed in the field), and fine-grained parallelism. From a technological perspective, FPGAs stand somewhere in between Application-Specific Integrated Circuits (ASICs) and general-purpose processors. One of the main advantages of FPGAs with respect to ASICs is that the first can be reprogrammed after the manufacturing process.

The clock's operating frequency of a given design depends on the synthesized circuit, but it is usually lower than other heterogeneous devices. FPGAs also offer lower peak floating-point performance than GPUs and even multi-core CPUs, and less memory bandwidth, but this may change at some point, as FPGA manufacturers are making big efforts to compete with GPU performance in these contexts.

Traditionally, FPGAs have been a good alternative in fixed-point, dataflow streaming applications, where they reach high speeds at excellent energy efficiency. Also, as opposed to CPUs and GPUs they natively support arbitrary precision bitwidths. However, their poor performance in floating-point arithmetic, in addition to the complex design flow kept them apart from the mainstream HPC world. This started to change recently, as modern high-end FPGA devices offer up to millions of logic elements, thousands of DSP blocks (that allow TFLOP performance) and high-bandwidth memory (HBM). These characteristics, in combination with the HLS tools available, are making these devices increasingly attractive in the HPC domain.

A brief review of the state of the art about the use of FPGAs to compute dense numerical algebra kernels can be found in F. Favaro et al. [15,16].

3 Evaluated Kernels

3.1 Vitis Libraries

Xilinx offers an extensive set of performance-optimized, open source libraries for use with Vitis software. Their repository includes common topics such as math, linear algebra, statistics, data management, and also domain specific libraries for image processing, computer vision, data compression, etc. For linear algebra, Xilinx developed Vitis BLAS Library, which is an FPGA implementation of the Basic Linear Algebra Subroutines (BLAS).

The library provides three levels of implementations (not to be confused with the BLAS levels organization): primitives (L1), kernels (L2), and software APIs (L3). L1 provides parametrized C++ implementations (to be compiled with HLS) of the basic operations found in BLAS. These primitives include modules for computations and for data movement. The first ones have streaming interfaces and carry out the operations, while the second ones move data between on-chip memory and the computation modules. This allows the programmer to construct high-performance logic by interconnecting computation and data mover modules. L2 offers kernel implementation examples aimed at host code developers. L3 provides C/C++ and Python APIs to allow software developers to accelerate BLAS operations using pre-built FPGA images.

For this work we evaluated the BLAS function kernels from L2. These kernels share the same top function, which has only two ports to communicate with external memory (DRAM, HBM or PLRAM). The kernels consist of an instruction processing block, a computation unit (e.g. GEMM), and a timer unit.

GEMM Basic: The architecture of this kernel is composed of the following blocks:

- Systolic array: Implemented using L1 primitives. Its size depends on the datatype and the memory interface. For single precision floating point and 512 bits interface it corresponds to 16×16.
- Data movers: These blocks get data from global memory and send it to the computation blocks, and vice versa.
- Transpose modules: One of the matrices must be transposed before entering the systolic array. This block also acts as a buffer to reuse data.

GEMM Multiple Compute Units (MCU): This kernel is implemented as two parallel instances (compute units) of the previous kernel. Each compute unit has its own dedicated HBM channel. The provided version of this kernel uses four compute units and its intended for the Alveo U250 board. In order to fit the design in the ALveo U50 board only 2 instances could be used. Also the DDR memory had to be changed for HBM.

GEMV Basic: This kernel follows the same structure as GEMM basic, but with a custom processing block to perform GEMV operation.

GEMV Streaming: This kernel does not follow the aforementioned BLAS kernels unique function architecture. Instead, it makes efficient use of the high-bandwidth memory. To maximize throughput, it instantiates 16 parallel GEMV compute blocks and connects each one to an individual HBM channel.

3.2 Matrix-Matrix Multiplication (MMM)

In order to obtain a point of comparison for the results of Vitis BLAS, we included in the evaluation a state of the art implementation for GEMM developed by J. de Fine Licht et al. [9]. They propose a matrix-matrix multiplication (MMM) implementation on FPGA aimed at minimizing off-chip data movement (by reusing data stored in fast on-chip memory) and maximizing performance (computations per I/O operation). They start with a general model for computation, I/O and resource utilization to create a hardware architecture that is highly optimized for the resource available on a target device.

Their I/O model assumes a parallel machine consisting on p processors, each one with S words of fast private memory. To perform an arithmetic operation, each processor must have all operands in its fast memory. They model the MMM algorithm as a computation directed acyclic graph (CDAG), where each vertex corresponds to a unique value during the execution and the edges represent data dependencies between them.

They constrain their model based on FPGA available resources and characteristics (number of ports and limited fan-out) to maximize the computation throughput and favour routability. They reach a logic hierarchy which encapsulates various FPGA resources and guides the implementation to minimize I/O and maximize performance. The implementation follows a systolic array architecture, were N_p processing elements (PE) consume pre-fetched elements of the matrices A and B in a stream-like fashion. Each PE holds N_c compute units (CU) and each one of them is capable of producing one output product (partial result of matrix C) every clock cycle. The PEs are encapsulated in compute tiles, which are in turn grouped in block tiles. On top, a memory tile encapsulates the block tiles, using all available memory blocks of the FPGA. The parallelism is determined by the number of compute units.

Their implementation is done in HLS C++, is flexible (parametrized), portable, scalable (adaptable to different FPGAs with different number of resources and with different characteristics) and open source (rare for highly tuned FPGA implementations).

They tested the implementation for different configurations of tiles size and number of CUs and for various data types, measuring performance and energy efficiency. Their design achieved 409 GOp/s 32-bit floating point performance, and 1.5 TOp/s 8-bit integer performance, utilizing more than 80% of hardware resources in a Xilinx VCU1525 accelerator board.

4   Experimental Evaluation

4.1   Setup

We used the following hardware for the experiments:

- An Alveo U50 FPGA accelerator card from Xilinx. The FPGA is based on the UltraScale+ architecture and includes 872K look-up tables, 1743K registers, 28 MB of internal RAM, and 5952 DSP blocks. The chip also has 8 GB of HBM RAM. The designs for this platform were compiled using Xilinx Vitis 2020.2.
- A system with an Intel Xeon Silver 4208 CPU with 8-cores running at 2.1 GHz, and 80 GB of RAM. The CPU implementations make use of Intel MKL library, using all 8 cores (8 threads) with SMT disabled and AVX2 instructions. This device is capable of AVX512, but we experimentally determined that using this feature in multicore execution severely limits the operating frequency of the cores, which degrades the performance.

We performed the characterization of performance and energy consumption as follows:

- In the Alveo U50 FPGA, the board has internal sensors that provide current, voltage, and temperature readings while the kernel is running. The driver Xilinx Runtime (XRT) sends these values to the host.
- In the Intel Xeon processor, we measured CPU and memory power consumption using RAPL (which provides an estimate of the dissipated power based on performance counters and a device power model).

- All power measurements were automated using PMlib [4]. Results are an average of readings collected during 2 min of execution, with an equal warm-up time before measuring.
- The runtime measurements are the average of multiple iterations of the kernels.

4.2 Experimental Results and Discussion

For the experimental evaluation, and as a baseline, we employ the BLAS implementations offered by MKL library on CPU.

All the results summarized in this section are the average of 10 independent executions. Also, in all cases we used single precision floating point.

The resource utilization of the implemented FPGA kernels is shown in Table 1.

Table 1. Resource utilization in percentage of available resources for the implemented FPGA kernels.

Type	Available	Utilization (%)				
		GEMV basic	GEMV streaming	GEMM basic	GEMM MCU	MMM
LUTs	870016	14.02	22.83	37.39	61.16	42.45
Registers	1740032	8.98	17.10	28.30	47.59	32.33
Block RAM	1344	16.22	16.07	18.34	22.84	53.27
DSPs	5940	0.29	9.87	20.94	41.82	46.13

In the first experiment we evaluate the computational performance reached by the different versions for the GEMV operation over square matrices of: 128, 256, 512, 1024, 2048, 4096 and 8192 columns. Specifically, Fig. 1 presents the GFLOPs achieved by all the evaluated variants.

Considering the obtained experimental results for the GEMV kernel, and with focus on the FPGAs variants, firstly we can say that the basic version is a non-competitive option. This implementation has very low levels of parallelism, because it performs the dot product on vectors of 16 elements. Also, due to a carried-dependency issue in the computation loop, it ends operating 4 times slower than intended. Next, for the small test cases the MMM reaches better runtimes than the Streaming variant, which has a poor performance for small matrices. However, for dimension bigger than 1024 the result is reversed. More in detail, the performance of the MMM variant is stagnant since matrices of 1024 while the Streaming counterpart is growing even for the largest matrices. The Streaming variant provides 16 times more parallelism than the basic version and takes advantage of the HBM on the Alveo board. The CPU version offers the best peak of performance for matrices of 1024 columns, but in the largest test

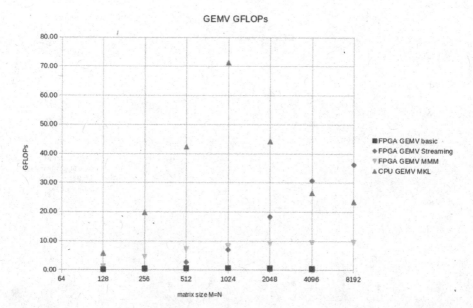

Fig. 1. Achieved performance (GFLOPs) of the GEMV kernels for different matrix sizes.

cases the performance is degraded. This result is reasonable taking into account the effects of the use of the cache memories.

Later, we evaluate the energy consumption implied by the different GEMV implementations. In this line, Fig. 2 presents the GFLOPs per watt achieved by the evaluated variants over the same range of matrices. Similar to the performance evaluation, the energy study allows us to conclude that the fastest GEMV version is, in general, the most energy-efficient option. However, in all cases the FPGAimplementations require less power than the CPU counterpart. Additionally, the MMM version uses, on average, less power than the Streaming variant. Finally, and as a remarkable aspect, the FPGA version outperforms (in the energy-consumption perspective) the CPU counterpart for the three largest dimensions.

The experimental results for the performance reached by the GEMM kernels is shown in Fig. 3. For this operation, the CPU variant is faster than the FPGA counterparts for all the evaluated matrix dimensions. With focus on the FPGA, the basic variant is far below the other versions in performance. For the basic and MCU GEMM kernels, performance climbs to a maximum around dimensions 1024 and then starts to degrade. The cause for this performance loss for the bigger sizes was not fully determined and needs to be further investigated. The MMM variant also peaks around size 1024 but the for bigger sizes the performance remains constant.

r

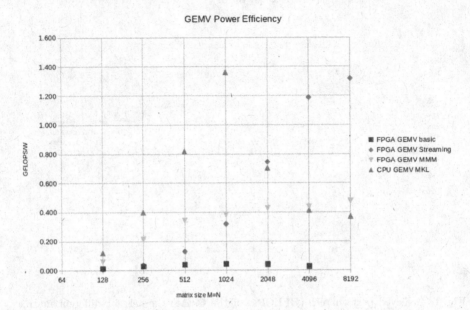

Fig. 2. Energy efficiency (GFLOPs/W) of the GEMV kernels for different matrix sizes.

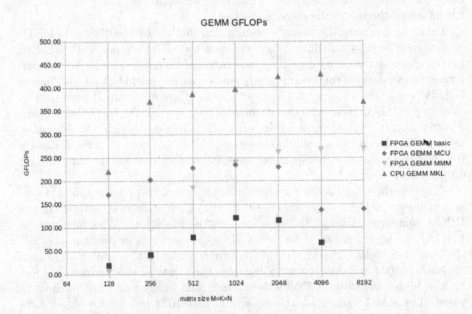

Fig. 3. Achieved performance (GFLOPs) of the GEMM kernels for different matrix sizes.

The energy consumption results for the GEMM kernels are summarized in Fig. 4. Contrary to the performance results achieved in the GEMV experiment, in this case the FPGA outperforms the CPU counterpart for six of seven matrix dimensions. This situation remarks the energy efficiency offered by the FPGA platforms, specially in this context where the CPU is faster than other versions. Neither of the Vitis BLAS versions manages to outperform the CPU in this case (except for the smallest matrix size). This is expected since the evaluated kernels for GEMM were designed for bigger FPGAs boards and are not optimized for the Alveo U50 platform (contrary to the Streaming GEMVwhich was designed for this board).

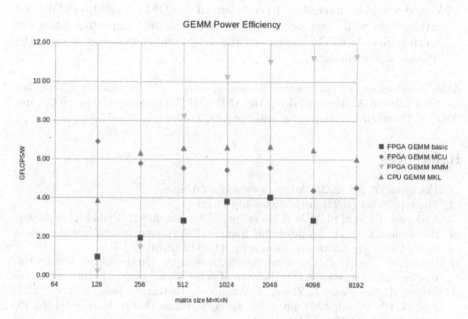

Fig. 4. Energy efficiency (GFLOPs/W) of the GEMM kernels for different matrix sizes.

5   Conclusions

In this article we have revisited the use of non-traditional HPC hardware to compute BLAS kernels. Specifically, we review the available kernels to compute the GEMV and GEMM kernels in FPGAs and also we extend and tune some other variants of these kernels. The experimental evaluation carried out over an Alveo U50 FPGA board shows that, in general, the CPU version outperforms in GFLOPs the FPGAs counterparts but the use of FPGAs offer more efficient variants from the energy consumption perspective. These results are very relevant. First, due to the importance of the energy consumption as a restriction in the HPC field and second, considering the years of development of CPU implementations compared to the recent focus on this kind of methods for FPGAs.

As a future line of work we identify several perspectives, following we describe the most important ones.

- Firstly, is mandatory to extend our study to include other FPGAs with different characteristics, among other Intel FPGAs.
- Secondly, the comparison should be done with other heterogeneous hardware platforms. In particular, comparing the FPGA kernels with implementations on cutting-edge GPUs and particularly low-consuming devices (such as ARM processors).
- Also, it would be interesting to complement the GFLOPs and GFLOPs per watt metrics with other perspectives, maybe the most important being the learning curve in FPGA design and the design and compilation times of the FPGAs implementations.

Acknowledgements. The researchers were supported by Universidad de la República and the PEDECIBA. We acknowledge the ANII – MPG Independent Research Groups: "Efficient Hetergenous Computing" with the CSC group.

References

1. The green500 list (2022). http://www.green500.org
2. The top500 list (2022). http://www.top500.org
3. Anderson, E., et al.: LAPACK Users' guide, 3rd edn. SIAM, Philadelphia (1999)
4. Barrachina, S., et al.: An integrated framework for power-performance analysis of parallel scientific workloads. Energy, pp. 114–119 (2013)
5. Benner, P., Ezzatti, P., Quintana-Ortí, E., Remón, A.: On the impact of optimization on the time-power-energy balance of dense linear algebra factorizations. In: Aversa, R., Kołodziej, J., Zhang, J., Amato, F., Fortino, G. (eds.) ICA3PP 2013, Part II. LNCS, vol. 8286, pp. 3–10. Springer, Cham (2013). https://doi.org/10.1007/978-3-319-03889-6_1
6. Bientinesi, P., et al.: Deriving dense linear algebra libraries. Formal Aspects Comput. **25**(6), 933–945 (2013)
7. Blackford, L.S., et al.: ScaLAPACK Users' Guide. SIAM, Philadelphia (1997)
8. Blackford, L.S., et al.: An updated set of basic linear algebra subprograms (BLAS). ACM Trans. Math. Softw. **28**(2), 135–151 (2002)
9. de Fine Licht, J., Kwasniewski, G., Hoefler, T.: Flexible communication avoiding matrix multiplication on FPGA with high-level synthesis. In: Proceedings of the 2020 ACM/SIGDA International Symposium on Field-Programmable Gate Arrays (FPGA), 23–25 Feb 2020, Seaside, CA, USA (2020)
10. Dongarra, J.J., Du Croz, J., Hammarling, S., Duff, I.S.: A set of level 3 basic linear algebra subprograms. ACM Trans. Math. Softw. **16**(1), 1–17 (1990)
11. Dongarra, J.J., Croz, J.D., Hammarling, S., Hanson, R.J.: An extended set of FORTRAN basic linear algebra subprograms. ACM Trans. Math. Softw. **14**(1), 1–17 (1988)
12. Dongarra, J.J., Luszczek, P., Petitet, A.: The LINPACK benchmark: past, present, and future (2002)

13. Dongarra, J., et al.: The international ExaScale software project roadmap. Int. J. High Perform. Comput. Appl. **25**(1), 3–60 (2011)
14. Ezzatti, P., Quintana-Ortí, E.S., Remón, A., Saak, J.: Power-aware computing. Concurrency Computa. Pract. Experience **31**(6), e5034 (2019)
15. Favaro, F., Dufrechou, E., Ezzatti, P., Oliver, J.P.: Energy-efficient algebra kernels in FPGA for High Performance Computing. **21** (2021)
16. Favaro, F., Oliver, J.P., Dufrechou, E., Ezzatti, P.: Understanding the performance of elementary NLA kernels in FPGAs. In: 2020 IEEE International Parallel and Distributed Processing Symposium Workshops (IPDPSW), pp. 479–482 (2020)
17. Lawson, C.L., Hanson, R.J., Kincaid, D.R., Krogh, F.T.: Basic linear algebra subprograms for Fortran usage. ACM Trans. Math. Softw. **5**(3), 308–323 (1979)

Improving Boundary Layer Predictions Using Parametric Physics-Aware Neural Networks

Antônio Tadeu Azevedo Gomes(✉) ⓘ, Larissa Miguez da Silva,
and Frédéric Valentin ⓘ

Laboratório Nacional de Computação Científica (LNCC), Av. Getúlio Vargas 333,
Quitandinha, Petrópolis-RJ, Brazil
{atagomes,lamiguez,valentin}@lncc.br

Abstract. *Physics-Informed Neural Networks* (PINNs) are machine
learning tools that approximate the solution of general partial differential equations (PDEs) by adding them in some form as terms of the
loss/cost function of a Neural Network. Most pieces of work in the area
of PINNs tackle *non-linear* PDEs. Nevertheless, many interesting problems involving linear PDEs may benefit from PINNs; these include parametric studies, multi-query problems, and parabolic (transient) PDEs.
The purpose of this paper is to explore PINNs for linear PDEs whose
solutions may present one or more *boundary layers*. More specifically, we
analyze the steady-state reaction-advection-diffusion equation in regimes
in which the diffusive coefficient is small in comparison with the reactive
or advective coefficients. We show that adding information about these
coefficients as predictor variables in a PINN results in better prediction
models than a PINN that only uses spatial information as predictor variables. Even though using these coefficients when training a PINN model
is a common strategy for inverse problems, to the best of our knowledge
we are the first to consider these coefficients for parametric direct problems. This finding may be instrumental in multiscale problems where the
coefficients of the PDEs present high variability in small spatiotemporal
regions of the domain, and therefore PINNs may be employed together
with domain decomposition techniques to efficiently approximate the
PDEs locally at each partition of the spatiotemporal domain, without
resorting to different learned PINN models at each of these partitions.

Keywords: Physics-informed neural networks · Boundary layer
problems · Multiscale methods

1 Introduction

Physics-Aware Neural Networks (NNs) are machine learning tools that approximate the solution of general partial differential equations (PDEs) by adding the

---

The authors are presented in alphabetical order.

ⓒ The Author(s), under exclusive license to Springer Nature Switzerland AG 2022
P. Navaux et al. (Eds.): CARLA 2022, CCIS 1660, pp. 90–102, 2022.
https://doi.org/10.1007/978-3-031-23821-5_7

physical laws these equations represent to some component of the neural network. The PINNs [19] are likely to be the most well-known of these NNs; the defining characteristic of a PINN is the inclusion of the strong form of a PDE (including its boundary and initial conditions) as terms of the loss/cost function.

Most pieces of work in the area of physics-aware NNs tackle *non-linear* PDEs [6,10,11,14,17]. Nevertheless, many interesting problems involving linear PDEs may benefit from physics-aware NNs; these include parametric studies, multi-query problems, and parabolic (transient) PDEs.

We are mostly interested in the solution of linear PDEs whose coefficients present high variability in small spatiotemporal regions of the physical domain. In this case, we say that the solution has a multiscale behavior. Standard numerical methods often present difficulties in approximating the solution to such PDEs with combined quality and computational affordability. Multiscale numerical methods (e.g. [9]) have emerged as an attractive option for dealing with such difficulties by rewriting the original formulation of the PDE in terms of: (i) local problems living each one in a partition of the physical domain; and (ii) a global problem that "glues together" the solution of the local problems. The price to pay is a potentially large number of local problems. Although said local problems are independent from one another, thus benefiting from massive parallel computations, they may still be computationally demanding.

The purpose of this paper is to investigate the potential of physics-aware NNs in general, and PINNs specifically, for efficiently solving local problems in multiscale numerical methods. We explore the particular case of linear PDEs whose solutions may present one or more *boundary layers*. More specifically, we analyze the steady-state reaction-advection-diffusion equation in regimes in which the diffusive coefficient is small in comparison with the reactive or advective coefficients. We verify that adding information about these coefficients as predictor variables in a PINN results in better prediction models than a PINN that only uses spatial information as predictor variables. Even though using these coefficients when training a PINN model is a common strategy for *inverse* problems, to the best of our knowledge we are the first to consider these coefficients for parametric direct problems. We believe this finding may be instrumental in multiscale problems, because it opens the path for PINNs to be employed together with domain decomposition techniques to efficiently approximate the PDEs locally at each partition of the spatiotemporal domain, without resorting to different learned PINN models at each of these partitions.

The remainder of this paper is structured as follows. In Sect. 2, we quickly review the related literature. In Sect. 3, we present the problem and the methodology for the proposed model. In Sect. 4, we examine two different cases of the target equation and the effectiveness of the proposed model. Finally, in Sect. 5, we report the conclusions of this work along with a discussion of future directions.

2 Related Work

In recent years, the use of algorithms that "learn" from data has caused great impact and change in several areas of science. Algorithms using NNs have been used in many problems governed by PDEs and presented satisfactory results [2, 15, 20, 21]. In particular, in [19] the methodology of PINNs was first proposed, combining the properties of universal approximation of NNs and the knowledge of physical laws described by PDEs. Since then, many pieces of work have been published on this topic [3, 16, 18]. However, problems with complex geometry domains have led to other methodologies based on domain decomposition methods and PINNs, including Extended PINNs (XPINNs) [12], Conservative PINNs (cPINNs) [11] and Variational PINNs (VPINNs) [14].

Although the aforementioned pieces of work have shown excellent results, there are still many theoretical gaps that need to be filled. The techniques are new and do not have a trivial application in the solution of physical problems. For instance, a particularly complex step in formulating deep learning problems and PINNs is the definition of the loss functional to be minimized. Additionally, there are many hyperparameters to be configured and, although the automatic selection of hyperparameters is possible, there is usually a large computational cost. Interestingly, this last problem also exists somehow in a handful of multiscale methods with regard to their configuration parameters (e.g. [7, 8]).

There is a growing number of papers relating multiscale methods and data-driven approaches [4, 5, 13, 22]. To the best of our knowledge, none of these pieces of work tackle the problem the way we do, which is by training a single machine learning model that may be parameterized for approximating the solution of a PDE with highly variable coefficients in the spatial domain.

3   Methodology

3.1   Boundary Layer Problem

The boundary layer problem can appear in many applications, including fluid dynamics, meteorology, atomic reactors, among others. This phenomenon occurs when the gradient is high in the region close to the boundary and can bring instability to the discrete solution of the problem. Next, we present an example for this case.

Consider the case in which the reaction-advection-diffusion problem has an exact solution which contains boundary layers. This happens when the reactive or advective coefficient dominates the diffusive one. We consider the following reaction-advection-diffusion problem: *Find $u \in H^1(\Omega)$ such that:*

$$
\begin{cases}
\nabla \cdot (-\mathcal{K}\nabla u + \alpha u) + \sigma u = 1 \text{ in } \Omega, \\
u = 0 \text{ on } \partial\Omega_D, \\
\nabla u \cdot \mathbf{n} = 0 \text{ on } \partial\Omega_N,
\end{cases}
\tag{1}
$$

where Ω is a unit square domain, $\partial\Omega_D$ corresponds to the boundaries $x = (0, y)$ and $x = (1, y)$, with $y \in (0, 1)$, where homogeneous Dirichlet conditions are to be enforced, and $\partial\Omega_N = \partial\Omega \backslash \partial\Omega_D$ corresponds to the boundaries where homogeneous Neumann conditions are to be enforced. The coefficients are such that $\alpha := (a, 0)^T$, $\mathcal{K} = k\mathcal{I}$, where $\mathcal{I}$ is the identity matrix and a, k, $\sigma \in \mathbb{R}$. If $\sigma > 0$, the analytical solution to this equation is:

$$u(x,y) = \frac{\sinh(\frac{\sqrt{4k\sigma}}{2k}(x-1)) - \sinh(\frac{\sqrt{4k\sigma}}{2k}x)}{\sinh(\frac{\sqrt{a^2+4k\sigma}}{2k})} + 1,$$

Otherwise, if $\sigma = 0$ and $a > 0$, then the exact solution becomes

$$u(x,y) = \frac{1}{a}\left(x - \frac{\sinh(\frac{\sqrt{a}}{2k}x)}{\sinh(\frac{\sqrt{a}}{2k})} e^{\frac{\sqrt{a}}{2k}(x-1)} \right)$$

We consider two experimental settings. First, in Subsect. 4.1 we will assume $\sigma = 1$ and $a = 0$. So, we will explore the case in which the reactive coefficient dominates the diffusive one. Next, in Subsect. 4.2 we will consider the case in which the advective coefficient dominates by assuming that $\sigma = 0$ and $a = 1$.

3.2 Architecture Design

To solve the problem presented in Subsect. 3.1, we use the PINN depicted in Fig. 1. A key feature of this PINN is the use of the diffusion coefficient k as a predictor variable together with the spatial data (x, y). This way, we aim at getting a model capable of making predictions for different diffusion coefficients.

We assume a feed-forward NN with the following structure: 4 fully connected layers each containing 24 neurons and each followed by a hyperbolic tangent activation function. Furthermore, we use one output layer of size 1 and a linear activation function. These hyperparameters as well as all other configurations not explicitly explained in the remainder of the text have been determined empirically.

For the sake of comparison, we establish two scenarios for the input layer, as will be further explained in the following section: (i) *Scenario 1*, with only 2 neurons, input k being taken out; (ii) *Scenario 2* with 3 neurons, exactly as shown in Fig. 1.

Also, we considered the loss function

$$\phi_\theta(X) := c_1\phi_\theta^{bd}(X^{bd}) + c_2\phi_\theta^{bn}(X^{bn}) + c_3\phi_\theta^r(X^r), \tag{2}$$

as a function of the training data, as also explained in the following section.

4 Experimental Results

In this section, we present some numerical results that show the performance of PINNs to solve the boundary layer problem.[1] In our simulations, we consider the following scenarios:

---

[1] The experiments presented in this paper can be reproduced in Google Colaboratory: https://colab.research.google.com/drive/1dzzK41xIrmi5ozzO4IzBnkktGjI90j_-.

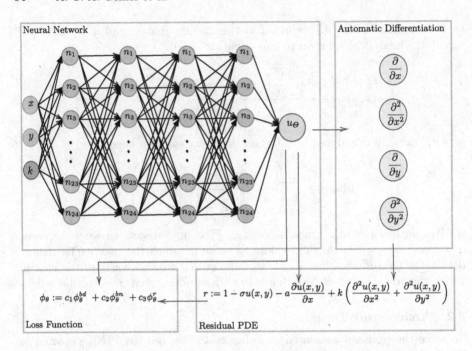

Fig. 1. PINN architecture for Reaction-Advection-Diffusion problem.

Scenario 1: We fix a diffusion coefficient k, train the network for some collocation and boundary points and predict others. Therefore, the input parameters of the network are (x, y) and the output is the solution u.

Scenario 2: We vary the diffusion coefficient k and train the network for some k to predict. Therefore, the input parameters of the network are (x, y, k) and the output is the solution u.

The collocation points are given by X_r, the boundary data is in X_{bd} and X_{bn}, where X_{bd} represents the data on the Dirichlet boundary Ω_D and X_{bn} the data on the Neumann boundary Ω_N. Respectively, on those boundary points, we have the solutions u_{bd} and u_{bn}. Additionally, the coefficients c_1, c_2 and c_3 representing the weights of each loss term are hyperparameters of the model, and their values have been chosen empirically based on the knowledge of the authors about the behavior of Eq. 1 for different values of its coefficients.

We assume that the collocation points X_r as well as the points for the boundary data X_{bd} and X_{bn} are randomly sampled from a uniform distribution.

4.1   First Setting: Reaction-Diffusion Problem

For this first problem, we began with a training data of size $N_{bd} = N_{bn} = 200$ and $N_r = 1000$, where N_{bd} is when we apply the Dirichlet boundary condition and N_{bn} when we apply the Neumann boundary condition. We illustrate this setting in Fig. 2.

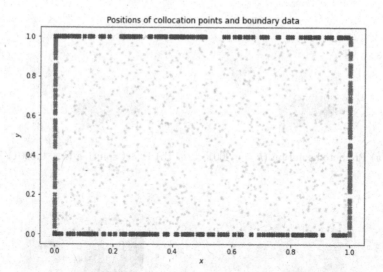

Fig. 2. The collocation points (red circles) and the positions where the Dirichlet boundary condition (blue cross marks) and the Neumann boundary condition (green cross marks) will be weakly imposed. (Color figure online)

Figure 3 depicts some experimental results for Scenario 1. We observe that as we shrink the diffusive coefficient k, the solution gets worse, with some undesired features when $k = 0.0001$ and $k = 0.00001$. (Nonetheless, we see in Fig. 6 that the PINN is able to approximate the solution with a small error when $k = 1.0$, $k = 0.1$, and $k = 0.01$.) Besides the difficulty of approximating the solution in the case where we have a very small k, another disadvantage of this approach is that the model needs to be retrained for each new k.

For Scenario 2, we add 20 different, randomly sampled $k \in (0.0001, 1.0)$ to the input data. First, we investigate the sensitivity of the PINN with respect to the amount and dispersion of collocation training points in Scenario 2. In Fig. 4, we show the exact solution and the solution field generated by a PINN with decreasing values of k, for different amounts of collocation and boundary points. We plot a cut for a fixed y; the exact solutions are represented by the solid lines and the predicted PINN solutions are represented by the dotted lines.

We can observe that the proposed PINN architecture for Scenario 2 interpolates quite well for values of k greater than or equal to 0.001, but for $k = 0.0001$ we have significant errors. Once more we see the impact of the boundary layer problem on the predictions.

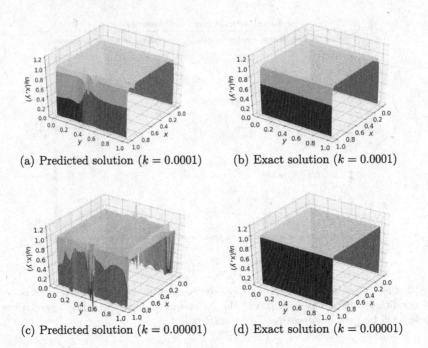

(a) Predicted solution ($k = 0.0001$)   (b) Exact solution ($k = 0.0001$)

(c) Predicted solution ($k = 0.00001$)   (d) Exact solution ($k = 0.00001$)

Fig. 3. Scenario 1, reaction-diffusion setting: predicted solution vs exact solution with respect to parameter k.

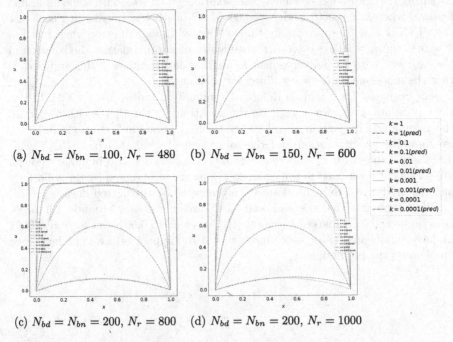

(a) $N_{bd} = N_{bn} = 100$, $N_r = 480$ (b) $N_{bd} = N_{bn} = 150$, $N_r = 600$

(c) $N_{bd} = N_{bn} = 200$, $N_r = 800$ (d) $N_{bd} = N_{bn} = 200$, $N_r = 1000$

$k = 1$
$k = 1(pred)$
$k = 0.1$
$k = 0.1(pred)$
$k = 0.01$
$k = 0.01(pred)$
$k = 0.001$
$k = 0.001(pred)$
$k = 0.0001$
$k = 0.0001(pred)$

Fig. 4. Scenario 2, reaction-diffusion setting: sensitivity analysis with respect to the size of the training data.

In the above experiments we trained the PINNs with $c_1 = 2$, $c_2 = 1$ and $c_3 = 0.01$ as the weights of the loss terms. In Fig. 5 we show the sensitivity of the model for Scenario 2 with respect to the loss weights.

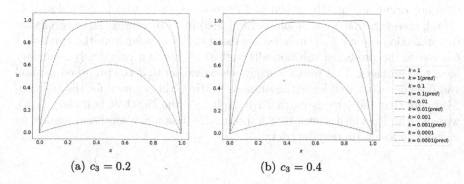

(a) $c_3 = 0.2$ (b) $c_3 = 0.4$

Fig. 5. Scenario 2, reaction-diffusion setting: sensitivity analysis with respect to loss weights.

For the cases presented in Fig. 5 we used $N_{bd} = N_{bn} = 100$, $N_r = 240$. The results are even more impressive because the PINN algorithm in Scenario 2 is able to reconstruct the solution field with high precision from a small number of points used for the training, even for the case where we have a very small k. Therefore, the results clearly show the impact of the loss weights on the training.

Finally, we compare the errors originating from Scenario 1 and Scenario 2. We use the Relative Mean Square Error (RMSE) to compare the results of the different scenarios, as presented in Fig. 6. We observe a significant error increase with a decaying k for Scenario 1, whereas for Scenario 2 this increase is much slower, specially for $k \in (0.001, 1.0)$. However, the much higher errors for Scenario 2 with larger values of k are still largely unexplained and motivates a series of investigations as part of our future work.

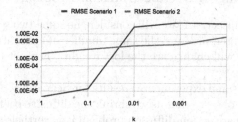

Fig. 6. Quality of prediction for the reaction dominant case (log-log scale).

Now, we take advantage of the fact that we can predict for different values of k in Scenario 2 and try to perform an extrapolation. The results are presented in Fig. 7, in which we plot two different cases. In Fig. 7(a), we extrapolate for an even smaller k, where the boundary layer problem is more evident. Even so, we still get a good approximation; we believe this is due to the fact that the diffusion coefficient is close to the range of k used for the training. The same does not occur in Fig. 7(b), when we try to extrapolate to a larger value of k. (Mind, however, that we have plotted Fig. 7(b) in a different scale, to emphasize the prediction error.) The curve for the exact solution is far from the curve that represents the predicted solution although this case is a completely boundary layer free problem. This result is likely an indication that the proposed method still does not work well for extrapolations far from the set used for the training. Also note that the error is particularly high near the Dirichlet boundary $(1, y)$, with $y \in (0, 1)$, which shows that imposing the boundary condition weakly by means of a loss term may be tricky.

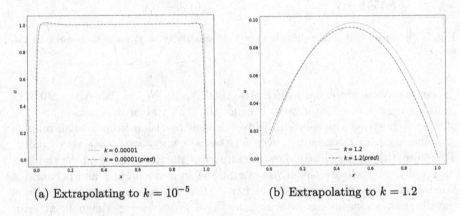

(a) Extrapolating to $k = 10^{-5}$ (b) Extrapolating to $k = 1.2$

Fig. 7. Scenario 2, reaction-diffusion setting: extrapolating for different values of k.

4.2   Second Setting: Advection-Diffusion Problem

Here, similarly to Subsect. 4.1, we will consider the same two scenarios, as well as the same PINN architecture, and the same number of collocation points already described. What we will change are the loss weights, now set to $c_1 = 1$, $c_2 = 1.2$ and $c_3 = 1$.

Figure 8 depicts some experimental results for Scenario 1. As in the reaction-diffusion setting, we observe that as we shrink the diffusive coefficient k, the solution gets worse. The advection-diffusion problem is nevertheless much tougher to approximate well than the reaction-diffusion problem. The figure clearly shows this, with completely wrong solutions when $k = 0.01$ and $k = 0.001$.

For Scenario 2, we add 20 different, randomly sampled $k \in (0.001, 1.0)$ to the input data. In Fig. 9, we show the exact solution and the solution field generated by a PINN with decreasing values of k for this scenario. The results are again

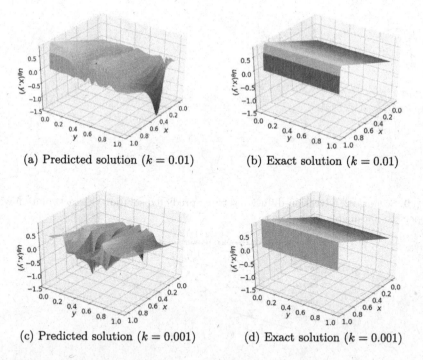

(a) Predicted solution ($k = 0.01$)   (b) Exact solution ($k = 0.01$)

(c) Predicted solution ($k = 0.001$)   (d) Exact solution ($k = 0.001$)

Fig. 8. Scenario 1, advection-diffusion setting: predicted solution vs exact solution with respect to parameter k.

impressive; the PINN algorithm in Scenario 2 is able to reconstruct the solution field with high precision from a small number of points used for the training, even for the case where we have a very small k.

Lastly, Fig. 10 presents the RMSE originating from Scenario 1 and Scenario 2. Again, for Scenario 2 the increase in the error is much slower than for Scenario 1. Nevertheless, as in the reaction-diffusion case, the much higher errors for Scenario 2 with larger values of k are still largely unexplained and motivates a series of investigations as part of our future work.

5   Summary and Outlook

The results presented herein clearly show the potential of PINNs for predicting the solution of PDEs with complex geometries and highly variable coefficients. Bringing physical coefficients into the training stage is key to avoiding the discrete solution's spurious oscillatory behavior in singularly perturbed regimes. In addition, it allows obtaining an accurate parameterization of the discrete solution concerning the physical coefficient in the interpolation scenario. However, when we extrapolate, we can observe that this methodology will hardly overcome the numerical methods to solve direct linear problems and, while automatic hyperparameter selection is possible, it can be expensive.

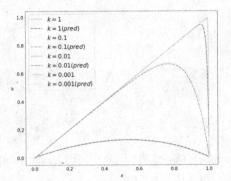

Fig. 9. Scenario 2, advection-diffusion setting: predicted solution vs exact solution with respect to parameter k.

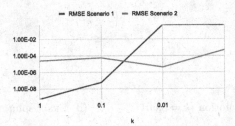

Fig. 10. Quality of prediction for the advection dominant case (log-log scale).

One way to solve this problem is to combine the strengths of numerical methods and data science by creating hybrid combinations of theory-based and data science models. We will focus on the family of Multiscale Hybrid-Mixed (MHM) methods [1,9] and their interaction with PINNs. The MHM methods are attractive because of their approximation properties and massive parallelization capability, which allows the physical properties of the model to be treated locally and efficiently, thanks to the concept of local multiscale functions. So, we envision PINNs being used within MHM as surrogate models to predict the shape of the multiscale basis functions in parallel, among other possibilities. This combination will be the subject for future work.

Other topics for future work include: (i) to explore alternatives to impose boundary conditions strongly (e.g. as in [6]); (ii) to apply the technique to other parametric studies, such as solutions with oscillatory behavior arising in oscillatory coefficient models or wave equation propagation problems; (iii) to consider the use of PINNs for other expensive linear problems, such as in multi-query scenarios.

Acknowledgment. The authors were supported by CAPES/Brazil under Project EOLIS (No. 88881.520197/2020-01). Frédéric Valentin was supported by Inria/France under the Inria International Chair, by CNPq/Brazil under Project No. 309173/2020-5, and by FAPERJ/Brazil under Project No. E-26/201.182/2021.

References

1. Barrenechea, G., Jaillet, F., Paredes, D., Valentin, F.: The multiscale hybrid mixed method in general polygonal meshes. Numerische Mathematik **145**(1), 197–237 (2020). https://doi.org/10.1007/s00211-020-01103-5
2. Berg, J., Nyström, K.: A unified deep artificial neural network approach to partial differential equations in complex geometries. Neurocomputing **317**, 28–41 (2018)
3. Cai, S., Wang, Z., Wang, S., Perdikaris, P., Karniadakis, G.E.: Physics-informed neural networks for heat transfer problems. J. Heat Transfer **143**(6), 060801 (2021)
4. Capuano, G., Rimoli, J.J.: Smart finite elements: a novel machine learning application. Comput. Methods Appl. Mech. Eng. **345**, 363–381 (2019)
5. Chan, S., Elsheikh, A.H.: A machine learning approach for efficient uncertainty quantification using multiscale methods. J. Comput. Phys. **354**, 493–511 (2018)
6. E, W., Yu, B.: The deep Ritz method: a deep learning-based numerical algorithm for solving variational problems. Commun. Math. Stat. **6**(1), 1–12 (2018). https://doi.org/10.1007/s40304-018-0127-z
7. Fabian, J.H.L., Gomes, A.T.A., Ogasawara, E.: Estimating the execution time of fully-online multiscale numerical simulations. In: Proceedings of the XXI Brazilian Symposium on High-Performance Computing Systems (WSCAD), pp. 191–202. Sociedade Brasileira de Computação (2020)
8. Fabian, J.H.L., Gomes, A.T.A., Ogasawara, E.: Estimating the execution time of the coupled stage in multiscale numerical simulations. In: Nesmachnow, S., Castro, H., Tchernykh, A. (eds.) CARLA 2020. CCIS, vol. 1327, pp. 86–100. Springer, Cham (2021). https://doi.org/10.1007/978-3-030-68035-0_7
9. Harder, C., Paredes, D., Valentin, F.: On a multiscale hybrid-mixed method for advective-reactive dominated problems with heterogeneous coefficients. Multiscale Model. Simul. **13**(2), 491–518 (2015)
10. Jagtap, A., Karniadakis, G.: Extended physics-informed neural networks (XPINNs): a generalized space-time domain decomposition based deep learning framework for nonlinear partial differential equations. Commun. Comput. Phys. **28**(5), 2002–2041 (2020). https://global-sci.org/intro/article_detail/cicp/18403.html
11. Jagtap, A.D., Kharazmi, E., Karniadakis, G.E.: Conservative physics-informed neural networks on discrete domains for conservation laws: applications to forward and inverse problems. Comput. Methods Appl. Mech. Eng. **365**, 113028 (2020). https://www.sciencedirect.com/science/article/pii/S0045782520302127
12. Jagtap, A.D., Karniadakis, G.E.: Extended physics-informed neural networks (XPINNs): a generalized space-time domain decomposition based deep learning framework for nonlinear partial differential equations. In: AAAI Spring Symposium: MLPS (2021)
13. Karpatne, A., Watkins, W., Read, J., Kumar, V.: Physics-guided neural networks (PGNN): an application in lake temperature modeling. arXiv preprint arXiv:1710.11431 (2017)
14. Kharazmi, E., Zhang, Z., Karniadakis, G.E.: Variational physics-informed neural networks for solving partial differential equations (2019). https://arxiv.org/abs/1912.00873

15. Lagaris, I.E., Likas, A., Fotiadis, D.I.: Artificial neural networks for solving ordinary and partial differential equations. IEEE Trans. Neural Netw. **9**(5), 987–1000 (1998)

16. Mao, Z., Jagtap, A.D., Karniadakis, G.E.: Physics-informed neural networks for high-speed flows. Comput. Methods Appl. Mech. Eng. **360**, 112789 (2020)

17. Liao, Y., Ming, P.: Deep Nitsche method: deep Ritz method with essential boundary conditions. Commun. Comput. Phys. **29**(5), 1365–1384 (2021). https://doi. org/10.4208/cicp.OA-2020-0219

18. Misyris, G.S., Venzke, A., Chatzivasileiadis, S.: Physics-informed neural networks for power systems. In: 2020 IEEE Power & Energy Society General Meeting (PESGM), pp. 1–5. IEEE (2020)

19. Raissi, M., Perdikaris, P., Karniadakis, G.: Physics-informed neural networks: a deep learning framework for solving forward and inverse problems involving nonlinear partial differential equations. J. Comput. Phys. **378**, 686–707 (2019). https:// www.sciencedirect.com/science/article/pii/S0021999118307125

20. Raissi, M., Karniadakis, G.E.: Hidden physics models: machine learning of nonlinear partial differential equations. J. Comput. Phys. **357**, 125–141 (2018)

21. Sirignano, J., Spiliopoulos, K.: DGM: a deep learning algorithm for solving partial differential equations. J. Comput. Phys. **375**, 1339–1364 (2018)

22. Yeung, T.S.A., Chung, E.T., See, S.: A deep learning based nonlinear upscaling method for transport equations. arXiv preprint arXiv:2007.03432 (2020)

Towards Fire Identification Model in Satellite Images Using HPC Embedded Systems and AI

Jhon Deivy Perez Arguello[1,2,4](✉) ⓘ, Carlos J. Barrios Hernández[1,2,4] ⓘ,
and Julián Rodriguez Ferreira[1,2,3,4] ⓘ

[1] Universidad Industrial de Santander (UIS), Bucaramanga, Colombia
jhon2198570@correo.uis.edu.co, {cbarrios,jgrodrif}@uis.edu.co
[2] High Performance and Scientific Computing Center (SC3UIS), Bucaramanga, Colombia
[3] Electronic Control, Simulation and Modelling Group (CEMOS), Bucaramanga, Colombia
[4] Advanced and Large Scale Computing Group (CAGE), Bucaramanga, Colombia

Abstract. Forest fires and environmental disasters that are rarely avoided due to Forest fires are environmental disasters is a crucial problem to resolve with High Performance Computing (HPC) due to the real-time need to avoid the reaction of the control agencies and the community. One of the strategies to support early warnings related to forest fires is using space technology and realtime image treatment. However, the large amount of data given by the satellite images, the cost of the satellite technology, and the difficulty of accessing remote places information make it challenging to deal with the problem. This project presents the development of a solution that fights fires through identification supported using artificial intelligence (AI), mainly Convolutional Neural Networks (CNN) and Computer Vision (CV). Space technology captures images in various spectral frequency ranges by optical instruments onboard artificial satellites. In addition, the solution deploys on a low-cost and easily accessible open-source embedded system, which allows its scope to be extended for use on mobile device applications such as robots, and uncrewed aerial vehicles, among others. This paper reflects the progress achieved within the project, mainly the creation of an open-source dataset of satellite images for fire classification, the election, conditioning, and training of the CNN.

Keywords: Satellite images · Computer vision · HPC embedded system · Artificial intelligence · Data analytics · Convolutional neural networks · Open-source

1 Introduction

The exponential development of the hardware required to execute algorithms and computational techniques has enabled the use of technologies such as Computer Vision (CV) or Machine Learning (ML) for solving specific problems [1]. These problems are notable for their intensive data handling in processes with high computational costs. However, advances in micro and nano electronics promote the use of compact (embedded) devices with low monetary cost and energy consumption as support for the solution to these

P. Navaux et al. (Eds.): CARLA 2022, CCIS 1660, pp. 103–115, 2022.
https://doi.org/10.1007/978-3-031-23821-5_8

problems [2]. One of these embedded systems, the NVIDIA Jetson Nano card [3], is widely used in prototyping and academic projects due to its good quality/price ratio.

One of these problems is finding fires from orbit. Although there are tools for this task [4], its identification continues to develop due to continuous improvements in algorithms, image processing, available instruments, and satellite communication.

Free access images from various satellites that observe the Earth at different wavelengths are used during this research. A dataset was created in which forest fires were observed from when they were small conflagrations until they became large fires. Finally, various characteristics are identified in the images, which using CNN and Computer Vision algorithms in embedded systems, allow the identification of said fires.

This paper presents the progress achieved in creating an alternative fire classification model to the current solutions, as an early warning so that the pertinent organisms act and evaluate the damage. For this, in the next Related Works section, a state of the art and some similar projects are exhibited resalting application goals, in this case, satellite imagery. The results section shows the creation of a dataset using images from the VIIRS sensor of the NOAA-20 and S-NPP satellites in which forest fires were analyzed from when they were small until they became large conflagrations, and later the performance of the CNNs in training with these images is shown. Finally, some conclusions and further work are presented.

2   Related Works

This section shows, firstly, a project that proposes a workflow for the identifying objects in satellite images with the help of machine learning technology, and secondly, a project to create small CNNs that reduce the computational load, useful to be deployed on embedded systems.

2.1   Satellite Imagery Multiscale Rapid Detection With Windowed Networks

Detecting small objects over large areas is a significant challenge in satellite imagery analysis. The main problems they face are a large number of pixels (more than 250 million), the geographical extension (more than 64 Km^2), or the tiny size of the objects of interest (less than 10 pixels). For which this research proposes a workflow called Satellite Imagery Multiscale Rapid Detection with Windowed Networks (SIMRDWN) [5], which evaluates satellite images of an arbitrarily large size at native resolution at speed greater than or equal to 0.2 km^2/s.

The SIMRDWN pipeline includes and compares the performance of some frameworks, where a version known as YOLT [6] is found, along with the TensorFlow object detection API models: SSD [7] and FASTER R-CNN [8]. This allows objects of very different scales to be quickly detected with relatively little training data across multiple sensors.

2.2 Lapped Convolutional Neural Networks for Embedded Systems

CNN has made numerous advances in many artificial intelligence applications. However, its complexity is quite relatively, usually requiring an expensive GPU (Graphics Processing Unit) [9] or FPGA (Field Programmable Logic Gate Array) [10] implementation, which is not cost-effective for many embedded systems. In this project, a new CNN or Lapped CNN (LCNN) architecture is developed that is suitable for resource-limited embedded systems [11].

The network is designed so that it can be decomposed into two or more stages. A hardware module can implement each with low complexity and low-resolution input.

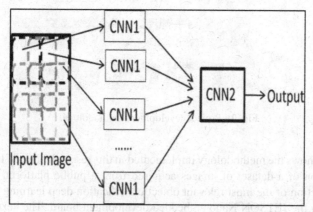

Fig. 1. Lapped convolutional neural networks.

Figure 1 show that the original input image is divide into some sub-images of the same size, with correctly designed overlaps with each other. The hardware module that implements the first stage of the CNN processes these sub-images sequentially. The outputs of different sub-images are merge and processed in the following low-cost hardware CNN module.

The result is the same as applying a larger-scale CNN to the entire image with higher resolution. Therefore, a lower-cost, larger-scale CNN system can be achieve by reusing inexpensive hardware CNN modules. Experimental results demonstrate the performance of the proposed scheme. This approach enables more cost-effective CNN solutions for some embedded systems. It is well suited for applications where basic deep learning capabilities are required but where constraints on computational cost and power consumption must also be met.

This proposal is in the convergence of the recognition of objects in satellite images with the deployment of CNNs in embedded systems. It seeks to present another solution to the identification of forest fires that contains the union of said technologies following an implementation methodology shown in the following section.

3   Workflow

The methodology used in this research work is based on the AI life cycle [12], grouping 19 development stages into 4 phases as seen in Fig. 2.

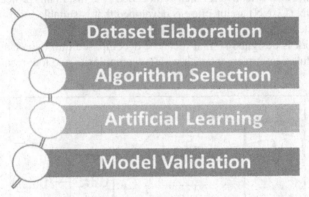

Fig. 2. Project development methodology.

Figure 2 shows the methodology implemented in this research project. It begins with the elaboration of a dataset of images acquired from a public platform. It continues with the selection of the most relevant object classification deep learning algorithm to implement on the JETSON Nano embedded development board. The next stage is the training of the neural network with the structured data set. The last activity corresponds to the validation of the model through its deployment in the embedded system.

3.1   Dataset Elaboration

The satellite images that make up the dataset were obtained from NASA's public access platform called WORLDVIEW [13], which shows photographs of the eEarthin a timeline with different wavelengths. From there, 1100 images were downloaded in various combinations of spectral bands generated by an optical sensor called VIIRS [14], present in satellites of the National Oceanic and Atmospheric Administration-20 (NOAA-20) [15] and the National Program of Association in Suomi Polar Orbit (S-NPP) [16]. These combinations of spectral bands are identified as "M3-I3-M11" [17], and their characteristics can be observed by analyzing the bands captured by the VIIRS sensor.

We chose the satellite images with this spectral combination due to the high contrast generated by the color of the thermal radiation of the fire, concerning the rest of the image and of the smoke given off by the fire for the clouds and other aerosols, allowing a more efficient identification with the algorithms used in this project (Fig. 3).

Fig. 3. Bands M3-I3-M11 left. Bands True Color, right.

The 1,100 images were divided into two packages. The first of 1000 images are used for the neural network training process, 500 with forest fires and 500 without fires. The second of 100 images are used for the classification process with the algorithms, 50 with forest fires and 50 without fires. The characteristics of these images are as follows:

- Training images size: 224 × 224 pixels
- Identification images size: 2048 × 2048 pixels
- Spatial resolution: 125 m
- Altitude: 200 km (Average altitude for microsatellites)

For the training images, 80% (800) were designated for training and 20% (200) for validation. Due to the low number of images and as a recommended practice in convolutional neural network training, a technique is applied to the first set of images (800) that allows us to increase our training data set caled "Data Augmentation" [18]. With this technique, we apply transformations to the original images, generating others with the reflected changes. The modifications applied in this case are Flip and Rotation. As a result, the 800-image set now has 2,230 images, and adding this with the 200-image validation set, leaves 2,430 images for the entire neural network training process.

3.2 Algorithm Selection

Two CNN models were chosen for training and evaluation to identify forest fires in satellite images: Inception V3 [19] and Mobilenet V2 [20]. These models are selected for their affinity with the project purposes, which implicitly entails generating a minimum expenditure of resources without losing effectiveness in the classification process.

The first model is inception V3 [21], which focuses mainly on consuming less energy and computational resources by modifying the previous models. We find factored convolutions, regularization, dimension reduction, and parallel calculations within the techniques used to optimize performance.

On the other hand, we have the mobilenet V2 model [22], designed for deployment on mobile devices; therefore, one of its characteristics is the low computational and energy consumption required for its operation. This model retains many of the features of its predecessor model, mobilenet V1 but introduces two new advances, such as linear bottlenecks between layers and shortcut connections between jams.

Regardless of the neural network model chosen to perform an classification process, good training performance requires a large number of images. Due to the difficulty of construction and the time needed to consolidate a large dataset, it is necessary to rely on a specific technique for these situations called transfer learning [23]. This technique take advantage of the knowledge acquired from previously trained models to train new models, which do not necessarily need to have a large number of images. For this project, it is necessary to carry out transfer learning using the pre-trained weights in the two neural models of the ImageNET image dataset [24].

The Inception V3 model used in this project is adapted from a development that detects fire in images captured by indoor and outdoor security cameras. On the other hand, the Mobilenet V2 model is adapted from a tutorial created by Tensorflow developers [25] and modified in the Roboflow platform [26] for flower classification. Data of this experiment are available for reproducibility in the project's GitHub repository [27].

4   Results

Now, the results obtained in the third methodological phase are presented below. In addition, the evaluation metrics that will be used are shown, although the model has not been validated on the embedded system.

4.1   Artificial Learning

This process begins with loading the structured dataset corresponding to the first methodological stage. The pre-trained CNN is also loaded, which works as a feature extractor by stacking the upper classification layers. Then the model is trained with our dataset and the parameters are saved as an "h5" file that will be used as input in the inference algorithm. The training results for each model were as follows:

In Fig. 4, the Inception V3 model in training shows an increase from approximately 83% to over 95% accuracy after five (5) epochs and oscillating between 94 and 96% in the remaining fifteen (15) epochs. The validation stage, the level of precision is between 90 and 93%.

Figure 5 shows that the inception V3 model during training presents a descending level of loss in a staggered manner from approximately 80% to 10% after eight (8) epochs, then stay there. In the validation stage, the level of loss always fluctuates between 20 and 30%.

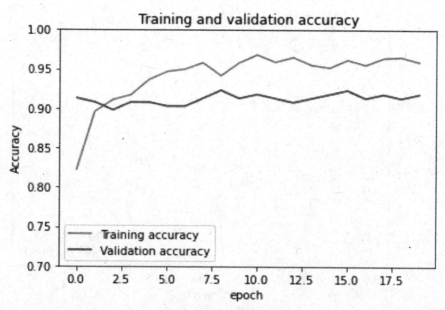

Fig. 4. Accuracy inception.

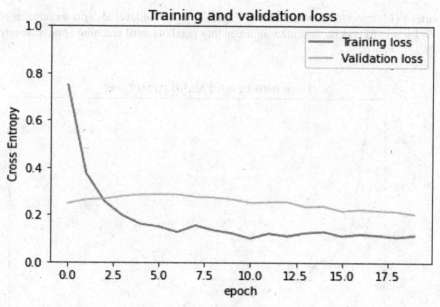

Fig. 5. Loss inception.

As can be seen in Fig. 6, the mobilenet V2 model in training presents a rectilinear ascent from approximately 87% to 96% accuracy after two (2) epochs, and then continues with a shallow ascending parabola until reaching 99% during the four (4) and following

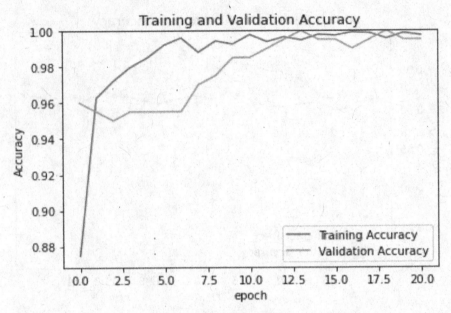

Fig. 6. Accuracy mobilenet.

fourteen (14) epochs. In the validation stage, the precision level also draws remains at 95% for six (6) epochs, and after an ascending parabola until reaching approximately 99%.

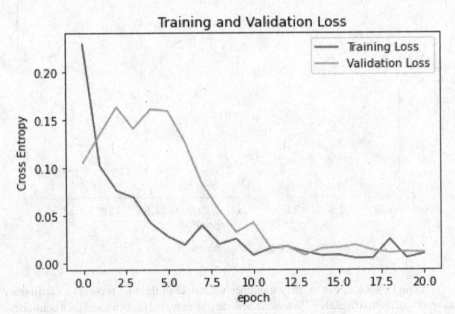

Fig. 7. Loss mobilenet.

Figure 7 shows that the mobilenet V2 model during training presents a level of loss through a descending curve from approximately 23% to 3% during six (6) epochs, to later mark a fluctuating line between 2 and 4%. In the validation stage, the level of loss draws a curve starting at 10%, rising to 16% for five (5) epochs, then falling and staying at 3% approximately.

For these two models, it is observed that the beginning of the precision is high because the training is supported by the characteristics extracted from the pre-trained model with the previous weights thanks to transfer learning. The same happens when we analyze the loss, although in the mobilenet model the training and validation start with higher percentages than in the inception model.

It is also observed that the increase in epochs in training and validation allows us to see more continuous values in the precision and loss metrics, as reflected in the curve of the mobilenet model, contrary to what is shown in the inception model.

4.2 Evaluation Metrics

4.2.1 Reliability

Reliability within the evaluation process allows determining the consistency level of the model through consecutive measurement events. For this, the Confusion Matrix will be used, which shows us the crossing of the true results with those obtained after the execution of the algorithm. Making use of the aforementioned prediction lists, the confusion matrix is created for each algorithm.

The results thrown by the confusion matrix are divided into 4 variables that reflect what happens when comparing the expected or real results with those received or generated by the algorithms (see Table 1).

Table 1. Confusion matrix result.

Real/Predicted	Positive	Negative
Positive	TP	FN
Negative	FP	TN

Where:

- TP - true positive: is real positive and predicted positive.
- FN - false negative: is real positive and predicted negative.
- FP - false positive: is real negative and predicted positive.
- TN - true negative: is real negative and predicted negative.

Based on these variables, the metrics that will allow evaluating the reliability of the algorithm are structured.

Precision: It is the resulting index between the true positives and the total positives generated by the algorithm.

$$TP/(TP + FP)$$

Accuracy: It is the resulting index between the successes, both positive and negative, and the total results generated by the algorithm.

$$TP + TN / (TP + FN + FP + TN)$$

Recall: It is the resulting index between the true positives and the total of real positives.

$$TP/(TP + FN)$$

F1-Score: Allows comparing two metrics into one, sensitivity and precision, and is widely used when the classes within the dataset are unequal.

$$2 * (Recall * Accuracy) / (Recall + Accuracy)$$

4.2.2 Efficiency

The different ML techniques require a large amount of computational and energy resources for their deployment, for this reason, in the development of this type of model, it is important to evaluate the consumption of said resources and, if possible, reduce it. This approach is called Algorithmic Efficiency. Although it is true that in any situation the saving of resources is a matter of great attention, in this particular case it is even more so, due to the limitations presented by embedded systems or integrated architectures.

The metrics to consider with the project models are:

- Energy Consumption: Measured in milliwatts (mW) and corresponds to the average consumption of the embedded card during the test with each algorithm.
- RAM consumption: Measured in megabytes (MB). The Jetson Nano card shares RAM with the GPU, that is, it is not separated.
- Device Temperature: Measured in degrees centigrade (°C) and corresponds to the temperature recorded by the entire card during the elapsed time.
- GPU consumption: Measured in percentage (%) and corresponds to the use of the GPU in its processing.

5   Conclusion

The results obtained in the progress of this research show that with a small dataset, adequate training of a convolutional neural network can be carried out, allowing an alternative proposal to be proposed as support in the surveillance of forest fires.

In addition, a dataset of 2430 satellite images with spectral bands M3-I3-M11 was structured, captured, and conditioned from within the WORLDVIEW platform. This dataset is available to the academic or scientific community in the respective repository.

The training through transfer learning of the CNNs used in this project facilitated the implementation process of the development, due to the decrease in time and data that these networks needed in their preparation compared to those carried out right from the start.

However, preparing an image dataset and building a model with convolutional neural networks presents several challenges for researchers, for example, the time spent developing prototypes that allow evaluating the behavior of a model, the reuse of these prototypes in other applications, and the adaptation of the resulting models to run on hardware with more limited specifications.

6 Future Work

Different proposals follow the outcomes of this project. First, the customization of the method to develop several fire classifications models, searching low-cost implementation, accuracy, and computing efficiency. Second, the growth of open access data sets to help researchers and agencies in the fire early aware forecasting. Finally, this project is under development and implementation for real use inside the Space Mission as A Service Model or SMMAS, an HPC-cloud computing model to space projects developed by the High Performance and Scientific Computing Center of the Universidad Industrial de Santander (SC3UIS),[1] and some of the following steps to be executed are:

- Execution Execution of the CNNs using minimal resources on the embedded system for inference with the images acquired.
- Measurement of the resources consumed during the execution process of the models on the embedded system to systems performance evaluation and characterization of the resources.
- Evaluation of the implemented models in the classification by a minimum expenditure of resources.

References

1. Feng, X., Jiang, Y., Yang, X., Du, M., Li, X.: Computer vision algorithms and hardware implementations: a survey. Integration **69**, 309–320 (2019)
2. Brozek, T., ed.: Micro-and nanoelectronics: emerging device challenges and solutions. CRC Press (2014)
3. Nano, N.J.: https://nvidia.com/en-us/autonomus-machines/embedded-systems/jetson-nano/. Accessed 23 Oct 2021
4. Petrescu, R.V., et al.: NASA satellites help us to quickly detect forest fires. Am. J. Eng. Appl. Sci. **11**(1), 288–296 (2018)
5. Van Etten, A.: Satellite imagery multi-scale rapid detection with windowed networks. In: 2019 IEEE Winter Conference on Applications of Computer Vision (WACV), pp. 735–743. IEEE (2019)
6. Van Etten, A.: You only look twice. Rapid multi-scale object detection in satellite imagery. arXiv preprint arXiv:1805.09512 (2018)

---

[1] More information in: https://www.sc3.uis.edu.co.

7. Liu, W., Anguelov, D., Erhan, D., Szegedy, C., Reed, S., Fu, C.-Y., Berg, A.C.: SSD: single shot multibox detector. In: Leibe, B., Matas, J., Sebe, N., Welling, M. (eds.) ECCV 2016. LNCS, vol. 9905, pp. 21–37. Springer, Cham (2016). https://doi.org/10.1007/978-3-319-464 48-0_2

8. Ren, S., He, K., Girshick, R.B., Sun, J.: Faster R-CNN: Towards Real-Time Object Detection with Region Proposal Networks. CoRR abs/1506.01497 (2015). http://arxiv.org/abs/1506. 01497

9. Graphic Processing Unit (GPU). https://www.intel.la/content/www/xl/es/products/docs/pro cessors/what-is-a-gpu.html. Accessed 13 July 2020

10. Field Programmable Gate Array (FPGA). https://www.arm.com/glossary/fpga. Accessed 14 July 2020

11. Wang, X., Ng, H.W., Liang, J.: Lapped convolutional neural networks for embedded systems. In: 2017 IEEE Global Conference on Signal and Information Processing (GlobalSIP), pp. 1135–1139. IEEE (2017)

12. De Silva, D., Alahakoon, D.: An artificial intelligence life cycle: From conception to production. Patterns, 100489 (2022)

13. National Aeronautics and Space Administration, data visualization application WORLD-VIEW. https://worldview.earthdata.nasa.gov/. Accessed 20 Oct 2020

14. Cao, C., Xiong, J., Blonski, S., Liu, Q., Uprety, S., Shao, X., Weng, F.: Suomi NPP VIIRS sensor data record verification, validation, and long-term performance monitoring. J. Geophys. Res. Atmos. **118**(20), 664–678 (2013)

15. Cao, C., et al.: NOAA-20 VIIRS on-orbit performance, data quality, and operational Cal/Val support. In: Earth Observing Missions and Sensors: Development, Implementation, and Characterization V, vol. 10781, p. 107810K. International Society for Optics and Photonics (2018)

16. Weng, F.: Advanced Technology Microwave Sounder Calibration and Validation. Liang, S.: Comprehensive Remote Sensing, pp. 42–63. Elsevier (2018). ISBN 9780128032213. https:// doi.org/10.1016/B978-0-12-409548-9.10393-8

17. National Oceanic and Atmospheric Administration. NOAA Technical Report NESDIS 142 (2017). https://ncc.nesdis.noaa.gov/documents/documentation/viirs-users-guide-tech-report-142a-v1.3.pdf. https://doi.org/10.1016/B978-0-12-409548-9.10393-8. Accessed 15 Apr 2020

18. Zoph, B., Cubuk, E., Ghiasi, G., Lin, T., Shlens, J., Le, Q.: Learning data augmentation strategies for object detection. arXiv (2019)

19. Szegedy, C., Vanhoucke, V., Ioffe, S., Shlens, J., Wojna, Z.: Rethinking the inception architecture for computer vision. In: 2016 IEEE Conference on Computer Vision and Pattern Recognition (CVPR), pp. 2818–2826 (2016)

20. Sandler, M., Howard, A.G., Zhu, M., Zhmoginov, A., Chen, L.: MobileNetV2: inverted residuals and linear bottlenecks. In: 2018 IEEE/CVF Conference on Computer Vision and Pattern Recognition, pp. 4510–4520 (2018)

21. D. Shah, «Early Fire detection system using deep learning and OpenCV,» 2020, https://tow ardsdatascience.com/early-fire-detection-system-using-deep-learning-and-opencv-6cb602 60d54a. Accessed 20 Jun 2021

22. Sahoo, S.: How to Train MobileNetV2 On a Custom Dataset (2021). https://blog.roboflow. com/how-to-train-mobilenetv2-on-a-custom-dataset/. Accessed 24 Jun 2021

23. Sarkar, D., Bali, R., Ghosh, T.: Hands-on Transfer Learning with Python: Implement advanced deep learning and neural network models using TensorFlow and Keras. Packt Publishing (2018)

24. Deng, J., Dong, W., Socher, R., Li, L., Li, K., Fei-Fei, L.: ImageNet: a large-scale hierarchical image database. In: 2009 IEEE Conference on Computer Vision and Pattern Recognition, pp. 248–255 (2009)

25. Pang, B., Nijkamp, E., Wu, Y.N.: Deep learning with tensorflow: a review. Journal of Educational and Behavioral Statistics **45**(2), 227–248 (2020)
26. Roboflow Platform. https://roboflow.com/. Access 30 Oct 2021
27. Github. https://github.com/jhonesis/Proyecto-IGNIS. Access 13 Jun 2022

A Machine Learning-Based Missing Data Imputation with FHIR Interoperability Approach in Sepsis Prediction

Cristian Fernando Toro Beltran[1,2], Erick Daniel Villarreal Ibañez[3], Vivian Milen Orejuela[2], and John Anderson García Henao[1,4(✉)]

[1] Nucleus-AI Research, Medellin, Colombia
jagh1729@gmail.com
[2] Central Unit of Valle del Cauca (UCEVA), Tuluá, Colombia
[3] Fundacion Oftalmologica de Santander (FOSCAL), Bucaramanga, Colombia
[4] ARTORG Center for Biomedical Research, University of Bern, Bern, Switzerland

Abstract. Sepsis is a dangerous infection that can affect different parts of the body. It is caused by the body's immune system overreacting to an infection. Therefore, hospitalized patients can benefit from having an Artificial Intelligence (AI)-based approach to alert healthcare professionals when the patient is at risk of sepsis. However, automating and diagnosing sepsis in hospitalized patients is difficult, as sepsis can present differently in each individual. However, although deep learning (DL) algorithms have demonstrated high accuracy and exemplary performance in different clinical categories, very few have been integrated into medical systems. In this paper, we introduce an interoperability platform to integrate electronic healthcare records (EHRs) and clinical modeling of mortality risk in patients with sepsis to support patient monitoring and early detection. Furthermore, we assess the training and evaluation of machine learning algorithms to classify the risk of a hospitalized patient getting sepsis using the EHRs from two hospitals released in the cardiology challenge 2019 for early sepsis prediction from clinical data. Additionally, we focus on structuring the data in units and building a clinical document architecture using the standard Fast Healthcare Interoperability Resources (FHIR) standard to enable the interoperability to train and deploy the model from different hospitals. We also present a dashboard for patient monitoring and support of early detection. We evaluated GradientBoosting, and LightGradientBoostingMachine (LightGBM) classifiers on two test sets, one by each hospital EHRs, using the F1-score represents the perfect accuracy and recall of the model and the area under the receiver operating characteristic curve (AUC). When trained on data from hospital A, the LightGBM yields an F1-score of 0.87 and 0.26 for the two test sets. The LightGBM trained from hospital B yields an F1-score of 0.20 and 0.88 for the two test sets, while using the data training combination of two hospitals improves the prediction accuracy with an F1-score of 0.93 and 0.94 for the two test sets. The accuracy

Supplementary Information The online version contains supplementary material available at https://doi.org/10.1007/978-3-031-23821-5_9.

of sepsis classification in hospitalized patients relies on the diversity of the training data since we identified variations in the values of the clinical characteristics used to represent each patient's condition. Therefore, we highlight that reliably composing a diverse and structured dataset improves the results. Also, adding a model for imputation of missing values improves the classification performance and deals with the missing data that often appear in hospitals.

Keywords: Sepsis prediction · Machine learning · BioInformatics

1 Introduction

In 2017, there were 48.9 million cases and 11 million deaths related to sepsis worldwide, which accounted for almost 20% of all global deaths [13]. Sepsis is a dangerous infection that affects different parts of the body. It is caused by the body's immune system overreacting to an infection. Therefore, hospitalized patients can benefit from having an Artificial Intelligence (AI)-based system to alert healthcare professionals when the patient is at risk of sepsis. However, automating and diagnosing sepsis in hospitalized patients is difficult, as sepsis can present differently in each individual. This adds to the methodological and engineering challenges of scaling up early warning systems in different healthcare centers, and hospitals [1,3]. Although early detection and appropriate treatment of sepsis help improve outcomes, professional intensive care societies have proposed new clinical criteria to aid in recognizing sepsis. Nevertheless, the fundamental need for early detection and treatment remains a challenging task [6,7,12].

The automation of Artificial Intelligence (AI)-based models for medical diagnostics are an indispensable tool to support the clinical decision process and increase the efficiency of care delivery in the diagnosis and care of patients in clinical settings. However, although deep learning (DL) algorithms have demonstrated high accuracy and exemplary performance in different clinical categories, very few have been integrated into medical systems. One of the main limitations is the scaling of medical applications with deep learning models built under a single clinical information system. Whose challenges are related to the different structures and semantics of the clinical information systems that hospitals may have; therefore, a model that works in hospital A does not scale directly to hospital B or C [8]). Therefore, In this paper, we introduce an interoperability platform to integrate electronic healthcare records (EHRs) and clinical modeling of mortality risk in patients with sepsis to support patient monitoring and early detection. Furthermore, we assess the training and evaluation of machine learning algorithms to classify the risk of a hospitalized patient getting sepsis using the EHRs from two hospitals released in the cardiology challenge 2019 for early sepsis prediction from clinical data. In this direction, this paper made the following contributions:

1. Transform patient clinical records with the HL7 FHIR standard. This stage is focused on structuring the data in units and building a clinical document

architecture using the standard Fast Healthcare Interoperability Resources (FHIR) standard to enable the interoperability to train and deploy the model from different hospitals.

2. Implementing an ML workflow from the data structure, adjusting the data imputation method according to the type of EHRs and their periodicity until assessing the ML algorithms to classify the risk of sepsis in hospitalized patients.

3. Build a dashboard for patient monitoring and support early detection. The patient dashboard presents the individual clinical records from vital and laboratory data and the predictions made by the machine learning models.

2   State of the Art

2.1   Machine Learning on Clinical Features for Sepsis Prediction

Given the increasing volume of data in healthcare systems, data mining is widely applied to extract patients' clinical features and characteristics. In addition, it is used with machine learning models to develop clinical decision systems. Specifically, this AI-based modeling can help clinicians to predict and prognosis the risk of hospitalized patients getting sepsis. Although the hospital could suffer a load and overload of hospitalizations and intensive care units, it becomes more challenging to identify the different symptoms that patients may present when they are at risk of sepsis, which can be difficult because of their different symptomatologies. On the other hand, they have the problem that some clinical results that are integrated into patient records are in incompatible formats, generating a diagnostic omission or poor ease of analysis and visualization of the data. For example Zhao et al. develops an early prediction of sepsis based on machine learning algorithm, where its main objective is to deliver sepsis predictions in patients, applying different classifiers and processing methods to make a prediction 6 h in advance. Feature generation methods are built by combining different features, including statistical strength features, window features and medical features. The Miceforest multiple interpolation method is applied to address large missing data problems. The results show that the feature generation method outperforms the average processing method. XGBoost and LightGBM algorithms are excellent in prediction performance, this paper contributed to model building and classifier training [15].

2.2   Interoperability of Healthcare Information Systems

The first difficulty for healthcare systems in transforming from data-driven healthcare to a knowledge-driven healthcare system is the health information exchange from a patient-centered perspective [4]. It was moving as a scalability difficulty for deep learning-based medical applications to integrate into new clinical settings. Thus, the model that works in hospital A does not work in hospital B due to the structure and semantics of the patient-related information required to feed the DL medical application [8]. The EHR interoperability challenges occur at different scales, from minimal communication and data exchange between several independent software within the same organization to the diversity of codes used to record the exact characteristics of the patient between internal units and external organizations. For example, Bender et al. build an agile and RESTful approach to healthcare information Exchange [2], in which they examine the potential for new Health Level 7 (HL7) standard Fast Healthcare Interoperability Resources (FHIR, pronounced "fire") standard to help achieve healthcare systems interoperability. HL7 messaging standards are widely implemented by the healthcare industry and have been deployed internationally for decades. HL7 Version 2 ("v2") health information exchange standards are a popular choice of local hospital communities for the exchange of healthcare information, including electronic medical record information [2]. While Greg et al., introduce a future-proof architecture for telemedicine using loose-coupled modules and HL7 FHIR, in which the majority of telemedicine solutions are proprietary and disease specific, which causes a heterogeneous and silo-oriented system landscape with limited interoperability. Solving the interoperability problem would require a strong focus on data integration and standardization in telemedicine infrastructures. Our objective was to suggest a future-proof architecture that consisted of small loose-coupled modules to allow flexible integration with new and existing services and the use of international standards to allow high reusability of modules and interoperability in the health IT landscape [9]. In this direction, we believe that the basis for building continuous machine learning approaches to the healthcare domain is to add a layer of standardization of EHRs through a standard medical model, such as those provided by the FHIR standard.

3 Materials and Methods

3.1 Study Design

Figure 1 presents the imputation interoperability scheme of a machine learning-based missing data for inpatient sepsis classification. The imputation interoperability scheme is implemented in four stages: Processing and transforming clinical data to the FHIR standard. First, the data corresponding to hospitals A and B will be split into training and validation sets. Next, the data corresponding to hospitals A and B will be used separately for the evaluation (MIMIC-III). Then, training the machine learning algorithms and automatic capture of metrics such as accuracy (F1-score) and an inspection of box plots such as AUC ROC. Finally, assess the machine learning algorithms using the test set corresponding to hospitals A and B.

3.2 Dataset Early Prediction of Sepsis from Clinical Data

The data used in the competition is sourced from ICU patients in three separate hospital systems. Data from two hospital systems will be publicly available; however, one data set will be censored and used for scoring. The data provided by

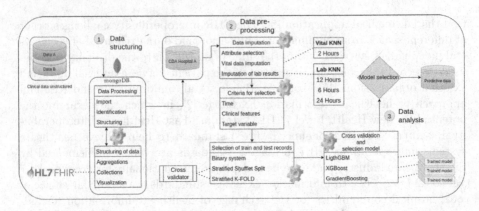

Fig. 1. Scheme of the machine learning-based missing data imputation interoperability approach for inpatient sepsis classification.

Early prediction of sepsis from clinical Data (PhysionetSepsis2019), are divided by one-hour time records of hospitalized patients, these data are separated into groupings of clinical records such as: vital signs with 8 different attributes, laboratory values with 26 different attributes, demographic data with 7 different attributes [12].

3.3   Processing and Transformation of Clinical Data to the FHIR Standard

To structure the EHRs, a non-relational database, such as Mongodb, was used because it allows the generation of patient information in JSON documents. This allows the creation of aggregations and different collections where the patients' medical records will be distributed, and the new engineering attributes, achieving the respective records of each patient, which provides speed in the search and grouping of data for future analysis [11].

Figure 2 hows the EHRs structuring pipeline. It begins from EHRs import, verifies it, inserts the time columns, and continues with the next patient. At the end of the import of the received patients, the aggregations of the engineering variables are started, generating different attributes based on health methods focused on the identification of sepsis in patients, the aggregations created on the dataset are SIRS (Systemic Inflammatory Response Syndrome) and SOFA (Acute Organ System Failure), These aggregations comply with different conditions of the methodology, identifying if the patient complies with the conditions for the SIRS or SOFA variable to be positive or negative, the SOFA conditions verifies to which group it belongs since it is in a specified range, giving us the SOFA variable in the group it is in [5].

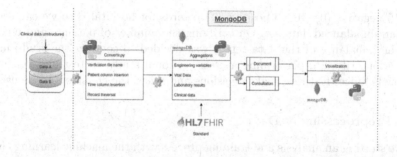

Fig. 2. EHRs structuring pipeline based on FHIR standard.

Use of the SIRS and SOFA Scales as Secondary Clinical Outcomes:
Different ways of studying the data set were verified to evidence the occurrence of sepsis in patients, by investigating different methods to identify the occurrence of sepsis in hospitalized patients, the concepts of Sepsis-2 and Sepsis-3 are studied, taking as a guide for analysis and study the SIRS and SOFA method [14].

SIRS is a clinical situation of general inflammatory response to an aggression, as a consequence of an infection. It is a complex set of pathological phenomena that produce clinical alterations in four elements: temperature, heart rate, respiratory rate and leukocyte count. An aggregation was performed for the sepsis-2 study method called SIRS in which the data evaluated by the method such as: hearth rate, temperature, White blood cell. These will be evaluated in the aggregation complying with some metric conditions [14]. See clinical conditions in the supplementary document.

SOFA (Sequential Organ Failure Assessment), which includes a series of clinical, laboratory and management criteria. SOFA, which includes a series of clinical variables, laboratory and management criteria. An aggregation was performed for the sepsis-3 study method called SOFA in which the data evaluated by the method will be verified such as: Respiration rate, Platelets, Bilirubins, Mean arterial pressure, Creatinine [14]. See clinical conditions in the supplementary document.

3.4 Data Distribution - Hospitals A and B

After obtaining the CDA data structuring, we verified the number of records and patients contained in the CDA in the elapsed time of hospitalization to verify how to approach the analysis of the data. When observing the dataset of hospitals A and B, we found the patients' hospitalization time and the imbalance in the clinical data of each hospital-obtaining a total of 20336 patients in hospital A and 20000 patients in hospital B. When verifying the number of patients throughout the hospitalization period, we obtained a total of 790215 records in hospital A and 761995 records from hospital B. In the count of the *Sepsis Label*, we can see that there are many patients classified as zero (0) negative, at different times, a total of 773079, and 17136 patients classified as (1) positive for hospital A, and

751215 negative (0), 10780 positive (1) records for hospital B so we can see we have an unbalanced data set. On verifying the number of patients and records, and the imbalance of the data set, it was decided to conduct the study under a selection criterion, performing a cross-sectional study, to test and verify the essential clinical features, make decisions and select the classifiers to be used.

3.5   Preprocessing of Data

Before starting an analysis and training process with the machine learning classifiers, it is necessary to perform a data preprocessing on the two data sets created, and to select different methods and attribute criteria to test the models to be generated.

Selection of Attibutes: Performing an analysis of different clinical variables and observing the amount of missing values, it was decided to reduce the number of attributes with which the training of classifiers is being performed, different articles were investigated which handled similar databases and several conclusions of these articles were taken into account, therefore it was decided to reduce the attributes to 27 clinical values delivered by the dataset and add 2 engineering values created for the CDA.

Data Imputation: It is observed that in addition to having an unbalanced dataset there is more missing data than the data delivered by the dataset, but it should be noted that these missing data are mostly clinical results which are taken every 12 or 24 h, generating that such data are with a very wide time distance, so the clinical records will be an important factor when performing an analysis for the Machine learning classifier, since these missing values generate that the training is spoiled and delivers wrong answers or a large margin of error. It is also observed that in some laboratory attributes the time range may vary depending on the patient's condition, these attributes may appear in a range of 3, 5, or 6 h, therefore the vital and laboratory values that are having these missing values are identified, and we proceed to perform a data imputation to obtain an accurate training with the 28 variables selected for training the classifier. To start this data imputation process, the division of the attributes of vital signs and laboratory records was made, for the classification attributes, such as patient records and demographic data, no missing values were found, Since this imputation would only be done for vital signs and laboratory data, it will be divided into two different functions since the vital signs attributes have few missing values and these records are taken every hour, but the laboratory variables have a wider range that can reach up to 24 h.

Imputation of Vital Signs: For the imputation of the vital signs attributes, some engineering variables were used, which were created in the CDA, such as the unit of measurement of time of the patient in hospitalization, and the days elapsed in such hospitalization, in order to achieve an interpolation of the data of each patient, in the course of 24 h, therefore it was decided to generate this interpolation of data for each elapsed day of hospitalization, where the vital signs were with missing values of a maximum of 2 h, so a function is created in python that analyzes the 24 h of hospitalization of the corresponding patient and for each missing value in a range of 2 h will generate the sum and the average of the closest values the value of the upper hour and now lower, recording the average of the analyzed data and replacing the missing value.

Vital signs, every two—2 h—Interpolation of data per patient every 24 h (1 day), calculated mean. Imputation (KNN) [15]

Imputation of Laboratory Results: For the imputation of the attributes of the laboratory results, we also used the time measurement variables of the patient's hospitalization and the days of hospitalization, in order to interpolate the values lost in the course of 24 h, for the laboratory results we had three different conditions, as some laboratories had a difference of 12 and 24 h, the first condition verified the number of records that were taken in the laboratory attribute in the course of the day for the patient analyzed, the next condition if the laboratory result is recorded on more than one occasion the summation and the average will be made to replace the missing values of the day in question with the average obtained, and as a last condition if the laboratory result is not recorded in the corresponding 24 h the missing values will be replaced by 0.

Laboratory results, every—12 h—or—24 h—Interpolation of data per patient every 24 h (1 day), calculated average. Imputation (KNN) If there is no record in the 24 h, the patient's attribute on the corresponding day is zero. Upon verifying the attributes of both vital signs and laboratory and that needed data imputation, the decision was made to perform this imputation to the complete Data set and not only to the study groups in order to correctly interpolate the records of the patient's days of hospitalization, upon interpolating and performing the data imputation in the complete Data set, the training and division of the data for a broader test is performed.

3.6   Experiment Dataset

The experimental dataset will not be divided by time criteria, since the selected criteria are the records of all patients who had sepsis at some time during their hospitalization, taking both positive and negative records, obtaining a total of 1790 patients and 104,964 records. The analysis corresponding to the dataset is performed, verifying the amount of missing data in both vital signs and laboratory results, performing the imputation process with knn, generating a change in the dataset without affecting the results of the clinical attributes, and initiating the training and analysis process.

3.7   Creation of Train Test

It was proposed to create a binary scoring system, in which the complete data frame will be traversed, verifying the records, and checking different attributes such as "SepsisLabel", "SepsisSirs", "SepsisSofa" which are classifications made

Table 1. Imputed test and training dataset measurement

Features	Hospital A Imp.	Hospital A No Imp.	Hospital B Imp.	Hospital B No Imp.
HR	88.04 ± 18.03	87.99 ± 18.17	88.44 ± 18.79	88.25 ± 19.01
O2SAT	97.37 ± 13.27	97.41 ± 2.84	97.08 ± 3.15	97.11 ± 3.25
TEMP	36.84 ± 13.11	37.14 ± 0.86	36.22 ± 12.10	37.11 ± 1.25
SBP	118.26 ± 130.62	122.54 ± 22.36	125.96 ± 26.28	126.54 ± 26.81
MAP	79.70 ± 115.18	79.76 ± 15.51	85.27 ± 16.23	85.452 ± 16.68
DBP	51.02 ± 125.51	61.11 ± 13.10	64.60 ± 13.73	64.58 ± 14.16
RESP	20.03 ± 15.82	20.07 ± 5.88	18.96 ± 5.82	19.29 ± 5.81
HCO3	24.16 ± 14.87	23.97 ± 4.73	22.19 ± 3.25	22.42 ± 3.65
Ph	3.96 ± 13.10	7.38 ± 0.07	4.82 ± 2.93	7.38 ± 0.09
PaCO2	21.50 ± 118.13	41.41 ± 9.60	25.09 ± 17.18	39.85 ± 10.49
AST	65.24 ± 1401.82	375.21 ± 1092.97	119.32 ± 495.39	281.16 ± 893.35
BUN	17.46 ± 118.67	30.021 ± 23.54	17.58 ± 18.55	28.53 ± 21.36
Alkalinephos	35.45 ± 165.36	112.26 ± 108.59	70.38 ± 68.30	98.09 ± 80.11
Chloride	67.26 ± 138.77	105.78 ± 6.33	72.56 ± 41.79	106.34 ± 5.22
Creatinine	0.96 ± 11.27	1.58 ± 1.54	1.14 ± 1.60	1.73 ± 1.81
Lactate	0.81 ± 11.23	2.42 ± 2.06	1.54 ± 1.78	3.13 ± 2.93
Magnesium	1.29 ± 10.78	2.06 ± 0.37	1.41 ± 0.77	2.17 ± 0.46
Potassium	2.58 ± 11.56	4.09 ± 0.62	2.59 ± 1.54	4.11 ± 0.67
Bilirubin total	0.78 ± 12.74	3.92 ± 6.99	1.31 ± 2.16	3.02 ± 5.14
PTT	22.35 ± 120.62	42.29 ± 24.56	33.84 ± 34.96	45.85 ± 37.31
WBC	8.04 ±17.43	12.49 ± 8.31	8.03 ± 7.53	12.50 ± 7.73
Fibrinogen	54.98 ± 1143.83	300.86 ± 189.30	224.30 ± 189.83	285.06 ± 167.28
Platelets	137.71 ± 1118.06	195.25 ± 118.80	125.81 ± 100.23	172.59 ± 102.93
Age	63 ± 115.82	63 ± 15.82	60 ± 16.57	60 ± 16.57

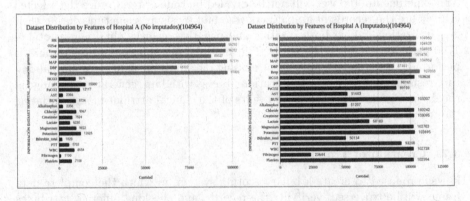

Fig. 3. Dataset Hospital A experiment missing data and Dataset imputed experiment.

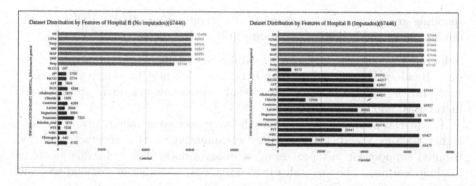

Fig. 4. Dataset Hospital B experiment missing data and Dataset imputed experiment.

by different clinical methodologies that were created in mongodb. This will deliver a classification referring to a binary table, assigning a score, depending on the result obtained for each attribute [10] (Table 1 and Fig. 3) .

After generating the dataset with the binary system for patients a validation will be performed, with a cross validator called "Stratified Suflet Split" and "Stratified KFold" that helped to provide training indices, with which we can split the datasets into training, and test, in a more equitable way based on the designated parameters. This Cross Validation object returns stratified random folds the folds are performed while preserving the percentage of samples from each class. With the binary scoring function and the use of the cross-validator, the issue of generating an equitable training and test data set is resolved (Fig. 4).

Once the identification and selection of all patients to be used in the training and test dataset, selected thanks to the binary classifier and cross-validators, has been obtained, the dataset is divided into "training" and "test", and the process of selection and implementation of the machine learning classifiers is started in order to check which of them offers the best result.

3.8   Implementation of Classifiers

The training process starts with three classifiers that provide ease in the analysis process and have different hyperparameters that can help in the analysis of the data: Logistic regression, Random Forest, K-Nearest Neighbor.

The 30 clinical features were preprocessed and selected to classify the target variable SepsisLabel. Each ML classifier training function is created for the dataset assigned for training and combined with a cross-validator called Grid-SearchCV; which is a class available in Scikit-learn that allows to systematically evaluate and select the parameters of a model by indicating a model and the parameters to be tested, or by managing to evaluate the performance of the former based on the latter through cross-validation. When evaluating the trained models, a better response is obtained by the Random Forest classifier, delivering better results both in time and reducing its margin of error in the four corresponding groups, so it was decided to investigate other classifiers that use the random forest methodology to obtain results with a better accuracy rate.

Selected Classifiers. The search for different classifiers is performed using the same Random Forest methodology but more efficiently to reduce the training time and the margin of error. As a result, three new classifiers are obtained: LigthGBM, and Gradient Boosting.

LigthGBM supports training for efficiency and has excellent advantages like higher training speed, lower memory consumption, better accuracy, and distributed support for fast processing of massive data. It is a durable model in machine learning. The main idea is to use a weak classifier or decision tree and iterative training to obtain the optimal model.

Gradient Boosting consists of a set of individual decision trees, trained sequentially so that each new tree tries to improve the errors of the previous trees. Finally, the prediction of a new observation is obtained by aggregating the predictions of all the individual trees that make up the model.

A great result is obtained by the three new models (LigthGBM, Gradient Boosting). It is decided to take the best classification model, which delivered better results in F1-score and AUC, taking LigthGBM to continue with the research and testing process.

4   Experiments and Results

4.1   Experiment Results

We evaluated GradientBoosting, and LightGradientBoostingMachine (Light-GBM) classifiers on two test sets, one by each hospital EHRs, using the F1-score represents the perfect accuracy and recall of the model and the area under the receiver operating characteristic curve (AUC). When trained on data from hospital A, the LightGBM yields an F1-score of 0.87 and 0.26 for the two test sets, and the LightGBM trained from hospital B yields an F1-score of 0.20 and 0.88 for the two test sets while using the data training combination of two hospitals improves the prediction accuracy with an F1-score of 0.93 and 0.94 for the two test sets (Fig. 5).

After obtaining the selected classifier, having the function that configures the hyperparameters necessary for the selected classifiers, and having the Dataset imputed with no missing values, training was performed with the clinical data under the selection criteria for both hospitals A and B. Generate the data sets for training and testing by creating one set for each hospital dataset A and B . The training of the different models was carried out, obtaining the following results in the statistical measures. It is observed that LigthGBM has a more accurate response in predicting the target variable. Different statistical measures and accuracy of the predictions made by each model were performed, F1 score and AUC graphs inf Figs. 7 and 8 (Fig. 6).

After running the training and creating the model, the corresponding tests were performed in the Dataset test, giving results for the model created, a good

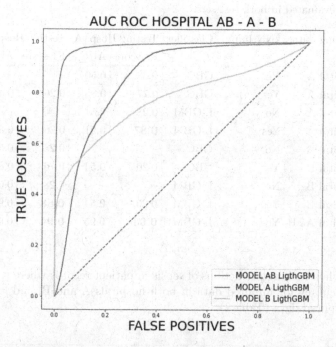

Fig. 5. AUC ROC comparison results between ML models evaluated on both test sets.

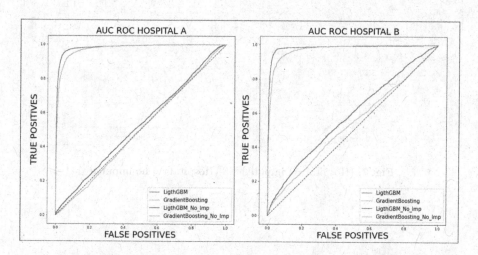

Fig. 6. AUC ROC comparison results between ML algorithms without and with data imputation, evaluated by each test set.

Table 2. Results of the comparison between ML algorithms without and with data imputation evaluated in both test sets.

Training data	kNN Impu.	Classifier	Testing Hosp. A		Testing Hosp. B	
			F1-score	AUC	F1-score	AUC
Hospital A	No	GBC	0.28	0.50	–	–
Hospital A	Yes	GBC	0.77	0.83	0.26	0.49
Hospital A	No	L-GBM	0.28	0.51	–	–
Hospital A	Yes	L-GBM	**0.87**	0.91	0.26	0.51
Hospital B	No	GBC	–	–	0.28	0.52
Hospital B	Yes	GBC	0.20	0.54	0.76	0.82
Hospital B	No	L-GBM	–	–	0.28	0.55
Hospital B	Yes	L-GBM	0.20	0.54	**0.88**	0.91
Hospital A&B	Yes	L-GBM	**0.93**	0.95	**0.94**	0.95

accuracy when making predictions of sepsis in patient records where it managed to have accuracy for imputed data in both hospitals A and B, and low results for non-imputed data (Table 2).

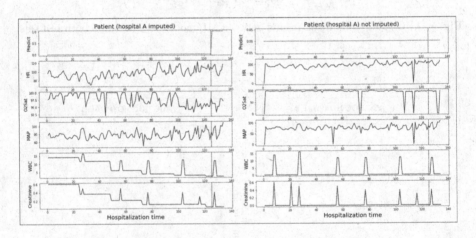

Fig. 7. (Hospital A) imputed VS (Hospital A) no imputed

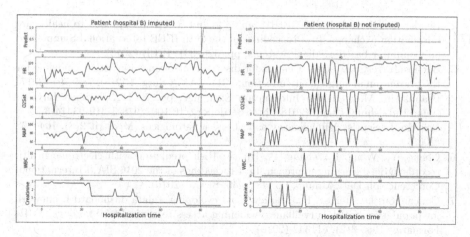

Fig. 8. (Hospital B) imputed VS (Hospital B) no imputed

5   Conclusions

The accuracy of sepsis classification in hospitalized patients relies on the diversity of the training data since we identified variations in the values of the clinical characteristics used to represent each patient's condition. Therefore, we highlight that reliably composing a diverse and structured dataset improves the results. Also, adding a model for imputation of missing values improves the classification performance and deals with the missing data that often appear in hospitals.

Our imputation interoperability approach successfully allows transforming and structuring of the EHRs into the HL7 FHIR standard for modeling machine learning-based missing data and integrating it into patient monitoring and early detection. Additionally, this study identified the essential attributes for developing ML models to classify sepsis in hospitalized patients, obtaining a reduction of 28 clinical features from 58 clinical features provided in the released dataset. As a result, the 28 clinical features were composed of eight vital attributes, 15 laboratory attributes, and five demographic attributes to obtain the best performance in both hospital test sets.

One limitation is that the dataset released in the cardiology challenge 2019 does not include patients' comorbidities, which makes it difficult to scale an ML model trained with data from a single hospital as sepsis can present differently in each individual. Therefore, future work will collect and compose more diverse and rich clinical data from Colombian hospitals.

References

1. Badgeley, M.A., et al.: EHDViz: clinical dashboard development using open-source technologies. BMJ Open **6**(3), e010579 (2016)

2. Bender, D., Sartipi, K.: Hl7 FHIR: an agile and RESTful approach to healthcare information exchange. In: Proceedings of the 26th IEEE International Symposium on Computer-based Medical Systems, pp. 326–331. IEEE (2013)

3. Berríos-Torres, S.I., et al.: Centers for disease control and prevention guideline for the prevention of surgical site infection, 2017. JAMA Surg. **152**(8), 784–791 (2017)

4. Braunstein, M.L.: Health Information Exchange, pp. 79–112. Springer International Publishing, Cham (2018). https://doi.org/10.1007/978-3-319-93414-3_5

5. Briceño, I.: Sepsis: definiciones y aspectos fisiopatológicos. Medicrit **2**(8), 164–178 (2005)

6. Cheng, Y., Wang, F., Zhang, P., Hu, J.: Risk prediction with electronic health records: a deep learning approach. In: Proceedings of the 2016 SIAM International Conference on Data Mining, pp. 432–440. SIAM (2016)

7. Concannon, D., Herbst, K., Manley, E.: Developing a data dashboard framework for population health surveillance: widening access to clinical trial findings. JMIR Formative Res. **3**(2), e11342 (2019)

8. Esteva, A., et al.: A guide to deep learning in healthcare. Nat. Med. **25**(1), 24–29 (2019). https://doi.org/10.1038/s41591-018-0316-z

9. Gøeg, K.R., Rasmussen, R.K., Jensen, L., Wollesen, C.M., Larsen, S., Pape-Haugaard, L.B.: A future-proof architecture for telemedicine using loose-coupled modules and HL7 FHIR. Comput. Methods Programs Biomed. **160**, 95–101 (2018)

10. Goh, K.H., et al.: Artificial intelligence in sepsis early prediction and diagnosis using unstructured data in healthcare. Nat. Commun. **12**(1), 1–10 (2021)

11. González López, D., Álvarez Barreras, L.M., Fernández Orozco, A.: Implementación de estándares DICOM SR y HL7 CDA para la creación y edición de informes de estudios imagenológicos. Revista Cubana de Informática Médica **6**(1), 71–86 (2014)

12. Reyna, M.A., et al.: Early prediction of sepsis from clinical data: the physionet/computing in cardiology challenge 2019. In: 2019 Computing in Cardiology (CinC). pp. Page-1. IEEE (2019)

13. Rudd, K.E., et al.: Global, regional, and national sepsis incidence and mortality, 1990–2017: analysis for the global burden of disease study. Lancet **395**(10219), 200–211 (2020)

14. Soto-Balán, J.C., Campo-Mercado, F.J., Fernández-Chica, D.A., Iglesias-Acosta, J., Salcedo-Mendoza, S., Mora-Moreo, L.: Escalas qSOFA, SOFA ẏ SIRS para evaluación del riesgo de sepsis y admisión hospitalaria. Med. Int. Mex. **38**(2), 258–267 (2022)

15. Zhao, X., Shen, W., Wang, G.: Early prediction of sepsis based on machine learning algorithm. Comput. Intel. Neurosci. **2021**, 1–13 (2021)

Understanding the Energy Consumption of HPC Scale Artificial Intelligence

Danilo Carastan-Santos[(✉)] and Thi Hoang Thi Pham

Univ. Grenoble Alpes, CNRS, Inria, Grenoble INP, LIG, Grenoble, France
`danilo.carastan-dos-santos@inria.fr`

Abstract. This paper contributes towards better understanding the energy consumption trade-offs of HPC scale Artificial Intelligence (AI), and more specifically Deep Learning (DL) algorithms. For this task we developed benchmark-tracker, a benchmark tool to evaluate the speed and energy consumption of DL algorithms in HPC environments. We exploited hardware counters and Python libraries to collect energy information through software, which enabled us to instrument a known AI benchmark tool, and to evaluate the energy consumption of numerous DL algorithms and models. Through an experimental campaign, we show a case example of the potential of benchmark-tracker to measure the computing speed and the energy consumption for training and inference DL algorithms, and also the potential of Benchmark-Tracker to help better understanding the energy behavior of DL algorithms in HPC platforms. This work is a step forward to better understand the energy consumption of Deep Learning in HPC, and it also contributes with a new tool to help HPC DL developers to better balance the HPC infrastructure in terms of speed and energy consumption.

Keywords: AI benchmark · AI energy consumption · HPC scale AI

1 Introduction

The current direction in Artificial Intelligence, and more specifically Deep Learning (DL), is clearly to orders of magnitude more compute [14], reaching High-Performance Computing (HPC) scale. That means more energy, which comes from sources such as fossil fuels, nuclear power, water dams, wind, *etc.* Fossil fuel is the main source, contributing to 36%[1] in the total energy sources mix. Fossil energy emits a significant amount of CO_2 into the environment. Under all of these observations, it is therefore important to monitor the energy consumption of DL, to master its energy demand and attenuate its contribution to climate change.

---

[1] https://ec.europa.eu/eurostat/cache/infographs/energy/bloc-3b.html?lang=en.

© The Author(s), under exclusive license to Springer Nature Switzerland AG 2022
P. Navaux et al. (Eds.): CARLA 2022, CCIS 1660, pp. 131–144, 2022.
https://doi.org/10.1007/978-3-031-23821-5_10

Typical DL research focuses mainly in the quality of the predictions of a trained DL model. As Deep Learning being a significant part of AI, understanding DL and its energy consumption will build us the path to better balance computing and energy resources needed for its proper operation, and thus being less energy demanding.

This paper is a step towards building this path. It addresses the following challenges:

- *For Deep Learning running in HPC platforms, how much energy are the current popular and widely used DNNs consume?*
- *Is it accurate to say that: More complex models will cost more energy?*
- *Does the model give higher accuracy, more energy will be consumed?*

In this work, we instrumented a Deep Learning benchmark with a software energy measurement tool to output the Benchmark-Tracker, which tracks the energy consumption of DNN models inside the DL benchmark. The results from running experiments with the developed instrument give us a better understanding of today's energy consumption for the widely used DNN models. From those insights, we can expand to further and more in-depth future studies on energy consumption issues. The available version of Benchmark-Tracker is on GitHub[2].

We organized the remaining of this paper in the following manner: Sect. 2 presents the related work. In Sect. 3 we present some preliminary background information. Section 4 briefly presents the instrumentation details to implement Benchmark-Tracker, and Sect. 5 present some preliminary results of our tool. Finally, in Sect. 6 we present our concluding remarks and our planned future works.

2   Related Work

2.1   AI and Climate Change

Climate change is a crucial issue for people all over the world. According to experts in the field, AI has the potential to accelerate the process of environmental degradation. For example, large-scale natural language processing models – specifically transformer [16] models – have a huge carbon footprint [13]. Alternatively, "There is a real need to think about how you're building these systems. Are you training a needlessly complex algorithm? How frequently are you retraining?" [13]. In order to understand energy consumption grounds, firstly, we have entered the background detailed in [8]. Secondly, we have to understand that not only using electrical energy to train an DNN creates CO_2, but also collecting and storing data. As DL becomes more complex, data centers are essential for storing large amounts of data needed to power DL systems, but require significant energy. "Data centers are going to be one of the most impactful things on the environment" [10]. Additionally, training advanced artificial intelligence systems, including deep learning models, may require high-powered GPUs running for days at a time and GPUs that use much power to run machine learning training have contributed to significant CO_2 emissions [3].

---

[2] https://github.com/phamthi1812/Benchmark-Tracker.

2.2   Energy-Aware AI

Many practical aspects were attempted by numerous works [6,7,12,15]. Besides focusing on reducing energy consumption in the training process, one of the possibilities is that we can have better energy management once its energy consumption can be modeled and predicted. Chen *et al.* [5] proposed the idea of using deep learning to model energy consumption. In technical points, the hardware provider has also tried to give the better compatible hardware or especially GPU, which gives the best performance in [17].

As some ideas have been outlined above, there are numerous efforts to better control energy consumption, but they still do not reduce the development and power of Deep Learning. We can consider when training models, such as controlling the number of parameters in the model or finding a better efficient way to store data which has mentioned in [2] or [11].

2.3   AI Benchmarks

There are many benchmarks available today for AI, for example, AI Benchmark[3] works for both mobile devices and desktops, Dynabench[4] mainly works on Natural language, Sentiment Analysis, or Cloud-Based AutoML[5], which can enable developers with limited machine learning expertise to train high-quality models specific to their needs. Each tool is developed with an emphasis on a fixed factor, notably the quality of the models' predictions.

2.4   Energy Measurement Tools

There are several tools based on three methodology points: Estimation from hardware characteristics (Green algorithms, ML CO2 Impact), External measures from outside the hardware (Wattmeters), or Software power models from hardware performance counters (CodeCarbon, Experiment-Impact-Tracker [8], CarbonTracker, Energy Scope [9]).

2.5   Positioning of This Paper

Our paper situates in two fronts: (i) Our paper bridges AI benchmarks and energy measurement tools, giving an out-of-the-box tool to help HPC DL developers to better balance the HPC infrastructure in terms of speed and energy consumption, and (ii) we go beyond only evaluating the prediction quality of AI models and algorithms, but we also evaluate the energy/complexity/performance trade-offs of popular AI models and algorithms, taking into consideration several HPC hardware.

---

[3] https://ai-benchmark.com/alpha.
[4] https://dynabench.org/.
[5] https://cloud.google.com/automl/.

3   Background

In this section we present information about the used tools. We start by bringing details about the AI Benchmark Alpha. We then bring some details about measuring/estimating the energy consumption and CO_2 emissions of HPC platforms, and we finish by presenting details about the Experiment-Impact-Tracker tool.

AI Benchmark Alpha. The AI Benchmark Alpha is an open-source[6] library, for evaluating the AI performance of various hardware platforms, including CPUs, GPUs, and TPUs. The benchmark relies on the TensorFlow [1] machine learning library and provides a precise and lightweight solution for assessing inference and training speed for widely used and popular Deep Learning models.

AI Benchmark treats the training and inference of the models as *tests*. The tests cover all major Deep Learning models and algorithms. They include: Classification (MobileNet-V2, Inception-V3, Inception-V4, Inception-ResNet-V2, ResNet-V2-50, ResNet-V2-152, VGG-16), Image-to-Image Mapping (SRCNN 9-5-5, VGG-19, ResNet-SRGAN, ResNet-DPED, U-Net, Nvidia-SPADE), Image Segmentation (ICNet, PSPNet, DeepLab), Image Inpainting (Pixel-RNN), Sentence Sentiment Analysis (LSTM), and Text Translation (GNMT).

Energy Consumption and Carbon Emissions in HPC Platforms. When we measure the energy consumption for training an AI model running in HPC platforms, we also have to consider the additional power used to run the platform that is not directly related to computing, such as cooling. We call this power overhead as Power Usage Effectiveness (PUE), which is a number that depends on the HPC platform cooling efficiency and is often slightly larger than 1, and acts as a multiplicative factor for the measured energy consumption of the computing nodes.

From the energy level consumed obtained at the computing nodes, and multiplied by the PUE, we can calculate the corresponding CO_2 emissions released into the environment as follows:

$$Emission_{carbon} = Energy_{computing} \times Intensity_{carbon}$$

The intensity of carbon is the number of grams of carbon dioxide (CO_2) that it takes to make one unit of electricity a kilowatt per hour (kWh).

---

[6] https://pypi.org/project/ai-benchmark/.

The quantity of carbon emission is just as substantial as the energy consumption because the higher the carbon intensity, the more polluting the energy consumption. The carbon intensity of electricity generation depends on the energy sources mix, and it varies from region to region[7]. For our experiments we adopted 55g CO2/kWh, which relates to France's typical carbon intensity[8].

The Experiment-Impact-Tracker. The Experiment-Impact-Tracker is a software tool[9] that provides a simple plug-and-play solution for tracking your system's energy use, carbon emissions, and compute utilization. It records: power consumption from CPU and GPU, hardware information, and projected carbon emission information on Linux computers with Intel CPUs that implement the Running Average Power Limit (RAPL) and NVIDIA GPUs.

Through the following example, we see how one can track the energy consumption by covering the process with the Experiment-Impact-Tracker:

```
from experiment_impact_tracker.compute_tracker import ImpactTracker
from experiment_impact_tracker.data_interface import DataInterface
os.mkdir("give_a_path")
tracker = ImpactTracker("given_path")
tracker.launch_impact_monitor()
Put_Your_Process_here()
tracker_results = {}
data_interface = DataInterface(["given_path"])
```

The Experiment-Impact-Tracker launches a separate Python process that gathers the energy consumption information in the background. Also, we can then access the information via the DataInterface. Moreover, like we mentioned before about how useful this Tracker is because of this context management, as illustrated in the listing below:

```
experiment1 = tempfile.mkdtemp()
experiment2 = tempfile.mkdtemp()

with ImpactTracker(experiment1):
    do_something()

with ImpactTracker(experiment2):
    do_something_else()
```

The combination of the AI Benchmark Alpha with the Experiment-Impact-Tracker that we did to produce Benchmark Tracker, which is used for running the experiments to understand the energy behavior of AI algorithms, is presented in the following subsection.

---

[7] https://app.electricitymap.org/map.

[8] https://app.electricitymap.org/map.

[9] https://github.com/Breakend/experiment-impact-tracker.

4 Benchmark Tracker

The essence of Benchmark-Tracker is in the instrumentation of the AI Benchmark Alpha with Experiment-Impact-Tracer, to also measure the energy consumption. For this task, we identified the code regions where AI Benchmark runs for each model's training and inference. From there, we instrumented the Experiment-Impact-Tracker in these code regions, intending to be able to measure not only the hardware benchmark from the AIBenchmark but also the energy consumption of each model running in this benchmark. We can control which process we would like to run in the primary run file. The process goes as follows:

1. Benchmark runs and starts calling the corresponding tests for each model.
2. The Experiment-Impact-Tracker is activated and starts measuring energy during the training process of that model.
3. The Tracker is turned off, and data logging occurs.
4. The inference process of the same model happens (if we run this tool for both training and inference).
5. Another test is called up to continue the process.

The inference process is shortly presented as follows:

```
for subTest in (test.inference):
    os.mkdir(PATH)
    with ImpactTracker(PATH):
        <<TRACKED_CODE>>
    tracker_INFERENCE_results = {}
    data_interface = DataInterface([PATH])
```

The advantage of using experiment-impact-tracker becomes evident, since we can easily instrument a code section using the Python context management (i.e., the with statement). In the case above, «TRACKED_CODE» refers to the code commands for an inference task. The same instrumentation procedure holds for the training tasks.

With the AI benchmark's dataset and our evaluated hardware (see Sect. 5.1), the AI benchmark runs approximately 60 s for one model. The Experiment-Impact-Tracker provides inaccurate estimations when the processing time is too short (in the order of 60 s). With this in mind, we artificially increase the size of the dataset to increase the processing time, and have accurate energy measurements. Artificially increasing the size of the dataset invalidate the accurate computed at the training tasks. That is why in the next section we compare the model's accuracy in terms of their reported accuracy in ImageNet[10]. We plan to release a new version of Benchmark-Tracker with an appropriate dataset in future work (see Sect. 6).

---

[10] https://ai-benchmark.com/tests.html.

5   Results

5.1   Experimental Setting

For the experiments, we used Grid'5000[11] High-Performance Computing test-bed. We used the Chifflet node (Model: Dell PowerEdge R730, CPU: Intel Xeon E5-2680 v4, Memory: 768 GiB, GPU: 2 x Nvidia GeForce GTX 1080 Ti (11 GiB)).

5.2   Experimental Results

We ran Benchmark-Tracker 10 times to achieve the below statistical results. The bar plots below represent an estimate of the central tendency for energy consumption with the height of each rectangle. It provides some indication of the uncertainty around that estimate using error bars. Intuitively, we see that the confidence intervals bar graph shows a slight error between 10 sets of the outcomes. It is also essential to remember that a bar plot shows only the mean value.

Let recall the definition of Training and Inference. We can say Training and Inference are the norm in DL. They are two key processes associated with developing and using AI:

- Training is "teaching" a Deep Neural Network (DNN) to perform the desired AI task (such as image classification or converting speech into text). We can express that it fits a model for training data. During the DL training process, the data scientist is trying to guide the DNN model to converge and gain the expected accuracy.
- The inference uses a trained DNN model to make predictions against previously unseen data and perform decision-making. The DL training process involves inference, because each time an image is fed into the DNN during training, the DNN tries to classify it. Given this, people usually deploy a trained DNN for inference. For example, one could make a copy of a trained DNN and start using it "as is" for inference.

Therefore, the results are grouped into training and inference phases.

With AI tasks, created DNN models can be large and complex, with dozens or hundreds of layers of artificial neurons and millions or billions of weights linking them. Normally, the bigger the DNN, the more computing, memory, and energy are consumed to execute it, and the longer will be the response time (or "latency") from when you input data to the DNN until you obtain an outcome.

Without losing generality, to better focus the analysis we only access the results of the classification task. It is important to remind that, thanks to AI Benchmark Alpha, Benchmark-Tracker also evaluates other kinds of tasks, such as (Classification, Image-to-Image Mapping, Image Segmentation). Table 1 presents the classification models' complexity, measured in the number of parameters.

---

[11] https://www.grid5000.fr/w/Grid5000:Home.

Table 1. Image classification model complexity, measured as the number of parameters [4]

Model	Number of parameter (M: millions)
MobileNet-V2	5M
Inception-V3	25M
Inception-V4	35M
Inception-ResNet-V2	60M
ResNet-V2-50	30M
ResNet-V2-152	70M
VGG-16	150M

Also, to give the reader an impression of the connection between the structure of the DNNs and the energy consumption, we briefly present the main ideas of the evaluated models for the image classification task:

– MobileNet-V2: Depth wise Separable Convolution which dramatically reduces the complexity cost and model size of the network.
– Inception-V3: Factorizing Convolutions, which reduces the number of connections/parameters without decreasing network efficiency, helps realize computational efficiency and fewer parameters.
– Inception-V4: A more uniform, simplified architecture and more inception modules than Inception-v3. It uses asymmetric filters.
– Inception-ResNet-V2: Use a part of Inception-V4 and replace connection by residual links.
– ResNet-V2-50: It introduces skip connection (or shortcut connection) to fit the input from the previous layer to the next layer without any modification of the input. This version has 50 layers and uses residual links.
– ResNet-V2-152: Same idea with ResNet-V2-50, but this one has the maximum number of layers 152. ResNet is the Winner of ILSVRC 2015 in image classification, detection, and localization, as well as Winner of MS COCO 2015 detection, and segmentation.
– VGG-16: by using 3×3 filters uniformly, VGG-16 reduces the number of weight parameters in the model significantly. It helps in reducing the complexity of computing.

We describe the results in inference belonging to each type of model. Additionally, the rectangle's color shows the reported accuracy on ImageNet for each of the evaluated models[12].

---

[12] https://ai-benchmark.com/tests.html.

Figure 1 presents the energy consumption in the inference process per image for classification, which shows us the amount of energy it will cost each time we input one more image into the trained relative model. The small number of parameters and the simple model structure are the main contributors to MobileNet-V2 having the lowest power level. However, this entails that it also has almost the lowest accuracy. The increase in the number of parameters increased the power consumption of Inception-V4 compared to Inception-V3.

With double the parameters, InceptionResNet-V2 offers 3% better accuracy than Inception-V3 and 1% in Inception-V4. However, it has an energy consumption of approximately the same as Inception-V4 or even lower. It can also be remarked that the relationship between model complexity and energy levels cannot be linear. Because if this happens, the energy consumption of InceptionResNet-V2 will probably double with the corresponding increase in the number of parameters. This result contributes to the hypothesis that the number of parameters of the model does not seem to be the only factor determining the energy consumption. The DNN model's structure also significantly influences the energy it consumes.

VGG-16 had the highest energy consumption among the evaluated models, but it did not offer better accuracy. It is even lower than MobileNet-V2, even though its parameters are approximately 30 times more.

Table 2 shows the energy consumption, estimated carbon emission and also the duration time for the inference process. We separately run the inference process on the same dataset with training. Usually, this is not the case when we run on the same dataset. However, it works to simulate the real-life process, and this result still contributes to the conclusion in comparing the energy consumption when we use trained models.

Table 2. Average energy consumption (EC), carbon emission (CE), duration (D) in inference for classification models

Model	EC (kWh)	CE (kgCO$_2$eq)	D (seconds)
MobileNet-V2	1.18×10^{-3}	0.66×10^{-4}	32,11
Inception-V3	1.96×10^{-3}	1.10×10^{-4}	32,26
Inception-V4	2.60×10^{-3}	1.45×10^{-4}	32,41
Inception-ResNet-V2	2.56×10^{-3}	1.43×10^{-4}	32,51
ResNet-V2-50	2.42×10^{-3}	1.35×10^{-4}	32,31
ResNet-V2-152	2.61×10^{-3}	1.46×10^{-4}	32,95
VGG-16	2.96×10^{-3}	1.66×10^{-4}	33,63

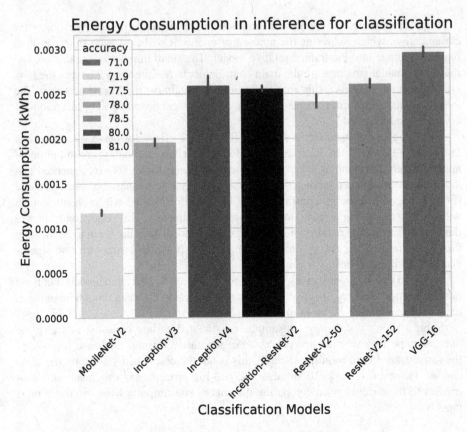

Fig. 1. Energy consumption in inference per image for classification models

Comeback with training, Table 3 gives the detailed energy consumption scores. From Fig. 2, 3, the complexity of the models explains that InceptionResNet-V2, with twice as many parameters for the model as Inception-V3, and Inception-V4, has the highest energy consumption level. Likewise, the training time for Inception-ResNet-V2 is the biggest among the three models mentioned above. The same goes for ResNet-152, which has twice the number of parameters ResNet-50 and has a higher power and time level than ResNet-50.

Nevertheless, it did not happen for VGG-16. Even though VGG-16 is the most significant one with 150M parameters, it has remarkably positive results by being the model that consumes the smallest amount of energy and runs in the shortest time. The belonging designed architecture idea of each DNN explains a part of why the energy consumption of VGG-16 and MobileNet-V2 are the best models in terms of energy consumption and training duration for Classification. They both have the same objective when trying to reduce the complexity cost. While MobileNet-V2 reduces the model size in order to run on mobile devices, VGG-16 decreases filter size. This observation shows evidence for the design of deep neural networks can reduce energy consumption and training time.

Table 3. Average energy consumption, carbon emission, duration in training for classification models

Model	EC (kWh)	CE (kgCO$_2$eq)	D (seconds)
MobileNet-V2	$1,75.10^{-3}$	$0,98.10^{-4}$	35,04
Inception-V3	$2,98.10^{-3}$	$1,67.10^{-4}$	52,09
Inception-V4	$3,93.10^{-3}$	$2,20.10^{-4}$	53,79
Inception-ResNet-V2	$4,06.10^{-3}$	$2,27.10^{-4}$	59,98
ResNet-V2-50	$2,29.10^{-3}$	$1,28.10^{-4}$	40,01
ResNet-V2-152	$4,01.10^{-3}$	$2,24.10^{-4}$	53,32
VGG-16	$1,83.10^{-3}$	$1,02.10^{-4}$	35,19

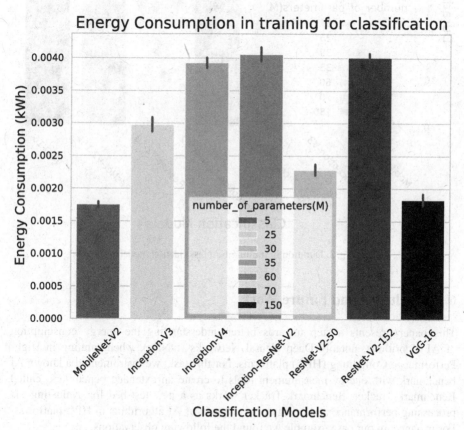

Fig. 2. Energy consumption in training for classification models

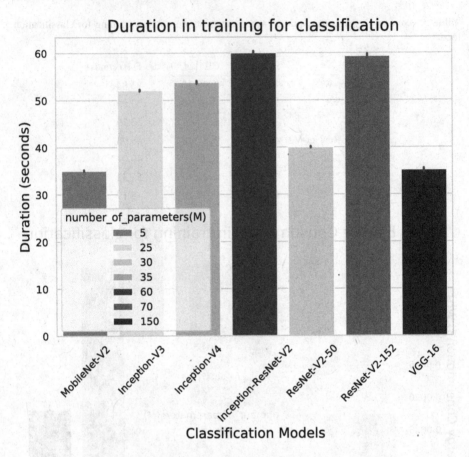

Fig. 3. Duration in training for classification models

6   Conclusion and Future Work

This paper presents a step towards better understanding the energy consumption of AI algorithms, notably Deep Neural Networks (DNNs), when running in High-Performance Computing (HPC) platforms. For this task, we instrumented a known AI benchmark with energy measurement tools to create an extended benchmark, called Benchmark-Tracker. Benchmark-Tracker works as a new test-bed for evaluating the processing performance and energy consumption of AI algorithms in HPC platforms. For instance, in our case example we found the following observations.

For a certain AI task (in our case example, for the image classification task), more complex DNN models can consume more energy, emit more CO2, and take longer time than simpler models to train. Nevertheless, there are exceptions, and they advise that the energy consumption likewise depends on the structure of the DNNs, and their relative function is not linear. A more accurate model does not necessarily consume more energy. Also, if we bring the connection between inference and training into the balance, the relationship becomes even more complicated. There are cases where the energy level for training is low but exceptionally high in inference and vice versa.

The choice of model selection and the HPC hardware is not a trivial decision, since it depends on the problem and resources specificities, which are not always well understood theoretically. Benchmark-Tracker can help to perform this decision by performing light-weight experiments to grasp how much energy a certain AI model will consume and how fast it will run, according to a certain HPC hardware.

6.1   Future Work

For future work, we will take into account calculating the accuracy belonging to the models for a specific dataset, besides the energy consumption. This will enable us to perform the following investigations.

1. If we reduce or increase the dataset size during training, we can consider how much energy the training will consume and how much accuracy we will get for each model to compare. Furthermore, doing that on a specific model will help understand the tradeoffs of dataset size, energy consumption, and resulting inference accuracy.
2. With the Benchmark-Tracker, we are going to set energy budgets during the models' training. We can control the training process for a specific objective by stopping the training when the total energy (measured by an energy measurement library) passes a defined budget. Furthermore, as a consequence, we can evaluate the performance behavior of the DNN models when we have limited energy budgets.
3. Following the energy budget idea, we are going to compare shallow learning algorithms for a selection of applications present in Benchmark-Tracker and whether these shallow learning algorithms outperform or not the deep learning algorithms when we have energy budgets.

Acknowledgements. This work was supported by the research program on Edge Intelligence of the Multi-disciplinary Institute on Artificial Intelligence MIAI at Grenoble Alpes (ANR-19-P3IA-0003), and the Energy Saving in Large Scale Distributed Platforms - Energumen project (ANR-18-CE25-0008). We also thank all institutions (INRIA, CNRS, RENATER and several Universities as well as other organizations) who support the Grid5000 platform.

Author contributions. Thi contributed to the source-code implementation, execution of experiments, data processing, analysis, and results interpretation with the guidance of Danilo. Danilo was the main writer of Sects. 1, 2, and 6, and Thi was the main writer of Sects. 3, 4, and 5. Finally, all the authors reviewed the final manuscript.

References

1. Abadi, M., et al.: TensorFlow: large-scale machine learning on heterogeneous systems (2015). Software available from tensorflow.org. https://www.tensorflow.org/
2. Avidon, E.: 'data for good' movement spurs action in fight for causes (2020). https://www.techtarget.com/searchbusinessanalytics/news/252487703/Data-for-good-movement-spurs-action-in-fight-for-causes

3. Avidon, E.: How much does it cost to run a GPU (2022). https://graphicscardsadvisor.com/how-much-does-it-cost-to-run-a-gpu/
4. Bianco, S., Cadene, R., Celona, L., Napoletano, P.: Benchmark analysis of representative deep neural network architectures. IEEE Access **6**, 64270–64277 (2018). https://doi.org/10.1109/access.2018.2877890
5. Chen, C., Liu, Y., Kumar, M., Qin, J.: Energy consumption modelling using deep learning technique - a case study of EAF. Procedia CIRP **72**, 1063–1068 (2018)
6. Ficher, M., Berthoud, F., Ligozat, A.L., Sigonneau, P., Wisslé, M., Tebbani, B.: Assessing the carbon footprint of the data transmission on a backbone network. In: 24th Conference on Innovation in Clouds, Internet and Networks, Paris, France, March 2021. https://hal.archives-ouvertes.fr/hal-03196527
7. García-Martín, E., Rodrigues, C.F., Riley, G.D., Grahn, H.: Estimation of energy consumption in machine learning. J. Parallel Distrib. Comput. **134**, 75–88 (2019)
8. Henderson, P., Hu, J., Romoff, J., Brunskill, E., Jurafsky, D., Pineau, J.: Towards the systematic reporting of the energy and carbon footprints of machine learning. J. Mach. Learn. Res. **21**, 1–43 (2020)
9. Jay, M.: How can we estimate the energy consumption of training an AI model? (2022). https://team.inria.fr/datamove/files/2022/02/220202-slides-mathilde-jay.pdf
10. Labbe, M.: Energy consumption of AI poses environmental problems. https://www.techtarget.com/searchenterpriseai/feature/Energy-consumption-of-AI-poses-environmental-problems
11. Labbe, M.: AI and climate change: the mixed impact of machine learning (2021). https://www.techtarget.com/searchenterpriseai/feature/AI-and-climate-change-The-mixed-impact-of-machine-learning
12. Mazouz, A., Wong, D.C.L., Kuck, D.J., Jalby, W.: An incremental methodology for energy measurement and modeling. In: Proceedings of the 8th ACM/SPEC on International Conference on Performance Engineering (2017)
13. Morgan, L.: AI carbon footprint: helping and hurting the environment (2021). https://www.techtarget.com/searchenterpriseai/feature/AI-carbon-footprint-Helping-and-hurting-the-environment
14. OpenAI: AI and compute (2018). https://openai.com/blog/ai-and-compute/
15. Schmidt, V., et al.: CodeCarbon: estimate and track carbon emissions from machine learning computing (2021). https://doi.org/10.5281/zenodo.4658424
16. Vaswani, A., et al.: Attention is all you need. In: Advances in Neural Information Processing Systems, vol. 30 (2017)
17. Walton, J.: Graphics card power consumption and efficiency tested (2021). https://www.tomshardware.com/features/graphics-card-power-consumption-tested

Using Big Data and Serverless Architecture to Follow the Emotional Response to the COVID-19 Pandemic in Mexico

Edgar León-Sandoval$^{(\boxtimes)}$ ⓘ, Mahdi Zareei ⓘ, Liliana Ibeth Barbosa-Santillán ⓘ, and Luis Eduardo Falcón Morales ⓘ

School of Engineering and Sciences, Monterrey Institute of Technology and Higher Education, Monterrey, Mexico
`leon.s.edgar@tec.mx`

Abstract. The emergence of the COVID-19 pandemic has led to an unprecedented change in the lifestyle routines of millions of people. Beyond the multiple repercussions of the pandemic, we are also facing significant challenges in the population's mental health and health programs. Typical techniques to measure the population's mental health are semiautomatic. Social media allow us to know habits and daily life, making this data a rich silo for understanding emotional and mental well-being. This study aims to build a resilient and flexible system that allows us to track and measure the sentiment changes of a given population, in our case, the Mexican people, in response to the COVID-19 pandemic. We built an extensive data system utilizing modern cloud-based serverless architectures to analyze 760,064,879 public domain tweets collected from a public access repository to examine the collective shifts in the general mood about the pandemic evolution, news cycles, and governmental policies using open sentiment analysis tools. We provide metrics, advantages, and challenges of developing serverless cloud-based architectures for a natural language processing project of a large magnitude.

Keywords: Sentiment analysis · Big data · COVID-19 · Machine learning · Mexico · Twitter

1 Introduction

On February 27, 2020, Hugo López-Gatell Ramírez, the head of the Undersecretaries of Prevention and Health Promotion at the Mexican Secretariat of Health, reported a patient in the INER (National Institute of Respiratory Diseases) as the first official case of COVID-19 reported nationwide [21]. From there, a general lockdown was mandated on April 21, 2020. Since then, the country has followed actions based on non-pharmaceutical interventions (NPI) to mitigate the effects of the pandemic on the general population. However, the COVID-19 pandemic also challenges individuals' emotional and psychological well-being.

P. Navaux et al. (Eds.): CARLA 2022, CCIS 1660, pp. 145–159, 2022.
https://doi.org/10.1007/978-3-031-23821-5_11

This challenge raises the need to incorporate emotional health-related data into organizations' decision-making processes and to build the appropriate dashboards showing critical information. Even though it is clear the importance of tracking the day-to-day data on the pandemic progression regarding ongoing infection rates and fatality, among other statistics, another important dimension, emotional health, needs a proper measuring instrument. These reasons point to the need to build, deploy, and maintain a large-scale, resilient system capable of performing sentiment analysis in large, continuous data sets, such as ongoing Twitter traffic.

Acquiring and processing this amount of information is not an easy task, as this is a task that presents all of the challenges described by the three Vs. of Big-Data: Volume, Variety, and Velocity [15]. For large-scale sentiment analysis systems, these challenges are explored in depth by [5] adopting a broader definition of big data. There are multiple definitions containing different aspects of these architectures, such as analysis, value, computer power, visualization, variability, and integrity, among others. An in-depth description of these definitions is described by [28], concluding that the challenges presented depend on the context of the task. However, as already defended by [15], this problem adheres to the extensive data domain in multiple dimensions beyond the original three dimensions proposed. Several challenges must be addressed as a big data problem, which is listed next.

1. Acquiring the emotional data of a large population of individuals, either in a traditional methodology or through social media, can be costly.
2. Processing this large amount of data in a short amount of time is difficult.
3. Handling heterogeneous data, such as those presented in tweets, is not trivial.
4. Building a system requires expertise from multiple dimensions: data science, big data, software engineering, systems engineering, and natural language processing.
5. Maintaining such systems is expensive for the software and infrastructure required.
6. Updating can be very difficult, depending on the coupling strategy chosen for the modules.

To solve point (1), we can recur to traditional survey methods, such as interviews or surveys. Still, we find them prohibitive, for, besides the high expense, they require a significant amount of time and effort to gather data on a smaller sample of the population. They can only provide information on discrete-time periods rather than a continuous flow. Thus we can look for data in the already public posts on social media. Twitter is a mature, well-established, and popular micro-blogging service that offers users a platform to share their conversations, reviews, and data. For this purpose, we collected a large corpus of heterogeneous COVID-19-related data [1], which we will refer to as *the COVID-19 Twitter chatter data set* and used as our primary source of information. *the COVID-19 Twitter chatter data set* includes raw text, tweet metadata, images, videos, URLs, popularity, and other types of metadata. This corpus is an excellent candidate for sentiment analysis to follow public opinion on any given topic or event as long as it is related to the COVID-19 pandemic. Still, it does present several challenges, such as the high computing resources needed for conducting the research work, but in return, it provides a curated, well-defined data corpus. In addition, sentiment analysis on a near-real-time basis is possible thanks to the big data technology stack, which is focused on handling and processing a large volume of data at a fast velocity, and from numerous heterogeneous sources [3].

Sentiment analysis refers to a group of natural language processing techniques that allow extracting affective indicators from raw text to determine the sentiment polarity of a given tweet, whether the tweet expresses a positive or negative emotion. To measure the sentiment polarity of tweets, we may employ several language models, each implemented using different technologies and having other characteristics. All implementations use nonlinear statistical models as language representations, in different ways, from massive attention-based deep learning architectures to more straightforward dictionary-based deployments, as is VADER (Valence Aware Dictionary and sEntiment Reasoner) [9].

VADER is an open-source, rule-based tool that recognizes standard terms, idioms, jargon, and more complex grammar structures such as punctuation, negations, abbreviations, etc., commonly employed in social media platforms. VADER uses a curated lexicon of over 7,500 standard terms rated by ten independent humans. VADER has been extensively validated for Twitter-based content, showing promising results in terms of accuracy for tweets in several sentiment analysis tools [2]. However, state-of-the-art language models are implemented by deep neural networks, allowing the use of a more sophisticated text representation space, context awareness, and powerful nonlinear statistical models to provide text classification. BERTweet [20] is based on BERT [4], using a pre-training procedure similar to that utilized by RoBERTa [17] and uses publicly available tweets in English for training and evaluation. TimeLMs [18] introduces a time concept into the language model by utilizing continuous learning and thus accounts for future and out-of-distribution tweets it might encounter.

This language model also uses publicly available tweets in English for training and evaluation. Thus, it is essential to have a system independent of the language model selected for the task, making it simple to choose and change the language model if needed. This work describes the architecture developed to perform this sentiment analysis study, already reported by [16], going in-depth on the design, advantages, and disadvantages of utilizing big data in serverless cloud-based architectures for a project of this size. Next, we present a brief exploration of related works, followed by the methodology followed in the study, the architecture implemented as well as infrastructure-related information, the experiments performed, and closing with a description of the results and a brief discussion of those results.

2   Related Work

Twitter has been widely used to perform sentiment analysis studies in the economic, social, and political domains [27]. Sentiment analysis research extensively uses Twitter-related traffic, partly due to the high volume [10], high availability, and the limit of 280 characters per entry [8]. A survey shows that building such systems running on private clouds is feasible, relying on the Hadoop tech stack. However, these systems are expensive: they require a significant up-front investment, require effort to set up and maintain and fail to scale properly according to the present demand [5].

Table 1. Summary of massively distributed systems for performing sentiment analysis over large volumes of tweets [16].

Reference	Tech	Batch/Stream	Features	Comments
Victor and Lijo, 2919 [26]	`Hadoop & Spark`	both	HBase interface	
Sathya et al., 2012 [22]	`Hadoop`	batch	classifier selection, pre-processing, sarcasm, VR	open source, needs self hosting
Bhuvaneswari et al., 2019 [2]	`Hadoop & Kafka`	both	Uses flume	
Cenni et al., 2018 [3]	`Hadoop`	batch	-	aggregation of 4 projects
Sehgal and Agarwal, 2016 [23]	`Hadoop`	batch	-	
Kummar and Bala, 2016 [14]	`Mahout`	batch	-	Less complex to build, experiments made on a single node
Kumamoto et al., 2014 [13]		batch	graphs	no details
Khuc et al., 2012 [11]	`Hadoop`	batch	HBase interface	nice UI for data cleanup
Marcus et al., 2011 [19]	`Hadoop`	batch	peak detection, sub-event selection	
this work	`cloud & serverless`	both	auto scaling, easy to consume, cloud native	uses remote hosting

Table 1 displays a summary of these systems, showcasing that Apache Hadoop technologies support most prototypes for streaming and batch data processing. While these systems all present good results, they also lack flexibility and scalability, resulting in high maintenance costs, and a robust up-front investment is required. Being self-hosted solutions, it is the responsibility of the implementing institution to procure equipment, networking, setup, and maintenance of the system. There is also waste in terms of regular under-utilization of the system, making this an expensive solution that requires a significant up-front investment. So, it can be mitigated by having dynamic scaling in place, thus providing the needed resources instead of having a fixed capacity regardless of utilization.

3   Method

We consumed a large dataset of tweets collected from an open-access repository of global COVID-19-related tweets, called the *COVID-19 Twitter chatter dataset* [1]. It is designed to collect every tweet posted that is somehow related to the pandemic in a diverse variety of geographic locations. This repository provides a list of tweet IDs, geographical location, and detected language using the following schema: [tweet_id, date, time, lang, country_code]. However, we encountered schema inconsistencies over time. For example, the annotation of country_code, which is necessary for filtering before requesting a tweet lookup, was not introduced until the second half of the year, and even so, a vast number of tweets lack this metadata annotation.

For this reason, we had to load them via Twitter's public API to filter out tweets originating from outside Mexico, which may leave data out from those users who choose not to share their location. We used this information to download each tweet in Mexico, discarding all other metadata provided by Twitter's API for privacy reasons. Specifically, we retrieved COVID-19-related tweets posted in Mexico from February 1, 2020, through December 31, 2020, processing $n = 760,064,879$ unique tweets. All tweets were scrubbed of any personally identifiable information to ensure the user's privacy and comply with ethical, social media use practices, resulting in the following simplified schema: full_text, id, timestamp. It is worth mentioning that this data set includes tweets in multiple languages, including both English and Spanish, for many of the population engage in social media in languages other than native Spanish.

Figure 1 summarizes the general data flow of the system. Tweets are consumed parallel to mitigate the official lookup API's rate limitations. The design of this system allows for this API to be easily swapped for other end-points, such as the search end-point, allowing data consumption as a near real-time data stream without the need to perform any other code or system changes. These tweets flow into a pre-processing stage, where they are cleaned up and made ready for consumption by the language models and further narrowed down to a total of over $n = 2,142,800$ unique tweets by discriminating tweets to include only the ones that are not retweets, and, posted from within Mexico. For a detailed definition of the schema returned by the lookup API, please consult the tweet object model definition [24]. Still, for this study, we strip down all

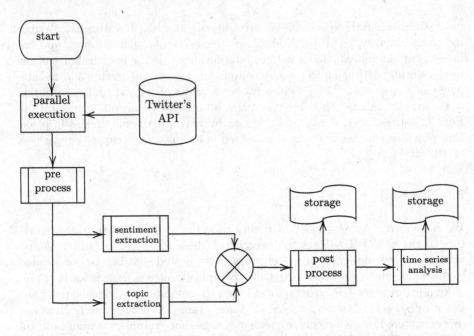

Fig. 1. *Data Flow Overview.* The data is processed in three main stages: first, we load the desired tweet IDs from the *COVID-19 Twitter chatter dataset*, then we consult them directly from Twitter using the official APIs. For pre-processing we clean-up and filter the data, then we process this data set in order to produce a time series of the perceived COVID-19 related sentiment.

the metadata to include only the ID, tweet text, and timestamp. For the pre-processing performed on the text, we follow the standard practices common in natural language processing projects: removing punctuations and emojis, URLs, stop words, converting the text to lower casing, tokenization, stemming, and lemmatization. We then perform sentiment analysis and a time series analysis on the remaining tweets to do the actual sentiment polarity tracking, better described by [16].

Next, a quick summary of the methodology followed by [16] is presented. Natural language processing has several architectures available to implement language models, each with their differences in robustness and accuracy for several tasks, such as sentiment polarity determination. These implementations use non-linear statistical models as language representations, in different ways, from vast attention-based deep learning architectures to more straightforward dictionary-based deployments, such as VADER. VADER [9] is an open-source rule-based robust language model that can handle complex grammar structures commonly employed in social networks. VADER is reliable, fast to deploy, and needs few resources to evaluate new text entries. However, for training, it utilizes a curated corpus evaluated by humans, making adapting it, or incorporating new data a difficult task. BERTweet [20] is based on BERT [4], using a pretraining procedure similar to that utilized by RoBERTa [17] and uses publicly available Tweets in English for training and evaluation.

We then utilize VADER for sentiment polarity determination, consuming a single tweet and providing three different metrics: positive and negative intensity, and a composed metric obtained by normalizing both the positive and negative scores and using an external factor to better approximate a 1 to −1 distribution [9],

$$norm\_score = \frac{sum\_polarities}{\sqrt{sum\_polarities^2 + \alpha}} \qquad (1)$$

where $sum\_polarities$ is the simple addition of positive and negative polarities, and α is initialized as $\alpha = 15$. We need to adjust this α for every operation based on a heuristic and the lexicon collected by the language model. We then use these three metrics to construct a smoothed time series, perform a daily average and calculate an ARIMA model where the box-test showed a $p-value < 2.2e^{-16}$ to estimate the trends and seasonality the series might show. Details on the results obtained are presented in the Results section.

3.1 General System Architecture

Implementing cloud technologies, a serverless architecture, and industry-standard ML-ops practices require three challenges to be properly addressed in order to be successful:

1. The system needs to ingest large amounts of data in the shortest possible time.
2. The system must maintain user privacy and keep the data secure.
3. Use state-of-the-art deep-learning-based language models and implementations with low-level hardware optimization for efficient data processing.

So, the system was implemented using Google's Cloud Platform (GCP)for its dynamic scaling of managed infrastructure and tight integration with the Tensorflow/Keras technology stack, enabling dynamic scaling, loose coupling, and managed micro-services/serverless technology. All while maintaining low-level hardware optimization over the use of multiple CPUs and GPUs in each managed instance.

Figure 2 summarizes the system's general architecture, which follows a flow somewhat similar to that described by Fig. 1. This flow is next described, but keep in mind we have observed some details out of the list, such as monitoring, logging, deployment pipelines, and general error handling.

1. Data is ingested from Twitter, using the identifiers provided by the *COVID-19 Twitter chatter dataset* and the public query API provided by Twitter.
2. The queried tweet is posted in PubSub. Then preprocessing is evaluated, writing the resulting clean tweet directly to disk storage and posted again to PubSub.

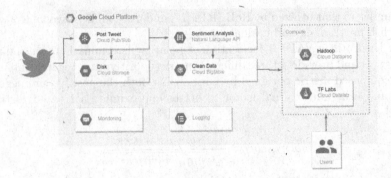

Fig. 2. *General Architecture implemented in Google Cloud Platform (GCP)* [16]. This cloud-based architecture ingests tweets using the official Twitter APIs, sending each one of these through Google's Pub/Sub, which uses as endpoints basic pre-processing, raw storage, and a serverless function to calculate the sentiment polarity. The results of this function is fed into BigTable through another Pub/Sub pipeline.

3. PubSub feeds this data entry into a service, which evaluates the polarity of the tweets using a language model implementation written in TensorFlow, and posts the results again in PubSub to be fed into BigTable for final consumption. Note that this evaluation greatly benefits from choosing instances with GPU support, or if hosting the model in another GCP service, this will happen automatically to use the CUDA technology.
4. The data is now ready for consumption by a managed Dataproc instance which can work under different approaches:
   (a) Periodic batch jobs that collect daily aggregations. These aggregations are also stored in cloud storage for easy access.
   (b) Jupyter notebooks for manual data exploration.
   (c) A third hook can be placed here for generating near-real-time visualizations of the gathered data.
   Here we decided on the daily aggregations generated by the batch jobs, but this can be easily changed, and the options are not mutually exclusive.

   This approach makes it easy to collaborate remotely and share progress or data. All the code was implemented using standard Python 3.7 and its data-focused libraries. The language models used for polarity calculation were implemented in TensorFlow. TensorFlow enables consuming state-of-the-art language models as a service, decoupling this architecture from the rest of the solution and allowing the implementation of an automated ML-ops flow to inject updates and model changes. Note the clear separation of operations performed on the ingested data. This flow allows for consuming data as streams, thus allowing using this solution as a decision-making tool by providing near real-time data processing.
   Remember that point (3) is the sentiment polarity evaluation triggered by PubSub and supports multiple endpoints. This makes it easy to swap solutions

or keep multiple language models evaluating data in parallel and putting results in different `BigTable` instances. We used for sentiment polarity evaluation the `VADER`, `BERTweet` and `RoBERTa` language models, for they cover both state-of-the-art implementations as well as rule-based, well tested systems. Both `BERTweet` and `RoBERTA` are based on `BERT`, which needs around 350M parameters to perform forward and back propagation, needed to evaluate sentiment polarity [4]. However, the system can keep up with tweet consumption by exploiting `CUDA` technology, both in the software and hardware layer, thus providing reliable results promptly.

For point (4), `Dataproc` provides a managed `Apache Hadoop/Spark` cluster that provides Big Data capabilities. We choose to perform data analytics on an extensive batch data set. However, `Apache Spark` also provides streaming capabilities, and this combined with infrastructure-as-code practices, makes trivial the decision of batch vs. streaming data analytics. This flexibility permits batch-processing large amounts of data or providing near real-time data results by processing it as it is consumed in a streaming fashion. Both are proven to be helpful in different use cases.

It is also worth mentioning the MLops practices used throughout this project and not described by Fig. 2. Besides hosting the utilized code in `GitHub`, we integrated and utilized `Google Cloud Deployment Manager` to describe as plain text files the services and infrastructure used, detect changes in them, and automatically propagate changes in the solution. More details on the infrastructure are provided in the next section. This practice, coupled with tagging and versioning of the utilized language models, allows for auto-deployments with a solid integration with `TensorFlow Serving` and infrastructure management as if it were code. While this practice requires robust up-front investment in development time, it provides flexibility and resources to maintain a high-quality standard in the development and experimentation cycle, such as pair programming, code reviews, and automated unit testing.

4   Experiments

This research work consumed a large dataset of tweets, collected from an open-access repository called the *COVID-19 Twitter chatter dataset* [1], and is composed of COVID-19-related tweets, in multiple languages and all over the world. From them, we downloaded $n = 760,064,879$ unique tweets using the official Twitter API, regardless of language but confined to the geographical region of Mexico and from February 1 to December 31, 2020. These were filtered down to $n = 2,142,800$ unique tweets and stripped of any metadata, with light text preprocessing to clean URLs and similar operations. The sentiment polarity was then calculated using several language models, from which a time series was generated, followed by a similar analysis to that of [16].

The system was designed following a serverless, cloud-based architecture as described in Sect. 3, Method. Our system was implemented entirely in the Google Cloud Platform, using `Python 3.7` for any code development, data transformation, or aggregation, as well as language model implementations.

Table 2. Summary of machine types provided by GCP. Note that there are multiple configurations for GPUs as well, but these are only available in A2 instances.

Instance type	CPUs	Memory	GPUs	SSD	interruptable
E2 (grl)	2~32	0.5~8 GB	0	no	yes
E2 (shared)	0.25~1	0.5~8 GB	0	no	yes
A2	12~96	7 GB	1~4	yes	yes
A2 (mega)	96	14 GB	1~16	yes	yes

However, there is a hard limit on Twitter's consumption rate, set to 450 requests per 15-min window, and a ceiling of total tweets consumed [25]. GCP offers multiple configuration options, considering the number of machines to be provided, although the load-balancer dynamically decides this and the type of machine. Table 2 summarizes the machines types [7], from which we set up three different environments:

1. Reduction costs by selecting the **E2** machine family, which has a low number of shared CPUs and no GPU option.
2. Providing a fast throughput by selecting the **E2** machine family, which comes with a fair number of dedicated CPUs and has multiple GPU options, and finally,
3. A hybrid approach, in which we utilize the data pipelines, but the processing is performed locally.

Table 3. Summary of performance of GPUs offered by GCP, in `TFLOPS`.

Metric	A100	T4	V100	P4	P100
FP64	9.7	0.25	7.8	0.2	4.7
FP32	19.5	8.1	15.7	5.5	9.3
FP16					18.7
INT8				22	
FP64	19.5				
TF32	156				
FP16	312	65	125		
INT8	624	180			
INT4	1248	260			

The local setup consists of a single laptop machine, with 8 CPU cores of Intel's i7-6700 at 2.6 GHz processors, 16 GB, and a 950 m GPU which provides 640 Maxwell GPU cores for a maximum of 1439 `GFLOPS` for FP32 operations and

44.96 `GFLOPS` for FP64 operations. The GPU options offered by GCP are summarized in Table 3, coming at higher costs and significantly better performance [6]. The language models were implemented using `Python 3.7` and `TensorFlow` with `Keras`, providing a tight hardware integration, allowing us to take advantage of the GPUs equipped fully. The following section summarizes and compares the results obtained in these configurations.

5   Results

Our system was built to be able to consume a large dataset of tweets collected from an open-access repository of global COVID-19-related tweets, called the *COVID-19 Twitter chatter dataset* [1]. The system was designed to collect every tweet posted related to the pandemic in various geographic locations, with over $n = 760,064,879$ unique tweets, all COVID-19 related and written in multiple languages. These tweets flow into a pre-processing stage, where they are cleaned up and made ready for consumption by the language models and further narrowed down to a total of over $n = 2,142,800$ unique tweets. Then, the algorithm goes into a sentiment analysis phase, where the tweet's sentiment polarity is calculated using multiple language models; in particular, the method utilized to evaluate the consumed tweets used the following implementations: `VADER`, `BERTweet`, and `RoBERTa`. Then, the data is analyzed as a time series, following the same methodology set by [16].

Note that the system could consume and process this large amount of tweets, storing partial results for each stage of the data flow and keeping separated versions running in parallel for the multiple language models utilized. One considerable limitation is Twitter's API rate limit, which is enforced to be 450 requests per 15-minute window, and comes with a low-ceiling cap on the total of tweets consumed. However, a particular academic rate helps these hard limits [25].

To keep costs low, the method utilized the E2 machines types provided by GCP [7] and summarized in Table 2, which comes with a low number of shared CPUs, reaching an evaluation rate of around 4 tweets per second using both `BERTweet` and `RoBERTa`. Keep in mind that these models depend on around 350M parameters. Still, this consumption rate is slightly faster than Twitter's rate limit, so this configuration provides a constant throughput while keeping the costs low. Also, note that these rates use low-cost E2 machine types with no GPU options. GPUs can be configured independently of the machine type, as long as it is in the A2 family [6].

A single GPU can provide performance of several `TFLOPs`, exploited well by the `TensorFlow` environment. Table 3 summarizes the performance achieved by the multiple GPU family types made available by GCP, all measurements are shown in `TFLOPs`. However, to keep costs further down, the method exploited the independence of the modules. We evaluated several of the sentiment analysis tasks in a local laptop, with 8 CPU cores of Intel's i7-6700 at 2.6 GHz processors, 16 GB, and a 950m GPU which provides 640 Maxwell GPU cores for a maximum of 1439 `GFLOPS` for FP32 operations and 44.96 `GFLOPS` for FP64 operations. While it is not ideal, the method did see a significant speed-up over the CPU-only evaluation of language models. Thus, choosing the language model based on the target performance and budget is recommended, which can be processed with CPUs and VADER with no issues whatsoever or use a powerful, yet expensive BERT architecture and GPUs.

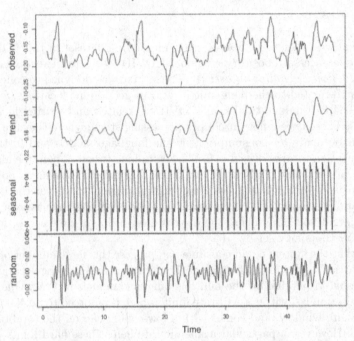

Fig. 3. *Year-long time series of daily averaged of compound sentiment polarity of COVID-19 related tweets, de-trended, in Mexico.* This represents a time series based on the same dataset collected by [1] and restricted to Mexico, from February 2 to December 31 2020. Data was smoothed over via a 7-day rolling means.

Figure 3 shows a summary of the study results. For more details, please refer to [16], but suffice to say that it was possible to perform on time. As can be observed, an almost zero trend is present in the time series, with a slope of $y = -2.2087107971 + 0.0001110643x$ and an ARIMA model fit with a very small p-value (of $2.2e^{-16}$). We also observe a robust weekly seasonality, which is expected from the Twitter data and was also observed by [12]. Another point to note is the change in tweet volume. Before the pandemic declaration, the average volume of tweets in Mexico was 20, 971 per day, adding to a total of 608, 170 tweets for the month. March presented an average of 46, 767 tweets per day and 1, 449, 768 tweets for the month alone. This represents an increase in the volume of 238.382% between these two months.

6   Conclusions

We presented a flexible system design that supports dynamic scaling and is capable of promptly consuming a large amount of data, which was then used to track the emotional well-being of the Mexican population from February to December 2020. For this, we consumed more than $n = 760,064,879$ unique tweets, all related to COVID-19 and written in multiple languages. We have shown that this system can process such a large amount of data, both in batch and streaming modes, while still being capable of swapping out multiple language models and facilitating data exploration and visualization. For the language models, we worked with both rule-based models, VADER, and state-of-the-art attention-based deep learning models, with BERTweet and RoBERTa, by simply plugging them into the appropriate stage in the data pipeline. It combined with modern MLops practices such as auto-deployments, model versioning, and infrastructure-as-code allows for a cost-effective solution for this big data problem. It mitigates common issues such as model performance degradation and adversary attacks and can gracefully handle data volume changes that occur naturally.

We have shown that it is possible to build a large-scale big data system for sentiment analysis using serverless technology and still achieve high performance. So near-real-time results by taking advantage of low-level code and hardware optimization. In our case by exploiting `Tensorflow` and its `CUDA` integration. This architecture presents additional advantages over traditional extensive data systems. For example, no significant initial investment is required, the software overhead and maintenance costs are significantly lower than those of `Apache's Hadoop`, and dynamic scaling is possible without any code changes. However, this system does present some drawbacks. The hosted services are off-site, with little to no control on our part, making security concern of the highest importance. To mitigate this concern, we have stripped the data of any metadata that could be used to identify a particular individual, such as account IDs. It's worth noting that the data utilized, while being a large corpus, is limited to a single year and country, that of 2020 in Mexico. There is no technical reason for having this limitation, and the system is fully capable of consuming an enormous amount of data. Also, in the future, we would like to develop visualization dashboards to provide instant feedback to decision-making organizations and to see a more extensive adoption in many organizations that include emotional data in their decision-making policies.

References

1. Banda, J.M., et al.: A large-scale COVID-19 twitter chatter dataset for open scientific research - an international collaboration, February 2021. https://doi.org/10.5281/zenodo.4540809
2. Bhuvaneswari, M., et al.: Handling of voluminous tweets and analyzing the sentiment of tweets. In: 2019 5th International Conference on Advanced Computing & Communication Systems (ICACCS), pp. 360–364. IEEE (2019)

3. Cenni, D., Nesi, P., Pantaleo, G., Zaza, I.: Twitter vigilance: a multi-user platform for cross-domain twitter data analytics, NLP and sentiment analysis. In: 2017 IEEE SmartWorld Ubiquitous Intelligence and Computing, Advanced and Trusted Computed, Scalable Computing and Communications, Cloud and Big Data Computing, Internet of People and Smart City Innovation, Smart-World/SCALCOM/UIC/ATC/CBDCom/IOP/SCI 2017, pp. 1–8 (2018). https://doi.org/10.1109/UIC-ATC.2017.8397589

4. Devlin, J., Chang, M.W., Lee, K., Toutanova, K.: BERT: pre-training of deep bidirectional transformers for language understanding. arXiv: Computation and Language (2018). MAG ID: 2896457183

5. El Alaoui, I., Gahi, Y., Messoussi, R.: Full consideration of big data characteristics in sentiment analysis context. In: 2019 IEEE 4th International Conference on Cloud Computing and Big Data Analysis (ICCCBDA), pp. 126–130. IEEE (2019)

6. Google: GCP's GPU offering (2022). https://cloud.google.com/compute/docs/gpus

7. Google: GCP's machine types (2022). https://cloud.google.com/compute/docs/machine-types

8. Heisler, Y.: Twitter's 280 character limit increased engagement without increasing the average tweet length (2018). https://bgr.com/2018/02/08/twitter-character-limit-280-vs-140-user-engagement/

9. Hutto, C., Gilbert, E.: Vader: a parsimonious rule-based model for sentiment analysis of social media text. In: Proceedings of the International AAAI Conference on Web and Social Media, vol. 8 (2014)

10. InternetLiveStats.com: Internet live stats (2019). https://www.internetlivestats.com/one-second/#tweets-band

11. Khuc, V.N., Shivade, C., Ramnath, R., Ramanathan, J.: Towards building large-scale distributed systems for twitter sentiment analysis. In: Proceedings of the ACM Symposium on Applied Computing, pp. 459–464 (2012). https://doi.org/10.1145/2245276.2245364

12. Kmetty, Z., Bokányi, E., Bozsonyi, K.: Seasonality pattern of suicides in the us-a comparative analysis of a twitter based bad-mood index and committed suicides. Intersect. East Eur. J. Soc. Polit. **3**(1), 56–75 (2017)

13. Kumamoto, T., Wada, H., Suzuki, T.: Visualizing temporal changes in impressions from tweets. In: ACM International Conference Proceeding Series, pp. 116–125, 04–06 December 2014. https://doi.org/10.1145/2684200.2684279

14. Kumar, M., Bala, A.: Analyzing twitter sentiments through big data. In: 2016 3rd International Conference on Computing for Sustainable Global Development (INDIACom), pp. 2628–2631. IEEE (2016)

15. Laney, D., et al.: 3D data management: controlling data volume, velocity and variety. META Group Res. Note **6**(70), 1 (2001)

16. León-Sandoval, E., Zareei, M., Barbosa-Santillán, L.I., Falcón Morales, L.E., Pareja Lora, A., Ochoa Ruiz, G.: Monitoring the emotional response to the COVID-19 pandemic using sentiment analysis: a case study in Mexico. Comput. Intell. Neurosci. **2022** (2022). https://doi.org/10.1155/2022/4914665. publisher: Hindawi

17. Liu, Y., et al.: RoBERTa: a robustly optimized BERT pretraining approach. arXiv: Computation and Language (2019). MAG ID: 2965373594

18. Loureiro, D., Barbieri, F., Neves, L., Anke, L.E., Camacho-Collados, J.: TimeLMs: diachronic language models from twitter. arXiv:2202.03829 (2022), http://arxiv.org/abs/2202.03829

19. Marcus, A., Bernstein, M.S., Badar, O., Karger, D.R., Madden, S., Miller, R.C.: Twitinfo: aggregating and visualizing microblogs for event exploration. In: Conference on Human Factors in Computing Systems - Proceedings, pp. 227–236 (2011). https://doi.org/10.1145/1978942.1978975
20. Nguyen, D.Q., Vu, T., Nguyen, A.T.: BERTweet: a pre-trained language model for English tweets. arXiv:2005.10200 (2020), http://arxiv.org/abs/2005.10200
21. Ramírez, H.L.G.: Twitter - undersecretaries of prevention and health promotion (2020). https://twitter.com/HLGatell/status/1233245568668966913
22. Sathya, V., Venkataramanan, A., Tiwari, A., Dev Daksan, P.S.: Ascertaining public opinion through sentiment analysis. In: Proceedings of the 3rd International Conference on Computing Methodologies and Communication, ICCMC 2019 (ICCMC), pp. 1139–1143 (2019). https://doi.org/10.1109/ICCMC.2019.8819738
23. Sehgal, D., Agarwal, A.K.: Sentiment analysis of big data applications using twitter data with the help of HADOOP framework. In: 2016 International Conference System Modeling & Advancement in Research Trends (SMART), pp. 251–255. IEEE (2016)
24. Twitter: Twitter's object model definition (2022). https://developer.twitter.com/en/docs/twitter-api/data-dictionary/object-model/tweet
25. Twitter: Twitter's public API access level policy (2022). https://developer.twitter.com/en/docs/twitter-api/getting-started/about-Twitter-api#v2-access-level
26. Victor, P., Lijo, V.: A big data processing framework for polarity detection in social network data. In: 2019 5th International Conference on Advanced Computing & Communication Systems (ICACCS), pp. 291–295. IEEE (2019)
27. Wang, H., Can, D., Kazemzadeh, A., Bar, F., Narayanan, S.: A system for real-time twitter sentiment analysis of 2012 US presidential election cycle. In: Proceedings of the ACL 2012 System Demonstrations, ACL 2012, pp. 115–120. Association for Computational Linguistics (2012)
28. Ylijoki, O., Porras, J.: Perspectives to definition of big data: a mapping study and discussion. J. Innov. Manage. 4, 69–91 (2016)

Multi-GPU 3-D Reverse Time Migration with Minimum I/O

Carlos H. S. Barbosa[✉][iD] and Alvaro L. G. A. Coutinho[iD]

High-Performance Computing Center, COPPE Federal University of Rio de Janeiro,
Rio de Janeiro, Brazil
{c.barbosa,alvaro}@nacad.ufrj.br

Abstract. Seismic imaging techniques based on two-way wave equations are computationally and data-intensive activities in the oil and gas industry. For instance, Reverse Time Migration (RTM) migrates a set of SEG-Y format data from the disk called a seismogram. Besides, during execution, the RTM application needs to store the forward-propagated wavefield (or source wavefield) on disk to build the final seismic image. Storing the source wavefield for multiple RTMs executing in parallel is even more challenging because the storage capacity can reach tens of Terabytes of information. Aiming to mitigate the storage demand, we develop a 3-D RTM with source wavefield reconstruction. The source wavefield is reconstructed by introducing a new wave equation to the problem and adjusting the initial and boundary conditions to take advantage of random boundary conditions' (RBC) properties. The RBC does not suppress unwanted waves coming from the artificial boundary enabling full wavefield recovery. We also develop a hybrid OpenACC/MPI implementation for the 3-D RTM on a multi-GPU machine. We test the RTM implementation on the 3-D HPC4E Seismic Test Suite. The numerical experiments show that the OpenACC/MPI 3-D RTM, which implements the wavefield reconstruction, presents the best execution times and hard disk demands.

Keywords: High performance computing · Reverse time migration · Wavefield reconstruction and OpenACC/MPI implementation

1 Introduction

Reverse Time Migration (RTM) is a depth migration technique that provides a reliable high-resolution representation of the Earth subsurface, useful for seismic interpretation and reservoir characterization [26]. RTM is based on the two-way wave equation and an appropriate imaging condition. Generally, the two-way wave equation is solved by numerical methods such as the Finite Difference Method (FDM) and the Finite Element Method (FEM). Besides, imaging conditions need the computational implementation of the forward-propagated wavefield (or source wavefield) for further access in reversal order to build the seismic image.

ⓒ The Author(s), under exclusive license to Springer Nature Switzerland AG 2022
P. Navaux et al. (Eds.): CARLA 2022, CCIS 1660, pp. 160–173, 2022.
https://doi.org/10.1007/978-3-031-23821-5_12

Advances in wave propagation algorithms and wavefield storage developments, and hardware acceleration implementations are some of the main challenges concerning RTM [26]. For instance, the most effective non-reflecting
boundary condition, Perfectly Matched Layer (PML), demands additional partial differential equations (PDEs) to be solved on artificial layers around the
domain [9,17] to deal with unwanted reflections due to truncated domains. A way
to overcome this issue is to use the random boundary conditions (RBC) proposed
by [6]. Thus, instead of suppressing unwanted waves by inserting new equations
into the problem, the methodology proposed by [6] is based on exploring low
correlations with non-coherent signals coming from an artificial boundary with
random velocities. On the other hand, the source wavefield in the RTM technique
is a bottleneck due to the amount of information that has to be stored on a disk
to build the imaging condition [26]. Strategies to diminish input/output (I/O)
related to the source wavefield storage or its reconstruction are presented by
[1,5–7,13,16,22,23]. Among them, [22] presented two strategies to reduce data
storage, where one is based on the Nyquist sampling theorem, and the second
one uses a lossless compression algorithm. In this sense, [1] studied the numerical
impact of applying lossless and lossy compression to the RTM source wavefield.
They show that the careful use of high levels of data compression can significantly reduce the storage demand without hampering the final seismic images.
However, instead of storing the wavefield, its reconstruction is a viable possibility. This can be done by checkpoint methods [7,23], using wavefield recording
around the boundary [5,16], or by initial value reconstruction (IVR) [6,13,16].

Independent of the RTM implementation strategy, all can use HPC techniques to boost their performance. [18] implemented the seismic modeling and
RTM on single and multi-GPUs using a hybrid MPI+OpenACC approach aiming
to develop portable high-level directive-based codes across heterogeneous platforms for seismic imaging applications. [20] evaluated three different computational optimizations based on multicore and GPU architectures and investigated
their codes' performance, energy efficiency, and portability. Nevertheless, the
storage demand issue remained in the RTM-based GPU implementations presented by the earlier research. For this, [15] implemented the RTM with RBC
to diminish the storage demand in migration algorithms showing that such a
strategy is beneficial for GPU implementations. The GPU computational implementation with the RBC technique was coded in CUDA and tested only for
2-D RTM applications. For 3-D environments, [2] developed a wave propagation
modeler and a RTM algorithm exploring the main RBC characteristics. It was
shown that RTM with RBCs performs better on vector processors and GPU
machines than CPU platforms.

In this context, we developed an RTM approach for 3-D environments that
explore the main characteristics of the RBC to mitigate calculations on the artificial boundaries and enable the source wavefield reconstruction. The RTM with
wavefield reconstruction takes advantage of the RBC's non-dissipative energy
property and implements the IVR technique to build the imaging condition with
minimum storage. Our implementation is particularly suited for GPUs because

we eliminate the need for storage for the whole source wavefield. We present the computational times and disk storage results for two algorithmic choices (with and without IO) in two different computational platforms: a CPU cluster and a CPU-GPU cluster. We show that our computational implementations are efficient, scalable, and portable with minimum interference on the optimized baseline code.

The remainder of the work is organized by introducing the RTM mathematical background in Sect. 2. Section 3 details the computational implementation along with optimizations for the NVIDIA V100 platform. In Sect. 4, we present numerical experiments, where we expose the execution time requirements, speedups, and hard disk demand for each computational implementation, as well as the RTM outcomes (seismic images). The paper ends with a summary of our main findings in Sect. 5.

2   Reverse Time Migration

Reverse Time Migration (RTM) is a depth migration technique based on the two-way wave equation, and an imaging condition [26]. Solving the wave equation twice to build the imaging condition is necessary. The first solution, called forward-propagated wavefield (source wavefield), can be obtained by solving the equation:

$$\nabla^2 p\left(\mathbf{r}, t\right) - \frac{1}{v^2\left(\mathbf{r}\right)} \frac{\partial^2 p\left(\mathbf{r}, t\right)}{\partial t^2} = f\left(\mathbf{r}_s, t\right), \tag{1}$$

where, p is the pressure, v the velocity for the compressional wave, $\mathbf{r}$ the spatial coordinates, t the time in $[0, T]$, and $f\left(\mathbf{r}_s, t\right)$ the seismic source at the position $\mathbf{r}_s$. The pressure p is defined in a domain $\Omega \subset \mathbb{R}^3$. The second-order differential equation (1) needs initial and boundary conditions. A natural initial condition is to define $p\left(\mathbf{r}, 0\right) = \partial p\left(\mathbf{r}, 0\right)/\partial t = 0$ for $\mathbf{r} \in \Omega$. Lastly, we set $p\left(\mathbf{r}, t\right) = 0$ on $\partial \Omega \in \mathbb{R}^2$, where $\partial \Omega$ is the domain boundary.

The second solution is obtained by solving the following equation:

$$\nabla^2 \bar{p}\left(\mathbf{r}, \tau\right) - \frac{1}{v^2\left(\mathbf{r}\right)} \frac{\partial^2 \bar{p}\left(\mathbf{r}, \tau\right)}{\partial \tau^2} = s\left(\mathbf{r}_r, \tau\right), \tag{2}$$

where, $\bar{p}$ is the backward-propagated wavefield (receiver wavefield), $s\left(\mathbf{r}_r, \tau\right)$ is the seismogram recorded at the receivers positions $\mathbf{r}_r$, and $\tau = T - t$ is the reversal time evolution defined as in [8], where $\tau \in [0, T]$. $\bar{p}$ is also defined in $\Omega \subset \mathbb{R}^3$, and corresponding initial, and boundary conditions should be set. Once we have the source and receiver wavefields, the imaging condition can be calculated as:

$$I\left(\mathbf{r}\right) = \frac{\int_0^T p\left(\mathbf{r}, t\right) \bar{p}\left(\mathbf{r}, \tau\right) \, dt}{\int_0^T \left[p\left(\mathbf{r}, t\right)\right]^2 dt}, \tag{3}$$

where $I\left(\mathbf{r}\right)$ is called source-normalized cross-correlated imaging condition. The source-normalized cross-correlation image in Eq. (3) has the same unit, scaling, and sign of the reflection coefficient [26].

3   Computational Implementation and Optimizations

Our RTM implementation employs the explicit Finite Difference Method (FDM) to solve the acoustic wave equation. The finite difference stencil for Eqs. (1) and (2) are 8th-order in space and 2nd-order in time. Thus, the numerical discretization leads to the discrete version of the velocity field, source wavefield, receiver wavefield, seismic source, and seismograms represented by the vectors $\mathbf{v}$, $\mathbf{p}$, $\bar{\mathbf{p}}$, $\mathbf{f}$, and $\mathbf{s}$, respectively. For the 3-D case, the vectors $\mathbf{v}$, $\mathbf{p}$, $\bar{\mathbf{p}}$ have the dimension $N = N_x \times N_y \times N_z$, where N_x, N_y and N_z are the number of grid points in each Cartesian direction. On the other hand, the seismogram is a vector of size $N_{rec} \times (N_t + 1)$, where N_{rec} is the number of receivers, and $N_t = T/\Delta t$, with Δt the time step. Lastly, the seismic source $\mathbf{f}$ has dimension N_t for each shot.

3.1   Classical Reverse Time Migration

Algorithm 1 presents the RTM implementation, which is one of the simplest ways to build the cross-correlated imaging condition. The colors in Algorithm 1 stand for host computations (black), data transfer (blue), and GPU calculations (red), which will be better explained in Sect. 3.3. The RTM needs as inputs a velocity field, a seismic source, and a set of seismograms, $\{\mathbf{s}_1, \cdots, \mathbf{s}_{N_{shots}}\}$ that contains information about the medium reflectivity. The computation of the imaging condition uses the source and receiver wavefield solutions to build the migrated seismic section that stacks the partial results over time $(\mathbf{I}_{\sum n_\tau})$, and over the number of seismograms $(\mathbf{I}_{\sum shot\_id})$. We compute the source wavefield by solving the wave equation with the independent term being the seismic source and storing it in disk for further access (step 10 in red). On the other hand, the recorded seismograms induce the computation of the receiver wavefield. At the end of Algorithm 1, we obtain the discrete seismic image $I \in \mathbb{R}^N$, where the amplitude variations represent physical properties changes. Both source and receiver wavefields can be obtained by solving the wave equation propagation over a temporal loop (the inner loops of Algorithm 1 - lines 7 and 14) for each $shot\_id$ (loop in line 4). The shot refers to the seismic source that starts the wave propagation, and each one is localized in the domain represented by the finite-difference grid.

   A computational implementation of absorbing boundary conditions (ABCs) leads to non-spurious reflections on the truncated domain. Among the several options in the literature, the Convolutional Perfectly Matched Layer (CPML) [9,17] and the damping factors for plane waves introduced by [4] are the most common. Although unusual in wave propagation simulation studies, the RBCs, first introduced by [6], can also be employed in seismic imaging methods based on the two-way wave equation, such as the RTM and FWI [5,6,13,16].

3.2   Reverse Time Migration with Wavefield Reconstruction

Storing and accessing the source wavefield into and from the hard disk is computationally demanding. For instance, the disk requirements to store the source

---

Algorithm 1. Reverse Time Migration

Require: $\mathbf{v}$, $\{\mathbf{s}_1, \cdots, \mathbf{s}_{N_{shots}}\}$, and $\mathbf{f}$
1: **function** RTM(vector $\mathbf{v}$, vectors $\{\mathbf{s}_1, \cdots, \mathbf{s}_{N_{shots}}\}$, vector $\mathbf{f}$)
2:     read $\mathbf{v}$, $\mathbf{f}$, and $\{\mathbf{s}_1, \cdots, \mathbf{s}_{N_{shots}}\}$
3:     initialize image condition $\mathbf{I}_{\sum shot\_id} = 0$
4:     **for** $shot\_id = 1$ to N_{shots} **do**
5:         initialize $n_t = 0$
6:         apply initial conditions for $i_t = 0$
7:         **for** $i_t = 1$ to N_t **do**
8:             $n_t = n_t + i_t * \Delta t$
9:             solve equation (1)   ▷ source wavefield
10:             store $\mathbf{p}_{n_t}$ for all n_t
11:         **end for**
12:         read $\mathbf{s}_{shot\_id}$
13:         initialize $n_\tau = 0$, and $\mathbf{I}_{\sum \tau} = 0$
14:         apply initial conditions for $i_\tau = 0$
15:         **for** $i_\tau = 1$ to N_t **do**
16:             $n_\tau = N_t - (n_\tau + i_\tau * \Delta \tau)$ ▷ reverse time
17:             read $\mathbf{p}_{n_\tau}$
18:             solve equation (2)   ▷ receiver wavefield
19:             calculate $\mathbf{I}_{\sum n_\tau} = \mathbf{I}_{\sum n_\tau} + (\mathbf{p}_{n_\tau} \bar{\mathbf{p}}_{n_\tau}) / (\mathbf{p}_{n_\tau} \mathbf{p}_{n_\tau})$ ▷ imaging condition
20:         **end for**
21:         stack $\mathbf{I}_{\sum shot\_id} = \mathbf{I}_{\sum shot\_id} + \mathbf{I}_{\sum n_\tau}$ ▷ stacking
22:     **end for**
23:     $\mathbf{I} \leftarrow \mathbf{I}_{\sum shot\_id}$
24:     store $\mathbf{I}$
25: **end function**

---

wavefield propagation for the 3-D case is $4 \times N_{shots} \times N_t \times N$ Bytes, where the value 4 stands for single precision representation of a real number. Considering a hypothetical scenario of the wavefield propagation in a grid of $200 \times 200 \times 200$ grid points during 6.0 s step-wised of 0.5 ms leads to a disk storage demand of ≈ 178.81 GB per shot. Executing the same example in parallel considering 20 shots elevates the disk requirements to 3.5 TB.

Although compression techniques [1,10,11,14], decimation strategies based on the Nyquist theory [22,25] and checkpoint methods [23] reduces persistent storage, applications of RTM for large scale for frequencies up to 20.0 Hz is still challenging [19]. Another way to overcome this issue, explored in this work, is to reconstruct the wavefield from information generated during the first RTM part, that is, forward wave propagation [16]. To reconstruct the source wavefield, we implement the IVR methodology first explored by [7] and [23]. The IVR proposed by [23] stores temporary states of the wavefield known as checkpoints. Such states are after used for recursive re-computations of the source wavefield. The complete reconstruction of the wavefield can be achieved by keeping all energy in the system. However, unwanted signals come from the boundary due to the absence of attenuated layers in truncated domains. This issue can be circumvented by generating incoherent signals coming from the boundary, as explored in [6], by introducing boundaries with randomized velocities.

The RBC proposed by [6] is based on the idea that what matters for the calculation of the RTM imaging condition is the coherent reflections coming from the boundaries. Thus, [6] proposed to introduce a random component to the velocity field at the boundaries. Notice that the random velocity field has to respect the numerical stability constraint of the FDM. It is expected that the random source wavefield coming from the boundaries does not coherently correlate with the receiver wavefield. Besides, a smoother transition from the inner domain to the boundaries is ideal. The smooth transition will avoid unwanted immediate reflections of the randomized area. One way to build a smooth transition area is by multiplying coefficients c_i to the random vector velocity $\mathbf{v}$ in the normal direction to the boundaries, where the index $i \in [1, \cdots, N_a]$ with N_a been the boundary thickness size. The coefficients are responsible for decreasing down the velocities values, and [21] suggested the values computed by linear and Gaussian functions.

Further, this strategy does not impose an extra cost on the wave equation calculation. An alternative way to avoid coherent signals coming from the boundaries is presented by [13], where they used an extra viscoacoustic wave equation in the boundaries to attenuate the wavefield. In this work, we employ the strategy presented in [21]. Details of the RBC algorithm can be observed in [6]. Here, we will describe the modifications for Algorithm 1 aiming to eliminate the storage requirements of the forward-propagated wavefield.

First, we need a third second-order wave equation as follows:

$$\nabla^2 p^R(\mathbf{r}, \tau) - \frac{1}{v^2(\mathbf{r})} \frac{\partial^2 p^R(\mathbf{r}, \tau)}{\partial \tau^2} = 0, \tag{4}$$

where p^R is the reconstructed source wavefield defined in $\Omega \subset \mathbb{R}^3$. Boundary conditions can be set as Eqs. (1), and (2), that is $p^R(\mathbf{r}, t) = 0$ on $\partial\Omega$. Lastly, the initial conditions are set as $p^R(\mathbf{r}, 0) = p(\mathbf{r}, T)$, and $\partial p^R(\mathbf{r}, 0)/\partial t = \partial p(\mathbf{r}, T)/\partial t$ after solving Eq. 1, and $\tau = T - t$ is the reversal time.

Algorithm 2 details the RTM that implements the source wavefield reconstruction. Again, the color pattern represents the host computations (black), data transfer (blue), and GPU calculations (red), which will be better explained in Sect. 3.3. We use the vector $\mathbf{p}^R$ to represent the finite difference discretization of Eq. (4). The first part of the RTM with wavefield reconstruction calculates the source wavefield, and the last two instants of the wavefield are stored (line 11). After reading the stored wavefield instants, the second part of the algorithm, that calculates the receiver wavefield, also computes the reconstruction of the source wavefield $\mathbf{p}^R$ by solving Eq. (4). Thus, the modified algorithm stores only two source wavefield panels instead of all panels for each n_t. This strategy comes with the additional cost of solving one extra wave equation.

Algorithm 2. Reverse Time Migration with Wavefield Reconstruction

---

Require: $\mathbf{v}$, $\{\mathbf{s}_1, \cdots, \mathbf{s}_{N_{shots}}\}$, and $\mathbf{f}$

1: **function** RTM(vector $\mathbf{v}$, vectors $\{\mathbf{s}_1, \cdots, \mathbf{s}_{N_{shots}}\}$, vector $\mathbf{f}$)
2:     read $\mathbf{v}$, $\mathbf{f}$, and $\{\mathbf{s}_1, \cdots, \mathbf{s}_{N_{shots}}\}$
3:     create a RBC as Algorithm 2 from [6]
4:     initialize image condition $\mathbf{I}_{\sum shot\_id} = 0$
5:     **for** $shot\_id = 1$ to N_{shots} **do**
6:         initialize $n_t = 0$
7:         apply initial conditions for $i_t = 0$
8:         **for** $i_t = 1$ to N_t **do**
9:             $n_t = n_t + i_t * \Delta t$
10:             solve equation (1)   ▷ source wavefield
11:             store $\mathbf{p}_{n_t}$ for N_{t-1}, and N_t
12:         **end for**
13:         initialize $n_\tau = 0$, and $\mathbf{I}_{\sum \tau} = 0$
14:         read $\mathbf{s}_{shot\_id}$
15:         read $\mathbf{p}_{N_t}$, and $\mathbf{p}_{N_{t-1}}$
16:         apply initial conditions for $i_\tau = 0$
17:         **for** $i_\tau = 1$ to N_t **do**
18:             $n_\tau = N_t - (n_\tau + i_\tau * \Delta\tau)$ ▷ reverse time
19:             solve equation (2)   ▷ receiver wavefield
20:             solve equation (4)   ▷ wavefield reconstruction
21:             calculate $\mathbf{I}_{\sum n_\tau} = \mathbf{I}_{\sum n_\tau} + \left(\mathbf{p}_{n_\tau}^R \bar{\mathbf{p}}_{n_\tau}\right) / \left(\mathbf{p}_{n_\tau}^R \mathbf{p}_{n_\tau}^R\right)$ ▷ imaging condition
22:         **end for**
23:         stack $\mathbf{I}_{\sum shot\_id} = \mathbf{I}_{\sum shot\_id} + \mathbf{I}_{\sum n_\tau}$ ▷ stacking
24:     **end for**
25:     $\mathbf{I} \leftarrow \mathbf{I}_{\sum shot\_id}$
26:     store $\mathbf{I}$
27: **end function**

3.3   Hybrid OpenACC/MPI Implementation

The GPU programming model based on OpenACC directives aims to provide an easier way for scientific applications coding [12,18]. Besides, compared to CUDA and OpenCL, OpenACC programming demands less coding efforts in heterogeneous environments with CPU+GPU [18,20]. The OpenACC implementation deals with three main issues: CPU (host) calculations, GPU calculations, and communications to and from the GPU. Thus, any computational implementation must maximize the GPU computations and prevent communications between the host and GPU.

Algorithm 1 also details the host and GPU calculations and the communication between them. Notice that we use three different colors to represent the host computations (black), data transfer (blue), and GPU calculations (red). The first operations made by the host are data allocation followed by disk reading and storage of the velocity field and seismic source information in the vectors $\mathbf{v}$, and $\mathbf{f}$. These steps are represented in line 2 of Algorithm 1. Lines 8 and 9 show the GPU operations for the wave equation calculation once the necessary information is transferred and allocated. Line 10 shows that the source wavefield needs to be moved during its calculation from the GPU to the host to be stored on the disk. In general, storing the source wavefield in a disk is needed because the GPU memory (or RAM) is insufficient to store it. The second part of the RTM algorithm (lines 12 to 21) moves back the source wavefield from host to GPU, calculates the receiver wavefield, and builds the imaging condition. The calculation of the receiver wavefield needs the seismograms stored on the disk. Thus, the host reads the seismogram from the disk and transfers it to the GPU. Algorithm 1 requires two data transfers for the velocity field and seismic source, N_{shots} data transfers for the seismograms, and $2 \times N_t$ data transfers for the source wavefield.

The OpenACC implementation based on Algorithm 2 follows the same strategy presented in Algorithm 1. Remember that Algorithm 2 implements the wavefield reconstruction, and one extra wave equation is required for that. Because of that, its computational implementation does not fully store the source wavefield, only the last two time-frames. The data transfer based on the OpenACC implementation occurs between the two main stages of the RTM technique and not during the temporal loops as the Algorithm 1. Thus, Algorithm 2 requires only four data transfers between the GPU and host for the source wavefield. We use for both Algorithms 1 and 2 the ACC DATA COPYIN directive for transferring the data from the host to GPU. ACC DATA COPYOUT directive transfers the data from GPU to host. ACC DATA CREATE allocates necessary vectors in the GPU. For parallelization, we use the ACC LOOP directive.

Message Passing Interface (MPI) library manages the execution of multiple shots, where batches of shots are assigned to different allocated MPI processes. We handle the set of shots per MPI process in lines 4 and 5 of the Algorithms 1 and 2, respectively. Each MPI process can be assigned to a GPU or CPU node.

4   Numerical Experiments

In this section, we present the performance analysis of the 3-D RTM using two different computational platforms: a CPU cluster and a CPU-GPU machine. Both belongs to the Santos Dumont system at the National Scientific Computing Laboratory at Petrópolis/Brazil[1]. The CPU cluster has Intel Xeon E5-2695v2 Ivy Bridge processors with 2.4 GHZ and 24 cores per node, where the nodes are connected by an FDR (Forteen Data Rate) infiniband network (56 Gb/s) All the 24 cores have been used for the CPU experiments. On the other hand, the CPU-GPU cluster has a CPU Intel Skylake GOLD 6148, 2.4 GHZ with 24 cores and $4 \times$ NVIDIA V100 per node. In this case, the nodes are connected by an EDR (Enhanced Data Rate) infiniband network (100 Gb/s). Both CPU and CPU-GPU nodes are supported by a Lustre filesystem v2.12.

We have chosen the MODEL AF provided by the HPC4E Seismic Test Suite[2] for the 3-D RTM experiments. Figure 1 shows the velocity field provided by the

---

[1] https://sdumont.lncc.br/support_manual.php?pg=support.

[2] https://hpc4e.bsc.es/downloads/hpc-geophysical-simulation-test-suite.

HPC4E benchmark defined as MODEL AF. The MODEL AF is a model designed as a set of 15 layers with constant velocity values and flat topography. Besides, the velocity parameter model (velocity field) covers an area of $10 \times 10 \times 4.5$ km. We have used a $501 \times 501 \times 235$ grid size with 25.0 m of grid space to represent the velocity field. Notice that the grid size for the 3-D cases includes $N_a = 50$ and half of the finite difference stencil length at the top of the velocity model to simulate the free surface. We used the Ricker seismic source [24] with 20 Hz cutoff frequency placed near the surface. The total acquisition time is 6.0 seconds step-wised of 1.0 ms. The experiments consist of running the RTM implementations for a single shot and a seismic acquisition and presenting the execution times, disk requirements, and speed-ups.

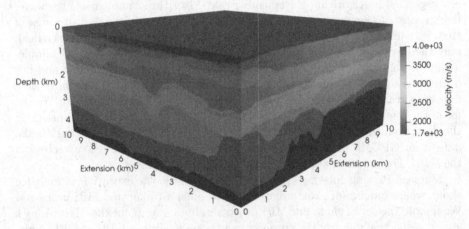

Fig. 1. 3-D velocity field provided by the HPC4E Seismic Test Suite.

Single Shot Experiment: The first experiment consists of executing the RTM applications for a single seismic source (single shot) located at $[5000, 5000]$ m. The RTM follows the implementations presented in Algorithms 1 and 2. The seismograms for the RTM are represented by the seismic signals recorded in a seismic survey. The receiver geometry of the seismogram follows the expressions:

$$r_x = 25.0(i - 1) + 1012.5 \text{ with } i = 1, \cdots, 320, \tag{5}$$
$$r_y = 25.0(j - 1) + 1012.5 \text{ with } j = 1, \cdots, 320, \tag{6}$$

where, the pair $[r_x, r_y]$ meters represents the receiver locations on the surface.

Table 1 shows the average time execution and the hard disk requirements for the 3-D RTM implementations. The RTM based on Algorithm 1 requires the full storage of the source wavefield. Nevertheless, instead of storing the source wavefield for every time step (Δt) based on the FDM, we took advantage of the

Nyquist theory as explored by [22] to store the wavefield at the Nyquist time step to reduce the amount of information. The Nyquist time step Δt_{nyq} is defined as,

$$\Delta t_{nyq} = \frac{1}{2(f_{max} - f_{min})}, \tag{7}$$

where f_{max} and f_{min} are the highest and lowest frequency of the seismic source. For the Ricker wavelet that we use for the RTM test case, $f_{max} = 100.0$ Hz and $f_{min} = 0.0$ Hz. Thus, the Nyquist time step based on Eq. 7 is $\Delta t_{nyq} = 10.0$ ms against to $\Delta t = 1.0$ ms, 10 times bigger than the FDM time step.

Hence, Algorithm 1 which implements the wavefield storage requires 132.062 GB of hard disk for NVIDIA V100 against 0.439 GB of the wavefield reconstruction implementation (Algorithm 2). The best average execution time refers to the RTM that implements the wavefield reconstruction. The RTM with wavefield reconstruction is $\approx 2.11\times$ faster than the wavefield storage implementation on NVIDIA V100. Although the storage demand decreases drastically from 132.062 GB to 0.439 GB, the same does not occur in the total execution time. We observe that in both Algorithms 1 and 2 the forward and backward solutions of the wave equation take 80.0 s. In Algorithm 1, all the remaining time is spent in I/O. However, in Algorithm 2, the wavefield reconstruction takes most of the additional execution time.

Table 1. Comparison of hard disk and time requirements for the 3-D RTM implementation with wavefield storage, and wavefield reconstruction.

Method	Platform	Hard disk (GB)	Av. time (s) [variance (s)]
Wavefield Storage	NVIDIA V100	132.062	256.166 [46.810]
Wavefield Reconstruction	NVIDIA V100	0.439	121.431 [1.371]

We also compare the RTM speedups across the platforms CPU Cluster and NVIDIA V100. For the OpenMP RTM implementation, we follow [1,3], where we implement an MPI/OpenMP+vectorization strategy on multi-core machines. The implementation takes advantage of OpenMP directives to explore multiple cores parallelism, it supports Single-Instruction-Multiple-Data (SIMD) model and memory alignment to ensure vectorization. We can see in Fig. 2 that the OpenMP implementation speedup is 12.09, and the OpenACC implementation speedup is 54.62. All the implementations for the platform comparisons are based on Algorithm 2 which describes the RTM with wavefield reconstruction and requires minimum I/O. Thus, the performance of the RTM implementation with OpenACC is $4.52\times$ OpenMP implementation.

Seismic Survey Experiment: The final experiments consider running the RTM for a survey geometry with 1681 seismograms. The geometry acquisition for the seismic survey follows the expressions:

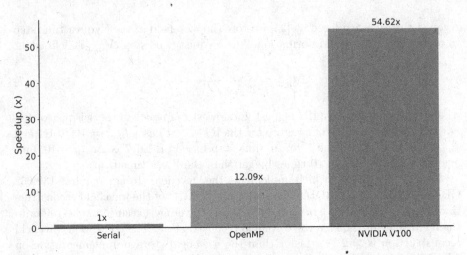

Fig. 2. Reverse Time Migration speedup across the platforms Santos Dumont CPU Cluster and NVIDIA V100 for the $501 \times 501 \times 235$ grid.

$$s_x = 200.0(i - 1) + 1000.0 \text{ with } i = 1, \cdots, 41, \qquad (8)$$
$$s_y = 200.0(j - 1) + 1000.0 \text{ with } j = 1, \cdots, 41, \qquad (9)$$

where, the pair $[s_x, s_y]$ meters represents the seismic source locations near the surface.

Firstly, we compare the total time of executing the RTM on CPU Cluster and NVIDIA V100. For the CPU cluster, we consider 16 nodes, where each node has 24 physical cores. Considering the GPU machine, we set 4 nodes because each one has 4 NVIDIA V100 adding up to 16 GPUs. Table 2 shows the total time of executing the RTM with wavefield reconstruction on CPU cluster and NVIDIA V100. We can see that the OpenACC implementation performs better than the OpenMP implementation for the same strategy which eliminates I/O related to the source wavefield. In this experiment, the RTM considering 16 NVIDIA GPUs is 7.62 times faster than the RTM running on 16 CPUs nodes.

Table 2. Comparison of the total execution time or the 3-D RTM implementation with wavefield reconstruction on CPU cluster and NVIDIA V100.

Method	Platform	Total time
Wavefield reconstruction	CPU cluster	1259 min 22.560 s
Wavefield reconstruction	NVIDIA V100	170 min 56.420 s

Figure 3 shows the stacked seismic image for one migrated shot of the 3-D HPC4E Seismic Test Suite benchmark. We generated the observed seismogram by simulating the wave propagation and recording the seismic signals at the locations following the Eqs. 5 and 6 near the surface at 25.0 m in depth. The survey acquisition follows the geometry expressed in Eqs. 8 and 9 and takes into account 1681 shots.

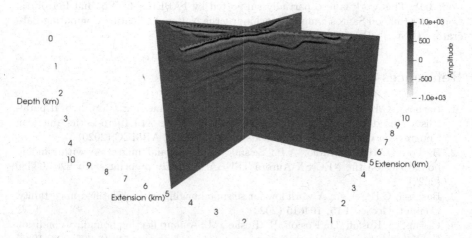

Fig. 3. Seismic image for the 3-D HPC4E Seismic Test Suite.

5 Conclusions

This work studies RTM algorithms for 3-D environments that mitigate the source wavefield's storage and explores hybrid architectures for speeding-up seismic applications. We eliminate the need of storing the source wavefield by reconstructing it through IVR based on the RBC. The RBC mitigates calculations on the artificial boundaries simplifying coding compared to versions with damping layers. Our algorithmic choices benefit computational architectures like GPUs. For instance, our numerical experiments show that the RTM based on the wavefield reconstruction performed better on the NVIDIA V100 than on Intel Xeon multi-CPUs platforms for 3-D applications. Besides, the 3-D RTM algorithms based on the wavefield reconstruction demand less storage and are faster than the classical RTM storing the source wavefield. We also compare the RTM execution time with wavefield reconstruction for a seismic survey with 1681 shots. In this case, the RTM takes advantage of multi-GPUs and multi-CPUs to run the entire application. The RTM for multi-GPUs is 7.62 times faster than the RTM for multi-CPUs platforms. We use high-level programming models such as OpenACC for the NVIDIA GPU and OpenMP for the Multi-CPU for all computational implementations. The high-level programming models allow code portability and little code interference on the optimized baseline version. We point out that the computational implementation based on the OpenACC library is one of the simplest ways to produce fast and portable codes maintaining high-performance rates. Nevertheless, further performance gains can be obtained by using tailored optimizations, sacrificing portability.

Acknowledgements. This study was financed in part by CAPES, Brazil Finance Code 001. This work is also partially supported by FAPERJ, CNPq, and Petrobras. Computer time on Santos Dumont machine at the National Scientific Computing Laboratory (LNCC - Petrópolis).

References

1. Barbosa, C.H., Coutinho, A.L.: Enhancing reverse time migration: hybrid parallelism plus data compression. In: Proceedings of the XLI Ibero-Latin-American Congress on Computational Methods in Engineering. ABMEC (2020)
2. Barbosa, C.H., Coutinho, A.L.: Seismic modeling and migration with random boundaries on the NEC SX-Aurora TSUBASA. arXiv preprint arXiv:2204.03380 (2022)
3. Barbosa, C.H., et al.: A workflow for seismic imaging with quantified uncertainty. Comput. Geosci. **145**, 104615 (2020)
4. Cerjan, C., Kosloff, D., Kosloff, R., Reshef, M.: A nonreflecting boundary condition for discrete acoustic and elastic wave equations. Geophysics **50**(4), 705–708 (1985)
5. Clapp, R.G.: Reverse time migration: saving the boundaries. Stanford Exploration Project 137 (2008)
6. Clapp, R.G.: Reverse time migration with random boundaries. In: SEG Technical Program Expanded Abstracts 2009, pp. 2809–2813. Society of Exploration Geophysicists (2009)
7. Faria, E.: Migração antes do empilhamento utilizando propagação reversa no tempo, January 1986. http://www.cpgg.ufba.br/pgeof/resumos/gfm/gfm0056a.html
8. Givoli, D.: Time reversal as a computational tool in acoustics and elastodynamics. J. Comput. Acoust. **22**(03), 1430001 (2014)
9. Komatitsch, D., Martin, R.: An unsplit convolutional perfectly matched layer improved at grazing incidence for the seismic wave equation. Geophysics **72**(5), SM155–SM167 (2007)
10. Kukreja, N., Hückelheim, J., Louboutin, M., Hovland, P., Gorman, G.: Combining checkpointing and data compression to accelerate adjoint-based optimization problems. In: Yahyapour, R. (ed.) Euro-Par 2019. LNCS, vol. 11725, pp. 87–100. Springer, Cham (2019). https://doi.org/10.1007/978-3-030-29400-7_7
11. Kukreja, N., Hückelheim, J., Louboutin, M., Washbourne, J., Kelly, P.H., Gorman, G.J.: Lossy checkpoint compression in full waveform inversion: a case study with ZFPv0. 5.5 and the overthrust model. Geosci. Model Dev. **15**(9), 3815–3829 (2022)
12. Kushida, N., Lin, Y.-T., Nielsen, P., Le Bras, R.: Acceleration in acoustic wave propagation modelling using OpenACC/OpenMP and its hybrid for the global monitoring system. In: Wienke, S., Bhalachandra, S. (eds.) WACCPD 2019. LNCS, vol. 12017, pp. 25–46. Springer, Cham (2020). https://doi.org/10.1007/978-3-030-49943-3_2
13. Li, Q., Fu, L.Y., Wu, R.S., Du, Q.: Efficient acoustic reverse time migration with an attenuated and reversible random boundary. IEEE Access **8**, 34598–34610 (2020)

14. Lindstrom, P., Chen, P., Lee, E.J.: Reducing disk storage of full-3D seismic waveform tomography (F3DT) through lossy online compression. Comput. Geosci. **93**, 45–54 (2016)

15. Liu, H., et al.: The issues of prestack reverse time migration and solutions with graphic processing unit implementation. Geophys. Prospect. **60**(5), 906–918 (2012)

16. Nguyen, B.D., McMechan, G.A.: Five ways to avoid storing source wavefield snapshots in 2D elastic prestack reverse time migration. Geophysics **80**(1), S1–S18 (2015)

17. Pasalic, D., McGarry, R.: Convolutional perfectly matched layer for isotropic and anisotropic acoustic wave equations. In: SEG Technical Program Expanded Abstracts 2010, pp. 2925–2929. Society of Exploration Geophysicists (2010)

18. Qawasmeh, A., Hugues, M.R., Calandra, H., Chapman, B.M.: Performance portability in reverse time migration and seismic modelling via OpenACC. Int. J. High Perform. Comput. Appl. **31**(5), 422–440 (2017)

19. Schuster, G.T.: Seismic Inversion. Society of Exploration Geophysicists, Tulsa (2017)

20. Serpa, M.S., et al.: Energy efficiency and portability of oil and gas simulations on multicore and graphics processing unit architectures. Concurr. Comput. Pract. Exp. **33**(18), e6212 (2021)

21. Silva, K.C.: Modelagem, mrt e estudos de iluminação empregando o conceito de dados sísmicos blended, January 2012. http://www.coc.ufrj.br/pt/dissertacoes-de-mestrado/112-msc-pt-2012/2265-karen-carrilho-da-silva

22. Sun, W., Fu, L.Y.: Two effective approaches to reduce data storage in reverse time migration. Comput. Geosci. **56**, 69–75 (2013)

23. Symes, W.W.: Reverse time migration with optimal checkpointing. Geophysics **72**(5), SM213–SM221 (2007)

24. Wang, Y.: Frequencies of the Ricker wavelet. Geophysics **80**(2), A31–A37 (2015)

25. Zand, T., Malcolm, A., Gholami, A., Richardson, A.: Compressed imaging to reduce storage in adjoint-state calculations. IEEE Trans. Geosci. Remote Sens. **57**(11), 9236–9241 (2019)

26. Zhou, H.W., Hu, H., Zou, Z., Wo, Y., Youn, O.: Reverse time migration: a prospect of seismic imaging methodology. Earth Sci. Rev. **179**, 207–227 (2018)

ParslRNA-Seq: An Efficient and Scalable RNAseq Analysis Workflow for Studies of Differentiated Gene Expression

Kary Ocaña[1]([✉]), Lucas Cruz[1,2], Micaella Coelho[1], Rafael Terra[1], Marcelo Galheigo[1], Andre Carneiro[1], Diego Carvalho[2], Luiz Gadelha[1], Francieli Boito[3], Philippe Navaux[4], and Carla Osthoff[1]

[1] National Laboratory of Scientific Computing, LNCC, Rio de Janeiro, Brazil
{karyann,lucruz,micaella,rafaelst,galheigo,andrerc,lgadelha,
osthoff}@lncc.br

[2] Federal Center for Technological Education Celso Suckow da Fonseca, CEFET-RJ,
Rio de Janeiro, Brazil
d.carvalho@ieee.org

[3] Univ. Bordeaux, CNRS, Bordeaux INP, INRIA, LaBRI, Talence, France
francieli.zanon-boito@u-bordeaux.fr

[4] Informatics Institute, Federal University of Rio Grande do Sul, UFRGS,
Porto Alegre, Brazil
navaux@inf.ufrgs.br
https://www.gov.br/lncc/pt-br

Abstract. RNA sequencing has become an increasingly affordable way to profile gene expression analyses. Here we introduce a scientific workflow implementing several open-source software executed by Parsl parallel scripting language in an high-performance computing environment. We have applied the workflow to a single-cardiomyocyte RNA-seq data retrieved from Gene Expression Omnibus database. The workflow allows for the analysis (alignment, QC, sort and count reads, statistics generation) of raw RNA-seq data and seamless integration of differential expression results into a configurable script code. In this work, we aim to investigate an analytical comparison of executing the workflow in Solid State Disk and Lustre as a critical decision for improving the execution efficiency and resilience in current and upcoming RNA-Seq workflows. Based on the resulting profiling of CPU and I/O data collection, we demonstrate that we can correctly identify anomalies in transcriptomics workflow performance which is an essential resource to optimize its use of high-performance computing systems. ParslRNA-Seq showed improvements in the total execution time of up to 70% against its previous sequential implementation. Finally, the article discusses which workflow modeling modifications lead to improved computational performance and scalability based on provenance data information. ParslRNA-Seq is available at https://github.com/lucruzz/rna-seq.

Keywords: High-performance computing · Transcriptomics · Scientific workflows

Supported by organization CNPq.

1   Introduction

RNA-Seq is a recently developed approach to transcriptome profiling that uses deep-sequencing technologies. In transcriptomics, the modeling, execution, and analysis of RNA Sequencing (RNA-Seq) experiments represent a challenge for managing the complexity and large volumes of biological and computational data. Differential gene expression (DGE) analysis is one of the most common applications of RNA-seq data, which allows for studying the behavior of a set of transcripts of differentially expressed genes across two or more conditions, such as a cell in a given physiological and developmental conditions or cancer. Despite technological advances, we still face many challenges in producing high-quality, reliable, and comparable DGE data [1].

Systems biology, omics technologies, artificial intelligence, machine learning, data science, data mining, and high-performance computing develop biological applications in RNA-Seq of differentially expressed genes from RNA-Seq and functional enrichment results. In addition, there is still no universal methodology that combines those approaches; then, bioinformaticians must develop their scripts to call several different approaches in the same code. However, scripting codes are not a guarantee that shows how large and complex RNA-Seq data affects the computational performance of execution and the data analytics of transcriptomic data.

Scientific workflows represent the flow of activities of an experiment [3], which makes it possible to establish better modeling, execution management, and analysis that will reinforce the experiment's reproducibility, reliability, and scalability. Scientific Workflows Management Systems (SWfMS) based on the web, such as Galaxy[1] and Statistical packages of R and Bioconductor (EdgeR, DESeq2) are used in DGE studies. Related to task automation, using distributed and parallel languages or SWfMS such as Nextflow, Tavaxy, Kepler, Pegasus, Swift, and Parsl are promising strategies [2].

The present work presents ParslRNA-Seq scientific workflow, its architecture and the validated performance by computational analysis, and discussions about transcriptomics DGE. The current implementation is composed of six main activities, where the formal modifications have been made to use the new update of the HTSeq program, which allows the partitioning of two input data for distribution and parallel executions in multiples cores [4]. Executions of the current implementation of ParslRNA-Seq reach a gain in computational time of up to 70%. The high-performance computing (HPC) environment used our tests is the Santos Dumont[2] (SDumont) supercomputer.

The remainder of this manuscript is structured as follows. Section 2 presents related works. Section 3 introduces terminology used throughout this paper. Section 4 describes the experimental framework used to evaluate the performance of the ParslRNA-Seq workflow algorithms. Section 5 describe the dataset, experi-

---

[1] https://galaxyproject.org/.
[2] https://sdumont.lncc.br/.

ment setup and computational environment. Section 6 describes the performance results of the workflow executions. Finally, Sect. 7 presents our conclusions

2   Related Works

Cruz et al. (2020) [4] traces the modeling and performance analysis of ParslRNA-Seq executed in the SDumont environment. The analyses involve Parsl management for the efficient use of two computational resources and a better exploration of the Bowtie2 multithread parameter, which significantly improves workflow performance. Other works for DGE analyses include the seveaseq pipeline managed by scripts and second as our investigations executed serially. RSEM is a package for identifying and quantifying transcripts in RNA-Seq analyses; it does not use reference genomes, uses Bowtie2 and a RSEM algorithm to calculate abundance; it was optimized in HPC environments.

WorkflowHub [13], an evolution of myExperiment, is a community framework that provides a collection of tools for analyzing workflow execution traces and simulating workflow executions. It follows an open-development model per FAIR principles to facilitate the discovery and re-use of workflows in an accessible and interoperable way. Galaxy is a web-based platform that features various RNA-Seq workflows, with parallelization options integrated with Taverna (Tavaxy). It is more similar to our ParslRNA-Seq, which has been intensively explored in supercomputing environments. Among other tools, we have Tximeta, Salmon, Sailfish, and featureCounts [5].

Bioworkbench [11] is a framework for collecting provenance and runtime information from workflows implemented in the Swift parallel scripting system [12], a predecessor of Parsl. The framework allows for executing queries on provenance data and predicting total workflow execution time and storage space used using machine learning techniques.

Wratten et al. [14] highlight the concepts that will become essential for data-driven research and applications in high-throughput biology. They introduce the advantages of workflow managers compared with traditional pipelines and compare some of the existing approaches. They review pipeline repositories that provide curated collections of pipelines to avoid re-implementing best-practice analysis workflows.

3   Background on Differential Gene Expression Analysis

Next-Generation Sequencing (NGS) technology revolutionizes the field of genomic and transcriptomic analysis due to massively large-scale sequencing. The technique known as RNA-Seq is based on the analysis of the DGE using statistical modeling tools of the data relating to the number of transcripts. RNA-Seq studies have facilitated the study of alternative splicing, Single Nucleotide Polymorphisms (SNPs), post-transcriptional modifications, and changes in gene expression over time or between treatment groups or disease progression. DGE analyses allow to elucidate the level of expression between different experimental conditions and establish whether there is a significant difference between them. Conducting studies of DGE indicates the formalization of a flow of activities that can be represented by the use of different software, being essential to verify a biological correlation for the resulting statistical results.

The sequence alignment of transcriptomic data is the task of determining the location in the reference genome that corresponds to each sequenced read. Given a file with aligned sequencing reads and a list of genomic features, a common task is to count how many reads map to each feature. DGE analysis is based in the detection and counting of RNA-seq data. Count data are stored in a tabular form with each sample related to the number of sequence fragments assigned to each gene. An important analysis issue is the quantification and statistical inference of systematic changes between conditions compared to variability within conditions. The DESeq2 package provides methods for testing the DGE by using negative binomial generalized linear models; the scatter and log shift estimates incorporate past data-based distributions.

4   ParslRNA-Seq: Workflow for DGE Analysis

4.1   Improvements in the Previous Implementation of the Workflow

Bowtie2 and HTseq are software activities that respectively aligns and counts sequencing reads and spend most of their time computing the CPU-bound processes. We assume that exploring multithreading and multiprocessing thread scaling in those critical activities are potential points for improvements the performance of the workflow. Bowtie2 and HTseq are the most representative CPU and time-consuming software of the workflow executed in SDumont and they were the main focus in our case studies. DESeq2 analyzed the DGE from the matrices of the counts of the alignment and the mapping of the sequences against the reference genome. These arrays (GTF file) contain the number of reads that were uniquely aligned (columns) with the exons of each gene in the samples (columns).

The previous implementation of the workflow cited in [4] is the first tentative of automating RNA-Seq processes in a structured scientific workflow. It was modeled with Parsl and presents three activities Bowtie2, HTSeq, and DESEq, as shown in Fig. 1(a). Parsl manages the execution of the script on clusters, clouds, grids, and other resources; orchestrates required data movement; and manages the execution of Python functions and external applications in parallel. The Parsl library can be easily integrated into Python-based gateways, allowing for simple management and scaling of workflows [8].

Bowtie2 calls a node and sets the *"-p/-threads NTHREADS"* performance option that launches the number of parallel search threads to process each FastQ. Bowtie2 threads option run on separate processors and synchronize the output alignments, which increases the alignment throughput by approximately a multiple of the number of threads. Users can set *"-p"* to increase Bowtie2 memory footprint making the execution highly parallel and the speedup close to linear [6]. As Parsl scales to hundreds of threads better than single processed workflows or pipelined approaches, we raise three modes of execution calling both Bowtie2 and Parsl to better understand if there is some kind of competition in the call of the numbers of threads by both of them. Our tests use: (a) The higher default buffer threshold for serialization Parsl with the Bowtie2 multithread option. (b) The Bowtie2 serial option with the Parsl multithread option. (c) The double parallelization of both Parsl and Bowtie2 multithreads options.

4.2   Multithreading and Multiprocessing

Multiprocessing (MP) is a system with more than one or two processors that assigns separate memory and resources for each of the processes. Multithreading (MT) is a program execution technique that allows a single process to have multiple code segments; then helps to create multiple threads inside a single process to increase computing throughput. We detect that modifications in some ParslRNA-Seq activities (mainly Bowtie2 and HTseq) can be exploited as potential points to MT or MP thread scaling, as they can increase the computing speed of the system.

The ParslRNA-Seq workflow code[3] shows the software command lines. While Bowtie2 creates MT processes, HTSeq *"–nprocesses"* (MP argument) only works to process different BAM files in parallel, i.e., htseq-count on one file is not parallelized. For instance, let us consider the following context in our ParslRNA-Seq processes. While we focus on making the best use of threads in a single process, an alternative is to run multiple simultaneous processes, possibly with many threads each. ParslRNA-Seq consumes six input FastQs, each deployed in parallel in an independent node.

For each node, Bowtie2 sets the performance option *"-p/–threads NTHREADS"* to launch the number of parallel search threads (default: 1) to process each FastQ. The threads will run on separate processors/cores and synchronize when parsing reads the output alignments, increasing alignment throughput by approximately a multiple of the number of the threads (linearly). The Split Picard's option *"SplitSamByNumberOfReads"* splits an input query-grouped SAM or BAM file into multiple (e.g., 24) BAM files while maintaining the sort order to parallelize alignment. The HTSeq *"–nprocesses"* processes those BAM files.

MP can suffer from load imbalance as some batches take longer to execute than others, and the job's duration is determined by the longest-running batch. Merge_HTSeq suffers this impact whereby some lock-holding threads are slow to finish their works (and release the lock) due waiting threads are using its resources. Finally, DESeq2 should wait for Merge_HTSeq finishes to be executed.

4.3   The Current Implementation of the ParslRNA-Seq Workflow

Bowtie2 multithreading was provided in the previous implementation of workflow; still with more improvements, we'll get to explore HTSeq in the current

---

[3] https://github.com/lucruzz/RNA-seq/blob/master/RNA-seq.py.

workflow implementation. HTSeq executes as default each file in an entire node, yet files are not parsed and no MT or MP strategies for execution were applied. The insertion of extra activities was required in the ParslRNA-Seq workflow modeling to (1) parse a SAM file in 24 blocks; (2) pass HTSeq the execution of a task for each SAM block in a thread; (3) manage the parallel distribution of tasks in CPU cores, applying in MP and MT approaches performed by Parsl.

The current implementation of the ParslRNA-Seq workflow presented in Fig. 1(b) is composed of six activities, including Sort, Split_Picard, and Merge_HTSeq that aim to improve performance over HTSeq. ParslRNA-Seq receives as input the reference genome of *Mus musculus*, the GTF (Gene Transfer Format) file with genomic metadata, and the sequencing files in FASTQ format. A CSV format file was created to relate the FASTQs and the experimental conditions: three control FASTQs and three Wnt condition FASTQs (Wingless pathway, Wnt transcriptional signaling metabolic pathway).

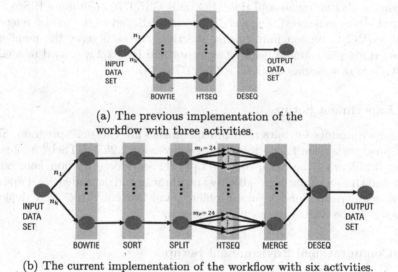

(a) The previous implementation of the workflow with three activities.

(b) The current implementation of the workflow with six activities.

Fig. 1. Conceptual modeling of the scientific workflow ParslRNA-Seq.

Activity 1 runs the program Bowtie2 which maps and compares the genome readings character by character. Activity 2 runs the program Samtools version 1.10 which sorts the readings. Activity 3 runs the program Picard version 2.25.0 used for manipulation and division of read files. Activity 4 runs the HTSeq program htseqcount from HTSeq version 0.13.5 to count the number of reads mapped by each gene. With n read files mapped, HTSeq sends each one to n cores, generating a single output file with $n + 1$ columns, where the first column represents the gene and the other columns represent counts performed on each file. Activity 5 (HTSeq-Merge) is a script in Python that merges the data generated by running HTSeq multicore, joining all the counts performed in a single column. Activity 6 runs the DESeq2 package that applies DGE statistics on the experimental conditions.

5   Methods and Infrastructure

5.1   Experiment Dataset

Maladaptive cardiac remodeling has been reported in the activation of the evolutionarily conserved Wnt pathway but the function of Wnt-transcriptional activation in the adult heart is yet unknown. RNA was isolated from mice cardiac tissue and RNA libraries were prepared for sequencing using standard Illumina protocols. The data belongs to a real RNA-Seq experiment[4], extracted from the public repository, Gene Expression Omnibus[5] (GEO) database. Data was divided into: (1) the control group: SRR5445794, SRR5445795, SRR5445796 and (2) the Wnt pathway condition group: SRR5445797, SRR5445798, SRR5445799. The organism is *Mus musculus* and the GEO.ID is GSE97763 (Illumina HiSeq 2000 Platform - *Mus musculus*). Sequence reads were aligned to the mouse reference assembly (UCSC version mm9) using Bowtie2. For each gene, the number of mapped reads was counted using htseq-count and DESeq2 was used to analyze the DGE. *Mus musculus* GEO.ID is GSE97763 [7].

5.2   Experiment Setup

The transcriptomics software used in experiments are Bowtie2[6] program, Samtools[7] program version 1.10, Picard[8] program version 2.25.0, HTSeq[9] framework version 0.13.5 with the htseq-count script, HTSeq-Merge Python homemade-script, and DESeq2[10] package. All software, libraries and dependencies, Parsl and Python components, Intel VTune Profiler[11], and Darshan[12] tool were deployed at the top of the Santos Dumont environment.

5.3   Computational Environment Setup

The SDumont is among the 500 most powerful machines in the world. It has a processing capacity of 5.1 Petaflop/s, with 34,688 multi-core CPUs distributed in 1,132 computational nodes that are interconnected by an Infiniband FDR/HDR interconnect network. The compute nodes have two Ivy Bridge Intel Xeon E5-2695v2 CPUs (12c @2.4 GHz) and 64 Gb of RAM and an Nvidia K40 GPU. The

---

[4] https://sfb1002.med.uni-goettingen.de/production/literature/publications/201.

[5] https://www.ncbi.nlm.nih.gov/geo/.

[6] http://bowtie-bio.sourceforge.net/bowtie2/index.shtml.

[7] http://www.htslib.org/doc/samtools.html.

[8] http://broadinstitute.github.io/picard/.

[9] https://htseq.readthedocs.io/.

[10] https://bioconductor.org/packages/DESeq2/.

[11] http://intel.ly/vtune-amplifier-xe.

[12] https://www.mcs.anl.gov/research/projects/darshan/.

executions were performed on compute nodes of two Intel Xeon E5-2695v2 Ivy Bridge CPUs, 24 cores (12 per CPU) and 64 GB of RAM. Software, algorithms, bioinformatics dependencies of Bowtie2, Samtools, Picard, HTSeq, DESeq2 and Parsl components were installed in the SDumont environment.

6   Experimental Results

This section analyzes the experimental results depicting workflow performance and scalability in the SDumont supercomputer environment. Besides the computational results, we also present some biological data showing the breakdown of RNA-Seq data, DGE analysis, and Multidimensional Scale Analysis.

6.1   Performance and Scalability Analyses

In order to understand workflow performance and scalability, Fig. 2 presents the execution time of different workflow versions (previous and current implementations), where we vary each execution from one to 24 threads in the SDumont environment. Although there is no substantial performance gain when increasing the number of threads beyond 12, we observe a noteworthy gain with the newly executed implementations depicted below.

Performance of the previous workflow implementation: improvements with Bowtie2. The Bowtie2 task implemented employs one of the three following strategies. (a) The higher default buffer threshold for serialization Parsl with the Bowtie2 multithread option. (b) The Bowtie2 serial option with the Parsl multithread option. (c) The double parallelization of both Parsl and Bowtie2 multi-threads option. Using n number of threads of Parsl and n number of threads of Bowtie2 led to a double parallelization.

Option (c) performs better than other strategies, and the Total Execution Time (TET) decreased from 643 min (1 node) to 75 min (6 nodes), which refers to 88.34% of improvement in terms of TET and 8,57 of speedup-after that, increasing the number of nodes does not show a significant improvement in TET. The double parallelization in both Parsl and Bowtie2 in Option (c) was the chosen strategy to be coupled into the current implementation of ParslRNA-Seq workflow.

Performance of current implementation of the ParslRNA-Seq workflow: Improvements with HTSeq. The workflow calls the most up-to-date version of the HTSeq activity that allows the multicore parallelization of inputs. Each entry was partitioned into 24 sub-entries so that each sub-entry was allocated and executed on a single SDumont CPU core. This strategy decreased the computational time of this activity from 305.3283 to 30.4161 min, representing approximately 90% of improvement in terms of TET and 10,03 of speedup (Table 1). The other activities of the workflow did not present any execution bottlenecks. Bowtie2 and Samtools use multi-threads parameters; besides Picard, HTSeq-Merge and DESeq are low-time and computationally expensive.

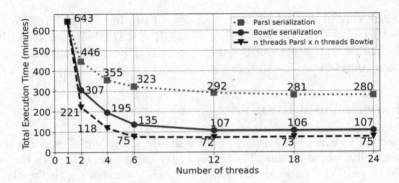

Fig. 2. Scalability of the previous implementation of the workflow with three activities. Performance is based on Bowtie2 TET in minutes.

Table 1 presents the results of serial execution of ParslRNA-Seq. Both ParslRNA-Seq versions, previous and current, were executed with the same configuration of libraries, software, number of cores, and type of CPU architectures. The TET of the previous workflow implementation was 326.07 min compared to the TET of 95.64 min of the current workflow implementation, representing a decrease in the TET of 70.67%. This result demonstrates that the gain is three times greater, even with the inclusion of the three activities: Sort, Picard, and HTSeq-Merge. Only, HTSeq improvements in ParslRNA-Seq of up to 90,04% decreased the TET from 305,33 to 30,42 min in 24 cores.

Table 1. Total Execution Time in minutes of the previous and current implementation of the ParslRNA-Seq workflow.

Workflow	Bowtie2	Sort	Split	HTSeq	Merge	DESeq	TET
Previous implementation	19,27	–	–	305,33	–	1,48	326,07
Current implementation		5,88	38,56	30,42	0,04		95,64

6.2 I/O Performance Results Using Darshan

The workflow was executed with the Darshan profiler to investigate the I/O behavior of each step. Figure 3 presents the distribution of step execution time—Bowtie2 on the top and Sort on the bottom—with two input sizes: 1.8 and 3 GB. Each bar plot presents the percentage of that step's execution time spent on each activity: POSIX read (in read, on the bottom of each bar), write (in green, in the middle), and others (in pink, on the top). The other steps—HTSeq, Split, DESeq2, and Merge_HTSeq—were omitted because they spent less than 10% of their time doing I/O. For both applications, increasing the input size increases the proportion of the execution time spent on I/O. That indicates that the I/O limits the scalability of these codes: as more data is treated, most time is spent on I/O, and thus the CPU-focused optimizations presented earlier may have less impact on performance [9,10].

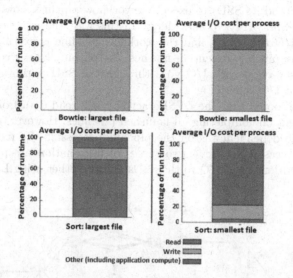

Fig. 3. Distribution of execution time of Bowtie2 and Sort, by activity, as reported by Darshan. (Color figure online)

I/O Analysis for Bowtie2. Changing the input from 1.8 to 3 GB increases the run time from 152 seconds (80% on write operations) to 263 seconds (90% on writes). This increase was only due to I/O, with the write time increasing practically linearly with the input size. The output size was 6 and 11 GB.

I/O Analysis for Sort. Time increased from 41 s (5% on reading and 15% on write operations) to 91 s (70% on reads and 10% on writes). While the writing time remained relatively constant (output size was 657 MB and 1.1 GB), the reading time of Sort increased over 30 times by doubling the input size, which indicates the reading portion of this code is a limiting factor for its performance.

HTSeq, Split, DESeq2, and Metge_HTSeq spend less than 10% of their time in I/O.

6.3 Performance Results Using SSD

To further improve the ParslRNA-Seq workflow's performance, we select the two most I/O intensive workflow tasks (Bowtie2 and Sort) as targets for improvements. Usually, all intermediate files, that are created by one task and consumed by the following one, are written to Lustre. Hence we decided to write intermediate files to Solid State Drive (SSD) storage devices, available in each of SDumont's compute nodes, instead.

We investigated different strategies for doing this, such as (i) to decouple the DESEq activity from the workflow since it gets only executed after the Merge activity has processed all data. The next was (ii) to use, in an isolated way, a compute node (and its SSD) to execute a workflow pipeline, now composed of: Bowtie2, Sort, Split, HTSeq, and Merge. In this way, the input data is copied from the Lustre to the SSD, and the workflow pipeline is executed only after that. When the pipeline execution finishes, the output data is copied back to Lustre. In this way, all raw I/O goes through the SSD during all tasks that present relevant I/O times (Fig. 4).

It should be noted that the DESEq activity will read data from Lustre and is still dependent on completing all launched pipelines. However, in distributed parallelism, the dependency is on the pipeline processing the most significant data. For this reason, in Fig. 4 two pieces of information are presented: one about the execution doing I/O to the SSDs and the other using Lustre.

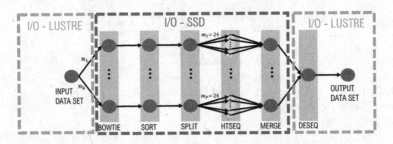

Fig. 4. Modelling of the current implementation of the ParslRNA-Seq workflow for I/O executions in SSD and Lustre.

Comparatively, in Table 2, which disregards the copy time, the execution time of the workflow decreased on average from 17 minutes to 15 minutes when using the SSDs for the intermediate files. This shows this idea of using node-local storage to avoid accessing the parallel file system is a promising one. Another approach, under development, is to not make copies from Lustre to the SSD and vice versa, but to have the Bowtie2 activity reading directly from Lustre and the Merge writing its output directly to the remote file system as well (while keeping the intermediate files in the SSDs).

6.4   Biological Results of RNA-Seq Data

The results of the analysis for the selection of differentially expressed genes under DESeq2 are presented in Fig. 5 (MA-Plot), Fig. 6 (MDS graph), and Fig. 7 (heatmaps). The comparative analyses of the Figures demonstrate that there is no evidence of difference in biological results obtained with the execution of the previous or current implementations of the ParslRNA-Seq workflow.

Table 2. Total execution time of the current implementation of the ParslRNA-Seq workflow in SSD and Lustre.

Executions using SSDs								
File	Size (GB)	Total execution time (min)					Avg.	Std. dev.
SRR5445797	1.8	10,07	10,03	10,08	10,20	10,08	10,09	0,06
SRR5445796	3.0	15,86	15,90	15,58	15,70	16,12	15,83	0,20
Executions using lustre								
File	Size (GB)	Total execution time (min)					Avg.	Std. dev.
SRR5445797	1.8	11,62	12,08	11,95	12,07	11,57	11,86	0,25
SRR5445796	3.0	17,60	17,40	17,77	17,77	17,63	17,63	0,15

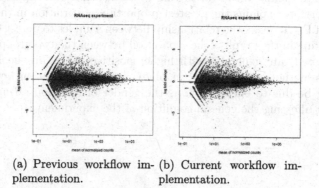

(a) Previous workflow im-   (b) Current workflow implementation.   plementation.

Fig. 5. Average normalized of the $log_2 foldChange$ gene/change counts.

DGE Analysis. DESeq2 uses the Negative Binomial probabilistic model for normalization to perform GDS analyses. DESeq2 normalizes data by estimating sample size and dispersion, fits data to a negative binomial Generalized Linear Model (GLM), and verifies the GDS using Wald's parametric test. DESeq2 calculates the functions $baseMean$ (average of normalized readings); $log_2 foldChange$ (proportion of readings as a function of log_2); $lfcSE$ (standard error); $stat$ (Wald); $pvalue$ and $padj$ (adjusted p and p values from DE transcripts).

In Fig. 5, the differentially expressed genes appear in red and the others in black. Some considerations are: (1) There will be differentially expressed genes (in red) above and below the line that delimits the $log_2 foldChange$ values. The genes above had more counts in the Control condition than in the Wnt condition, and the points below the opposite. (2) The higher the average counts (further to the right of the graph), the differentially expressed genes will be closer to the limit line, influenced by $log_2 foldChange$, that the higher the averages, although they are different, the logarithm will be less different and therefore the threshold for determining that a gene is differentially expressed will be lower. (3) There is a tendency for there to be no differentially expressed genes to the left of the graph. The further to the left of the graph, the lower the counts observed for the genes, and when there are almost no counts, almost no difference can be shown.

MA-Plot plots the average of the normalized readings of each gene against the log_2 of the doubled change (Fig. 5). Points corresponding to genes identified as differentially expressed (adjusted p value less than 0.05) are highlighted in red. Points outside the window are plotted as open triangles pointing up or down, depending on whether the value of $logFC$ is greater than 2 or less than -2, respectively.

Multidimensional Scale Analysis (MDS Graph). It is a multivariate technique that allows visually analyzing the proximity between samples from the same study, placing them in certain dimensions. In an MDS plot, the first dimension represents the magnitude of the initial change that best separates the samples and therefore explains the greatest proportion of variation in the data. The MDS plot of Fig. 6 shows the relationship between samples to detect GDS. What is most striking in the graph is the separation between the two groups. The Wnt samples (in red) are generally with higher positive values on the X-axis than the samples in the control group (in blue). The approximation between some groups may be due to effects such as the gender of the mouse (male/female), but without affecting the general condition of the experiment.

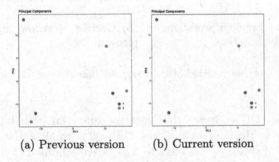

(a) Previous version   (b) Current version

Fig. 6. Multidimensional scale of distances from the relationship between samples.(a) Previous workflow implementation. (b) Current workflow implementation. (Color figure online)

Heatmaps. The dendrogram in Fig. 7 allows viewing the grouping of samples based on a hierarchical group along with the expression levels of individual genes. The variance in each of the lines of the $log_2 - CPM$ matrix was previously calculated and the number of genes to be displayed was established. The selection of the 1000 most variable genes grouped the samples according to the experimental group. The overexpressed genes are represented in red, downregulated genes in blue, and the white color indicates the absence of expression change. Each row of the grid represents a gene and each column a sample.

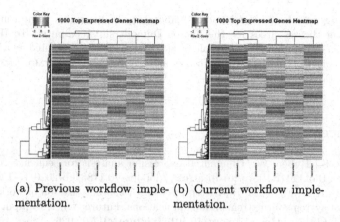

(a) Previous workflow imple- (b) Current workflow implementation. mentation.

Fig. 7. Heatmaps of the 1000 most variable genes. (Color figure online)

7 Conclusion

In this work, we have presented a real-world workflow analysis for data-intensive transcriptomics applications to enable performance optimization of HPC systems. We introduce a current implementation of the ParslRNA-Seq workflow tailored to the needs of tracking a workflow execution and identifying potential issues to improve performance. Our experiments demonstrate that this optimized workflow can accurately orchestrate computation resources, helping to pinpoint relevant metrics to help identify performance problems. Our results show performance improvements of up to 70.67% from 326.074 min with the previous implementation of the ParslRNA-Seq workflow to 95.64 min with the current implementation of the ParslRNA-Seq workflow, both executed in 24 cores. This result demonstrates that the gain is three times greater, even with the inclusion of the three activities: Sort, Picard, and HTSeq-Merge.

Additionally, we characterized the Bowtie2 improvements in the previous implementation of the ParslRNA-Seq workflow of up to 88.34% decreased the TET (8,57 of speedup) from 643 min (1 node) to 75 min (6 nodes) with a double parallelization option. HTSeq improvements in the current implementation of the ParslRNA-Seq workflow of up to 90,04% decreased the TET (10,03 of speedup) from 305,33 to 30,42 min in 24 cores. Further, we characterized the I/O behavior of the workflow components, identifying I/O problems in two of them, which will be the focus of future optimization efforts.

The next steps involve performance analyses of massive (terabytes datasets) RNA-Seq data in parallel and distributed executions of the optimized ParslRNA-Seq. The code will be made available to the scientific community through scientific gateways as Bioinfo-Portal[13], hosted at LNCC, aimed at strengthening research in the bioinformatics community.

---

[13] https://bioinfo.lncc.br/.

Acknowledgement. To the National Laboratory of Scientific Computing (Brazil) for providing the resources for the Santos Dumont supercomputer. To HPCProSol project (Next-generation HPC PROblems and SOLutions), represented by a joint team (équipe associée) between Inria, in France, and the National Laboratory for Scientific Computing (LNCC), in Brazil.

References

1. Anders, S., Huber, W.: Differential expression analysis for sequence count data. Genome Biol. **11**(R106) (2010). https://doi.org/10.1186/gb-2010-11-10-r106
2. da Silva, R.F., Filgueira, R., Pietri, I., et al.: A characterization of workflow management systems for extreme-scale applications. Future Gener. Comput. Syst. **75**, 228–238 (2017). https://doi.org/10.1016/j.future.2017.02.026
3. Mattoso, M., Werner, C., Travassos, G., et al.: Towards supporting the life cycle of large-scale scientific experiments. Int. J. Bus. Process. Integr. Manag. **5**, 79–92 (2010). https://doi.org/10.1504/IJBPIM.2010.033176
4. Cruz, L., Coelho, M., Gadelha, L., et al.: Avaliação de Desempenho de um Workflow Científico para Experimentos de RNA-Seq no Supercomputador Santos Dumont. In: Anais Estendidos do XXI Simpósio em Sistemas Computacionais de Alto Desempenho, SBC 2020, pp. 86–93 (2020). https://doi.org/10.5753/wscad_estendido.2020.14093
5. Liao, Y., Smyth, G., Shi, W.: featureCounts: an efficient general purpose program for assigning sequence reads to genomic features. Bioinformatics **30**(7), 923–930 (2014). https://doi.org/10.1093/bioinformatics/btt656
6. Anders, S., Pyl, P.T., Huber, W.: HTSeq-a Python framework to work with high-throughput sequencing data. Bioinformatics **31**(2), 166–169 (2014). https://doi.org/10.1093/bioinformatics/btu638
7. Iyer, L., Nagarajan, S., Woelfer, M., et al.: A context-specific cardiac β-catenin and GATA4 interaction influences TCF7L2 occupancy and remodels chromatin driving disease progression in the adult heart. Nucleic Acids Res. **46**(6), 2850–2867 (2018). https://doi.org/10.1093/nar/gky049
8. Babuji, Y., Woodard, A., Li, Z., et al.: Parsl: pervasive parallel programming in Python. In: Proceedings of the 28th International Symposium on High-Performance Parallel and Distributed Computing 2019, pp. 25–36 (2019). https://doi.org/10.48550/arXiv.1905.02158
9. Cruz, L., Coelho, M., Galheigo, M., et al.: Parallel performance and I/O profiling of HPC RNA-Seq applications. Computación y Sistemas (2022, Submitted)
10. Bez, J.L., Carneiro, A.R., Pavan, P., et al.: I/O performance of the Santos Dumont supercomputer. Int. J. High Perform. Comput. Appl. **34**(2), 227–245 (2020). https://doi.org/10.1177/1094342019868526
11. Mondelli, M.L., Magalhães, T., Loss, G., et al.: BioWorkbench: a high-performance framework for managing and analyzing bioinformatics experiments. PeerJ **6**, e5551 (2018). https://doi.org/10.7717/peerj.5551
12. Wilde, M., Hategan, M., Wozniak, J.M., et al.: Swift: a language for distributed parallel scripting. Parallel Comput. **37**(9), 633–652 (2011). https://doi.org/10.1016/j.parco.2011.05.005

13. Goble, C., Soiland-Reyes, S., Bacall, F., et al.: Implementing FAIR digital objects in the EOSC-life workflow collaboratory. Zenodo **2**(5), 99–110 (2021). https://doi.org/10.5281/zenodo.4605654
14. Wratten, L., Wilm, A., Göke, J.: Reproducible, scalable, and shareable analysis pipelines with bioinformatics workflow managers. Nat. Methods **18**, 1161–1168 (2021). https://doi.org/10.1038/s41592-021-01254-9

Refactoring an Electric-Market Simulation Software for Massively Parallel Computations

Franco Seveso, Raúl Marichal, Ernesto Dufrechou[✉], and Pablo Ezzatti

Instituto de Computación (INCO), Universidad de la República,
Montevideo, Uruguay
{franco.seveso,rmarichal,edufrechou,pezzatti}@fing.edu.uy

Abstract. In the last two decades, Uruguay has been immersed in the process of significantly changing its energy generation matrix, especially by the introduction of wind and solar sources. In this context, Sim-SEE, a simulation and optimization software designed to help decision-making in generating and distributing electrical energy, is extensively used. The design of this tool is conceived for conventional CPUs and follows a sequential execution paradigm. This paper focuses on a refactoring of SimSEE that enables leveraging massively-parallel hardware platforms, seeking to adapt the tool for the increasing size and complexity of Uruguay's electric market. We extend our previous ideas about reorganizing the software architecture to exploit the parallelism in each time-step of SimSEE's simulation. In more detail, we present two variants following this parallelism pattern, a straightforward parallel version that requires replicating the used memory and a variant that implies limited performance restrictions but requires a minimal memory overhead.

Keywords: Coarse-grained parallelism · Electric energy generation · Stochastic dynamic programming · Memory usage

1 Introduction

In the last two decades, the Uruguayan electricity generation matrix experienced important changes, mainly due to the constant incorporation of new generation sources such as wind and solar farms [16]. This brings important challenges to efficiently using and distributing the available resources, making demand and generation capacity prediction necessary. The SimSEE (Electric Power Systems Simulator) is a software tool that allows users to make customized simulations of an electric energy generation system. Its principal purpose is to aid in the decision-making process, both in the long term (investment planning) and in the short term (system operation and market simulation) [7]. It was developed at the Universidad de la República, by engineers of the Instituto de Ingeniería Eléctrica (IIE) of the Facultad de Ingeniería (FING), between the years 2006 and 2008, maintaining a constant evolution up to now [6,10]. The tool is tailored

P. Navaux et al. (Eds.): CARLA 2022, CCIS 1660, pp. 190–204, 2022.
https://doi.org/10.1007/978-3-031-23821-5_14

to represent the reality of Uruguay's electric market. Hence, its most intensive users are the Uruguayan public agency managing the electricity generation market, called ADME [3] and the Uruguayan public company that generates and distributes electric energy (UTE).

This work's motivation is to adapt the simulation tool to increase the number of actors (e.g., power sources) and complexity of the models while maintaining the accuracy levels and simulation runtime constraints, such as keeping bounded simulation times. For this purpose, we aim to leverage the computational power offered by modern massively parallel hardware platforms, such as heterogeneous servers equipped with GPUs. These platforms have shown an impressive evolution in the last decades and have become a vital piece of the HPC landscape [4,5,11].

This effort is an extension of [13], where we identify the SimSEE bottlenecks by evaluating different realistic cases and propose a new software architecture design for the SimSEE to exploit the massively parallel computations. Specifically, this work presents two different variants of SimSEE following the previously described parallelism pattern. First, a direct parallel version that requires replicating the used memory, and second, we design a new variant that implies concrete performance restrictions but requires a minimal memory overhead for each simulation trajectory computed in parallel. In other words, a parallel version that offers scalability in memory use.

The rest of the work is organized as follows. Section 2 synthesizes the arrived results of the previous work. In Sect. 3 we present different variations to implement the previously proposed and discussed parallel design. Next, in Sect. 4, the experimental evaluation results of the implementations are summarized. Finally, Sect. 5 presents our conclusions and some future lines of work.

2   The SimSEE and Previous Results

As we stated previously, SimSEE (Electric Power Systems Simulator) is a software tool that allows users to make customized simulations of an electric energy generation system. It is based on Stochastic Dynamic Programming techniques, it allows to simulate the contribution of multiple energy sources, including thermal, solar, hydro-electric or wind energy, to a specific electrical network. For this reason in the simulation different and random realizations of these stochastic processes, called trajectories, are executed, and the results are expressed in terms of the expected value or as distributions or probabilities of exceedance. Its principal purpose is to aid in the decision-making process both in the long term (investment planning) and in the short term (system operation and market simulation) [7]. It was developed at the UDELAR, by engineers of the Instituto de Ingeniería Eléctrica (IIE) of the Facultad de Ingeniería (FING) in the Pascal programming language [12].

In the previous work were designed and evaluated different realistic test cases, varying the scenarios between three classes: hourly, daily, and weekly (i.e., short, mid, and long-term). Since the SimSEE is a legacy complex system developed in

Pascal and is being used by ADME, the main goal of these tests was to exhibit the most resource-consuming procedures in the simulation routine and then, with a fine-grain approach, efficiently implement a parallel version of those procedures. This approach avoids re-implementing the entire simulation routine, a task of serious difficulty and resource demand. The experimental results showed that none of the procedures represent an important bottleneck since a single execution of these procedures is not demanding enough, deriving that the cost came from the number of calls or invoked. Nevertheless, we found that an important part of the simulation runtime is invested in Simplex resolution routines. In Fig. 1, for example, we can see the proportion of Simplex-related operations (middle green rectangle), and Table 1 shows how many times some of these procedures are called into the simulation. Based on this, we propose a strategy to exploit parallelism by designing a new simulation scheme focused on a coarse-grain approach instead of including fine-grain parallelism.

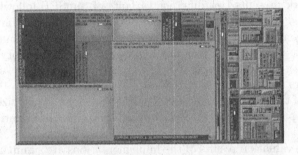

Fig. 1. Graphical representation of simulation call map with a daily playroom. The area of each rectangle is proportional to the runtime of the corresponding procedure.

Table 1. Top 5 procedures for the daily playroom simulation.

Procedure	Perc. (%)	CPU cycles	Calls	Unit
PASOBUSCARFACTIBLEIGUALDAD4	29.0	3.349×10^{11}	1.348×10^6	USIMPLEX
LOCATE_ZPOS	20.3	2.344×10^{11}	5.991×10^7	USIMPLEX
INTERCAMBIAR	15.4	1.780×10^{11}	8.258×10^6	USIMPLEX
MEJORPIVOTE	6.1	6.991×10^{10}	5.972×10^7	USIMPLEX
CAMBIO_VAR_COTA_SUP_EN_COLUMNA	4.1	4.719×10^{10}	5.670×10^{10}	USIMPLEX

The simulation algorithm can be divided into two main loops. The first and outer loop iterates through the trajectories, line (3) in Algorithm 1, and for each of these trajectories, there is a second loop (5) that sets up and solves, for each time step (7), an optimization problem using the Simplex algorithm, represented by a matrix, based on the work of Rutishauser et al. [14]. Since each trajectory is independent, in [13] we redesigned the routine interchanging the loops and structures related to solving, for the different trajectories, the simplex matrices associated with each time step in parallel. Note the (parallel) **for** of trajectories in line 11 of the Algorithm 2, solving independent simplex matrices.

Algorithm 1. Simular + cargarSala

```
 1  room = cargarSala ( room_file )
 2  // Simulation
 3  prepare ( room )
 4  for Trajectories :
 5     Traj_Init ( room )
 6     for time_steps :
 7        simplex_matrix = simplex ( room )
 8        solve ( simplex_matrix )
 9     end
10  end
```

Algorithm 2. Simular' + cargarSalas

```
 1  rooms = cargarSalas ( room_file )
 2  // Simulation
 3  for i in Trajectories :
 4     prepare ( rooms [ i ] )
 5     Traj_Init ( rooms [ i ] )
 6  end
 7  for time_steps :
 8     for Trajectories :
 9        spx_array [ i ] = simplex ( rooms [ i ] )
10     end
11     ( parallel ) for Trajectories :
12        solve ( spx_array [ i ] )
13     end
14  end
```

Pseudocode of the original SimSEE simulation scheme (Algorithm 1) and the reorganization proposed in [13] (Algorithm 2).

3   Proposal

As discussed in the previous section, the strategy behind the massively parallel version of the simulation is to process independent trajectories at the same time, solving in parallel multiple simplex matrices. To implement this design, the data associated with each trajectory must stay independent from the others. In other words, each trajectory needs its *playroom*, which is a data structure that holds all the information about the electrical system being simulated, including the state variables of each power source, such as the water level of hydroelectrical plants. In the original version, the playroom is created by the procedure `cargarSala` reading a configuration file associated with the room line by line. This room is instantiated once and used throughout the whole simulation. Therefore, the cost of the `cargarSala` in the original algorithm is constant for any number of trajectories, which is why it was not taken into account in the previous work evaluation. Depending on the room, this procedure can take several computation cycles, mainly conditioned to the number of entities and historical information. Then, in the simulation phase, as trajectories are run sequentially for each time step, the state variables of the playroom can be reset for each new trajectory. If trajectories run in parallel, sharing the state variables is impossible, so a certain degree of data replication is necessary.

In the following sections, we propose different implementations to load multiple playrooms and, considering the cost of in/out and file reading [9], we advance in implementing routines that use the playroom file once and create multiple rooms. On the other hand, it is important to highlight that memory usage multiplication is a very limiting strategy when trying to massively parallelize systems. In other words, one of the essential characteristics to reach in parallel patterns is the scalability in memory usage [8,9]. We design, implement and evaluate a version where the different rooms share certain structures through pointers or references, using SimSEE native classes. Later we present another version with a simple structure to store the reference pointers for the shared units between the rooms, avoiding the list searches of the first.

3.1   Loading the Playrooms for Massively-Parallel Trajectories, naive

A straightforward strategy to address the problem of independent playrooms is to create a collection of rooms, with a size equal to the number of trajectories, by calling the procedure `cargarSala` multiple times. As an early result, Table 2 shows the outcome of this implementation. The table shows the elevated cost of instantiating these rooms, with linear growth of the elapsed time to load the rooms and simulation time due to the preparation of the rooms in the `Simular'` procedure.

Table 2. Elapsed time (ms) of room load (`cargarSala`) and simulation (`Simular`) comparison for both strategies in hourly playroom (see Sect. 4.2 for details about test cases and the runtime environment).

# of trajectories	cargarSala	Simular	Loop of cargarSala	Simular'
256	4125	27828	968844	161094

For reasons previously described, we studied the procedure `cargarSala` in detail and evaluated the possibility of implementing a new procedure capable of instantiating multiple rooms efficiently.

3.2   Improving the Playrooms Replication, base

Although the previous implementation returns the expected collection, it needlessly repeats procedures when loading the different rooms. Since all rooms are equal and loaded from the same file, we can improve this implementation in different ways, such as refactoring some of the procedures or optimizing the access to the file for reading. Considering the above, we modified the strategy initially used to load the rooms, deriving this procedure in `cargarSalas`. Unlike `cargarSala`, this implementation reads the text file associated with the room once, line by line, and instantiates simultaneously many structures and units as rooms are needed.

Although `cargarSalas` is also a naive version, it allows fulfilling the task of loading multiple rooms, avoiding multiple file reads and the implied runtime overhead. However, this strategy implies a large memory usage since it instantiates every single structure for the room N times.

The memory used in the simulation is mainly given by the initialization of each room. For example, the sizes of the evaluated rooms (hourly, daily and weekly) result in around 90 MB, 3.8 MB, and 2.4 MB, respectively, when mapped to Pascal objects. Therefore, simulating 1000 trajectories of a hourly playroom will require around 90 GB of memory, making this `cargarSalas` implementation not scalable and unfeasible when the number of trajectories grows for devices with limited memory resources.

3.3   Sharing References to Avoid Memory Allocations, RefCat

A reasonable conclusion from the previous discussion, can be that the main restriction for the inclusion of massively parallel techniques in the SimSEE is the multiplication of the memory usage. This motivated a detailed study of the units created in `cargarSalas`, looking for possible instances unchanged between the different trajectories. The *Dynamic Parameters record* or simply *record* are particular cases of a valid structure for this approach. Based on [15], the dynamic *records* can be defined as the system allowing the various playroom entities to change their parameters at runtime. A dynamic *record* consists of a start date, a periodicity, and a set of parameters depending on the type of entity that it belongs to. The actors or other entities that require parameters that may vary over time must specify in their *records* what those parameters are, and the system automatically updates them when the indicated date is reached, both in simulation and in optimization. Each *record* will be valid from its start date until another replaces it. In other words, if an actor has a single *record* at the beginning of the simulation, it will be valid for the entire simulation horizon. If the actor has a *record* at the beginning and another in the middle, the first *record* will be valid until half of the simulation, then it will be replaced by the second one that will follow until another replaces it or the simulation finishes. Basically, represent historical states of the entities, and remain invariant through the simulation.

In the particular case of the hourly room (VATES [1]), it has about 2000 *records* associated with the entities that must be instantiated when loading the room, which, in the worst case, implies having to instantiate 2000 × *NTrajectories records*. The simplest solution would be for the same entities from the different rooms to point to a single instance of the *records* and somehow share them. The problem that arises is that many of these *records* have references or pointers to the entities within the same room. Due to this, it is impossible to directly share the *records* since these references are accessed when computing the variables to prepare, for example, the simplex matrix at each time step. So, to share the *records* it is necessary to have the information of the different references corresponding to each room and switch those references when computing with them. Figure 2 shows this problem; while the entities of different rooms must be independent, the *records* remain constant through the simulation (red box), and the main problem is the references to entities in the same room (yellow arrows).

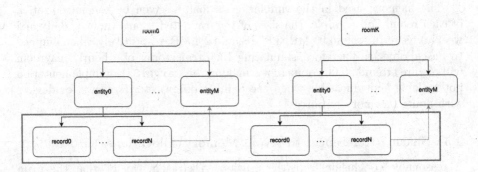

Fig. 2. Simplified scheme of multiple playrooms. Entities in different rooms must be different instances, but the files remain the same for the same entity in different rooms except by the references. (Color figure online)

Considering the previously described situation, we implemented a "Reference Catalogue", which is responsible for containing the information of references and maintaining the consistency of the ones for the room when the simulation needs to use it. The main idea is to map the excessive memory usage of rooms related to the *records*, to simple pointers stored in the "Reference Catalogue", representing a critical memory usage reduction. The new simulation scheme sharing *records* is presented in the Algorithm 3, where the procedure `ChangeReferences` is added to set the correct references to entities of different rooms when a trajectory calculates and prepares, for example, the simplex matrix. Note that this procedure is called twice in the Algorithm 3, in first place (line 3), due to the preparation of the rooms, initializing the actors, sources and variables of the playrooms previous to the true simulation stage. The second call (line 9) in the simulation stage, is needed to set the correct references before the simplex creation for each time step.

Algorithm 3. Simular' sharing room's objects

```
1    rooms, catalogue = cargarSalas(room_file)
2    for i in Trajectories:
3        ChangeReferences(rooms[i], catalogue)
4        prepare(rooms[i])
5        Traj_Init(rooms[i])
6    end
7    for time_steps:
8        for Trajectories:
9            ChangeReferences(rooms[i], catalogue)
10           spx_array[i] = simplex(rooms[i])
11       end
12       (parallel) for Trajectories:
13           solve(spx_array[i])
14       end
15   end
```

3.4   Enhancing the Access to Shared References in the Simulation, RefDicc

In the previously described strategy, when a reference needs to be changed, it is necessary to search for the new reference within the list of entities and the "Reference Catalogue" in simulation time. This operation implies a complexity proportional to the number of references and entities the room has, which can be substantial depending on the room. To avoid these searches, we propose to introduce a dictionary (a matrix of pointers), responsible for saving the already resolved references for all the rooms.

This strategy avoids the unnecessary task of iterating over the list of entities looking for a reference and then resolving it. By applying these changes, we convert the complexity of the operation that changes a reference to a constant order, significantly reducing the computation cost and its impact on the simulation. In other words, we sacrifice memory consumption to store the already solved references for each room to avoid repeated operations in simulation time.

4   Experimental Evaluation

This section presents the experimental evaluation of our proposal.

4.1   Test Cases

To evaluate how the proposed algorithm schemes perform, we vary the simulation scenarios between hourly, daily, and weekly playrooms, which are representative workloads of the SimSEE. Based on VATES [1] the hourly playroom runs to calculate the optimal energy dispatch in the following week and incorporates the forecasts of hydraulic contributions to the dams, the forecast of wind and solar generation, and the forecast of demand for every hour. It has 168 time steps, composed of three hydro generators with reservoirs and one without, twelve fuel-fired generators, one wind and one solar generator representing all the country's farms, and a CEGH source, that states for modeling multi-variable stochastic processes, working as a time series synthesizer having common characteristics with the available time series measures, with two hydrologic state variables.

The daily playrooms are mostly used for seasonal programming, with a CEGH source for the contribution to basins that also has two hydrologic state variables, and there are still three hydro generators with reservoirs. This kind of playroom is the most required by SimSEE users [2].

4.2   Runtime Environment

This section contains the environment specification where all the executions and results proposed in this work were carried out. This environment has an 8-core processor Intel(R) Core(TM) i7-4770 CPU @ 3.40 GHz, 16 GB of RAM with Linux operating system.

4.3   Experimental Results

The time measurements of the simulation were presented in scale to obtain an abstraction for the number of trajectories used, but in the same way, the computation time required by the simulation with the strategy of loading multiple rooms is still a bit distant from the original in terms of efficiency.

As mentioned in the previous section, Table 2 shows how the time of loading many rooms (repeating the file read) is significantly high, converting this into a non-viable implementation strategy, and in terms of memory use, it replicates all the rooms. The first proposed idea to mitigate this problem was reading the file once, with the implemented procedure `cargarSalas`. In the new idea, the runtime is not a problem, but the issue of memory usage keeps present.

Table 3. Peak memory usage (MB) for the different strategies simulating 100 trajectories of hourly, daily and weekly rooms.

	Original	Full independent	Reference catalogue
Hourly	500	9560	970
Daily	401	780	750
Weekly	142	630	363

In this line, the Vates playroom is the worst case in memory usage due to its large size and number of *records*, but for the same reason, it represents an opportunity to see the profits of the optimization strategy of sharing *records* between the rooms. Table 3 reflects the results of this approach. It shows that the new variant that shares structures using the references catalogue improves the rooms' loading stage, using considerably less memory. On the other hand, for the hourly scenario, with 100 trajectories, the principal disadvantage of this strategy can be seen in the last columns of Table 4, where the computational cost is now transferred to the simulation, with the procedure `ChangeReferences` implemented with the a "Reference Catalogue", native system class mainly used for the playroom's load.

Table 4. Elapsed time (ms) of `Simular`, `Simular'` and `ChangeReferences` with 100 trajectories for Hourly, Daily and Weekly playroom, using the reference catalogue.

Playroom	Simular	Simular'	ChangeReferences
Hourly	7875	274406	261711
Daily	43996	180896	128596
Weekly	14929	36312	19856

Finally, the last version of the refactored SimSEE is evaluated. Specifically, Table 5 presents the results of applying the structure share techniques between rooms in terms of memory usage.

Table 5. Peak memory usage (MB) for the different strategies simulating 100 trajectories of hourly, daily and weekly rooms.

	Original	Full independent	Reference catalogue	Reference dictionary
Hourly	500	9560	970	1068
Daily	401	780	750	760
Weekly	142	630	363	407

The first observation is that, although the Reference Catalogue technique employs less memory to store the references that need to be changed between rooms (2K references for VATES), they are solved every time in simulation when a room needs to make a computation. This resulted in poor performance, negatively affecting the simulation, as shown Table 4. On the other hand, the strategy that uses a matrix of pointers to store the already solved references requires little more memory since it employs as many rows and columns as trajectories and references, respectively, to store the correct pointers. Moreover, it significantly reduces the overhead introduced to the simulation by the previous technique.

When it is not the worst case (for example, Daily Room) and the number of referenced *records* contained in the room is not so large, the efficiency of loading the rooms with this implementation of shared *records* is not as noticeable as the Hourly room, but severely impacts on the simulation time. Like the previous one, the weekly playroom contains few *records*, and the improvement is not so noticeable. Despite this, both daily and weekly playrooms present very good performance loading rooms.

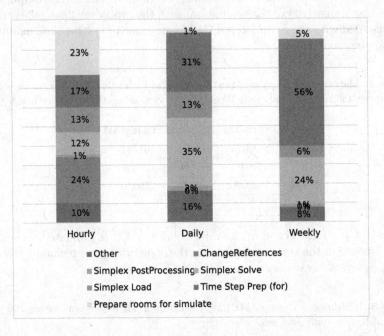

Fig. 3. Stages percents associated with the simulation of 100 trajectories sharing references with a dictionary, for hourly, daily and weekly playrooms.

Figure 3 shows the ratio between the simplex resolution time and the whole simulation time for the three evaluated scenarios. The first stage (Prepare rooms for simulation), which performs settings and initializations of the variables necessary for each trajectory during the simulation, consumes 23%, 1% or 5% of the total of the simulation for the hourly, daily, and weekly respectively. The second stage, as shown in Fig. 3, is composed of "Time Step Preparation", "ChangeReferences", Loading, Solving and Post Processing Simplex, and "Others". Those stages take the largest part of the time within the simulation. The final stage prints the results of all the simulations in an output file, which is almost negligible compared to the other stages from the computational point of view.

Carrying out an analysis of the simulation times with the different strategies, we can conclude that a large part of the difference between the times occurs in handling the references. This confirms that the last strategy to optimize simulation implementation, using a matrix of pointers instead of another complex structure as a Reference Catalogue, can lead to important savings.

Although this modification does not fully cover the time difference between the simulations, another important factor is that, in the first stage, certain variables are initialized, and memory is reserved for each room. These procedures have a heavy computational weight. Since in the initial version of the simulation, only one room is needed, these initializations are done once, whereas, in this version, they must be done as many times as rooms are needed. Line 3 in Algorithm 2 sets a lower bound to optimize the elapsed time of the first simulation stage. Considering this, the settings and initialization in the first stage and the ChangeReferences procedure in the second determine this implementation's overhead. Therefore, depending on the room, the overhead varies, allowing rooms with less overhead to be more efficient in the future.

In rooms where the time taken by solving the Simplexes is high, parallelizing the Simplexes solution in a massively parallel architecture (for example, a GPU) can save significantly more time than the overhead implied by our change in the simulation design, accelerating the original model.

Tables 6, 7 and 8 show, for each playroom (Hourly, Daily and Weekly), a comparison of the elapsed simulation times for the developed strategies.

Table 6. Simulation times (ms) for Hourly playroom (VATES) with different implementations.

# of trajectories	Original	Refs. Catalogue	Refs. dictionary
2	179	5432	295
4	337	11251	590
8	649	22749	1184
16	1308	43431	2401
32	2590	89255	4913
64	5131	175247	10066
100	7875	274406	15880
128	10280	351584	22119
256	20106	701891	45542

As seen in the previous tables, the implementation obtained after the different optimizations specified throughout this work is just above the sequential strategy, especially for rooms containing many *records*. Thus, as previously mentioned, the time it takes to solve the simplex in these rooms is constant in all the implementations, but unlike before, there is now an infrastructure that allows solving trajectories in parallel, creating the opportunity of solving many Simplexes in parallel using a GPU in the future.

Table 7. Simulation times (ms) for Daily playroom with different implementations.

# of trajectories	Original	Refs. catalogue	Refs. dictionary
2	902	3567	933
4	1743	6934	1804
8	3574	13806	3673
16	7168	28041	7483
32	14138	56802	15209
64	28256	114822	31219
100	43996	180896	49113
128	56452	233024	63320
256	113594	480108	128958

Table 8. Simulation times (ms) for Weekly playroom with different implementations.

# of trajectories	Original	Refs. catalogue	Refs. dictionary
2	312	714	315
4	616	1412	613
8	1205	2809	1212
16	2406	5585	2398
32	4794	11211	4847
64	9562	22780	9895
100	14929	36312	15657
128	19174	46688	20324
256	38091	94600	40868

5   Conclusion and Future Work

In this work, we have refactored a large legacy computational system to expose
parallelism and create the opportunity of accelerating it using GPUs shortly,
extending our initial effort to introduce modern parallelism techniques on the
SimSEE tool. Considering our previous results, we study the principal challenges
and constraints to implementing the proposed massively-parallel version of the
SimSEE.

Concretely, we successfully implemented and evaluated versions of the system that allow simulating multiple trajectories in parallel by instantiating as
many playrooms as the number of trajectories. The evaluation involved different
temporal scenarios, facing various problems for some of these cases. The principal difficulty was the memory scalability, i.e., the memory footprint related to
the rooms' instantiation. Therefore, we propose multiple optimizations. In the
first place, and common to all the strategies, we instantiate all the rooms by
reading the playroom's file once, reducing unnecessary serialized I/O activity.

The true optimizations focused on understanding playrooms' structures, identifying units that remain invariable through the different trajectories' room, to instantiate them once, for all rooms. We successfully implemented a version of the room's loading and simulation procedures, considerably more suitable for a massively-parallel implementation, with a scalable shared-memory variation, reducing 88% the memory footprint of the hourly case. The downside of this strategy is the introduction of certain overhead in the simulation routine. To reduce this overhead, we propose two different variations, one using a native structure implemented with classes and the other using a simple pointer matrix. We significantly reduced the overhead introduced by the first technique by sacrificing a very small percentage of memory. For example, in the hourly case, compared to the fist technique we improved the simulation time by a factor of $17\times$, by increasing memory usage by only 10%.

In future work, we intend to address the GPU parallelization of the Simplex solved for all the trajectories in each time step. Additionally, it is interesting to evaluate the parallelization of other stages of the simulation.

Acknowledgement. The authors of this article were partially financed by project ANII FSE_1_2018_1_153060 Aceleración del SimSEE utilizando GPUs (SimSEE-MP).

References

1. ADME: VATES. https://latorre.adme.com.uy/vates/
2. ADME: Usos del SimSEE. https://www.simsee.org/simsee/usos.html. Accessed 31 July 2021
3. ADME: Administración del Mercado Eléctrico (2022). https://adme.com.uy/. Accessed 10 June 2022
4. Baya, R., Pedemonte, M., Gutiérrez Arce, A., Ezzatti, P.: An asynchronous computation architecture for enhancing the performance of the weather research and forecasting model. Concurr. Comput. Pract. Exp. **32**(19) (2020). https://www.scopus.com
5. Baya, R., Porrini, C., Pedemonte, M., Ezzatti, P.: Task parallelism in the WRF model through computation offloading to many-core devices. In: Merelli, I., Liò, P., Kotenko, I.V. (eds.) 26th Euromicro International Conference on Parallel, Distributed and Network-based Processing, PDP 2018, Cambridge, United Kingdom, 21–23 March 2018, pp. 596–600. IEEE Computer Society (2018). https://doi.org/10.1109/PDP2018.2018.00100
6. Camacho, V., Chaer, R.: Hourly model of a combined cycle power plant for SimSEE. In: 2020 IEEE PES Transmission & Distribution Conference and Latin America (T&D LA), pp. 1–5. IEEE (2019)
7. Coppes, E., Tutté, C., Maciel, F., Forets, M., Cornalino, E., Chaer, R.: SimSEE Proyecto ANII FSE 2009 18 Mejoras a la plataforma SimSEE (2012). https://iie.fing.edu.uy/publicaciones/2012/CTMFCC12
8. CORDIS: REfactoring Parallel Heterogeneous Resource-Aware Applications - a Software Engineering Approach (2014). https://cordis.europa.eu/project/id/644235

9. Dennis, J.M., Loft, R.D.: Refactoring scientific applications for massive parallelism. In: Lauritzen, P., Jablonowski, C., Taylor, M., Nair, R. (eds.) Numerical Techniques for Global Atmospheric Models. LNCSE, vol. 80, pp. 539–556. Springer, Heidelberg (2011). https://doi.org/10.1007/978-3-642-11640-7_16

10. Flieller, G., Chaer, R.: Introduction of ensemble based forecasts to the electricity dispatch simulator SimSEE. In: 2020 IEEE PES Transmission & Distribution Conference Latin America (T&D LA), pp. 1–6. IEEE (2019)

11. Igounet, P., Alfaro, P., Usera, G., Ezzatti, P.: GPU acceleration of the `caffa3d.MB` model. In: Murgante, B., et al. (eds.) ICCSA 2012, Part IV. LNCS, vol. 7336, pp. 530–542. Springer, Heidelberg (2012). https://doi.org/10.1007/978-3-642-31128-4_39

12. Jensen, K., Wirth, N.: PASCAL User Manual and Report: ISO PASCAL Standard. Springer, Heidelberg (2012)

13. Marichal, R., Vallejo, D., Dufrechou, E., Ezzatti, P.: Towards a massively-parallel version of the SimSEE. In: 2021 IEEE URUCON. IEEE (2021). https://doi.org/10.1109/urucon53396.2021.9647142

14. Rutishauser, H., Gutknecht, M., Gautschi, W., Schwarz, H., Henrici, P., Läuchli, P.: Lectures on Numerical Mathematics. Birkhäuser, Boston (1990)

15. Fichas Dinámicas. https://simsee.org/simsee/simsee/ayuda/fichas-parametros-dinamicos.htm

16. UTE: Wind Energy in Uruguay (2022). https://portal.ute.com.uy/composicion-energetica-y-potencias. Accessed 18 June 2022

Nearly Quantum Computing
by Simulation

Gilberto J. Díaz T$^{1(\boxtimes)}$ ⓘ, Carlos J. Barrios H.^{1}ⓘ, Luiz A. Steffenel^2ⓘ,
and Jean F. Couturier^2ⓘ

^{1} High Performance and Scientific Computing, Universidad Industrial de Santander,
Bucaramanga, Colombia
{gjdiazt,cbarrios}@uis.edu.co
^{2} LICIIS Laboratory, Université de Reims Champagne-Ardenne, Reims, France
{angelo.steffenel,jean-francois.couturier}@univ-reims.fr
https://www.sc3.uis.edu.co , https://www.univ-reims.fr/

Abstract. Quantum computing has ceased to be an exotic topic for
researchers, moving its treatment today from theoretical physicists to
computer scientists and engineers. Recently, several real quantum devices
have become available through the cloud. On the other hand, different
possibilities on-premises allow having quantum computing simulators
using High-Performance Computing (HPC) capabilities. Nevertheless,
they did not expect to be very limited, in the near term, the number and
quality of the fundamental storage element, the **qubit**. Therefore, software quantum simulators are the only widely available tools to design and
test quantum algorithms. However, the representation of quantum computing components in classical computers consumes significant resources.
In quantum computing, a state composed of n qubits will be a union of
all possible combinations of n 0s and 1s. That is to say, the size of the
information is 2^n. The amplitude is the magnitude associated with every
variety and is composed of a complex number. This paper shows a survey
of different implementations to simulate quantum computing supported
by classical computing, highlighting important considerations for implementing and developing solutions.

Keywords: Quantum computing · Parallelism · Simulation

1   Introduction

An innovative model was developed in the second half of the 20th century by
scientists who combined two remarkable theories: Information Theory [1] and
Quantum Mechanics [2]. The first one is about the study of the transmission,
processing, extraction, and utilization of information. The second one is about
the behavior of matter and its interactions with energy on the scale of atoms
and subatomic particles. The result was a new point of view of computation and
information, the Quantum Information Theory [3–9].

P. Navaux et al. (Eds.): CARLA 2022, CCIS 1660, pp. 205–219, 2022.
https://doi.org/10.1007/978-3-031-23821-5_15

Information theory has abstracted away the physical part of the devices used for computation and communication in such a way that it is possible to talk about the efficiency of an algorithm or the robustness of a communication protocol without understanding the details of the underlying physics. Quantum information Theory applies concepts of quantum mechanics directly to the way of doing computing. The contribution of quantum mechanics to developing new computing devices has been highly significant. Until a few recent decades, the influence of quantum mechanics was only in low-level implementation; it did not affect how the computation or communication. However, the Quantum Information Theory provides a new paradigm of computing, where the model of quantum mechanics is not only limited to hardware but is applied directly to information processing and transmission.

Recently, several quantum devices, with up to tens of *qubits* on universal quantum computers (UQC) and thousand qubits on annealer (QA) devices, have become available through the cloud, enabling the possibility of using real quantum hardware to solve simple problems. In the near term, those devices are expected to be very limited in the number and quality of qubits. Therefore, using them for practical applications is challenging, requiring thousands of qubits [10]. Nevertheless, the production of software for quantum computing, which runs on classical computers, has increased substantially. A list of developments can be found in [11–13].

For all this, quantum computing simulators are the only widely available tools to design and test quantum algorithms. However, the simulation of quantum computing models in classical computers requires exponential time and involves highly complex memory management. Using conventional techniques to simulate an arbitrary quantum process significantly more extensively than existing quantum prototypes requires massive memory on a classical computer. For instance, to simulate a 60 qubits quantum state, the process would take about 18.000 petabytes of classical computer memory. Therefore, researchers try to reduce such challenges by proposing efficient simulators.

Several initiatives are trying to reduce the consumption of classical resources by quantum simulators. For example, Jianxin Chen et al. [12] work on a technique based on Google's model for variable elimination in the line graph that implements a single-amplitude simulator. Aidan Dang et al. [13] studies how the entanglement structure of Shor's algorithm [14] is suitable for a particular matrix product state representation, that quantifiable reduces the computational requirements for simulation, and Xin-Chuan Wu et al. [15] implements a loss compression algorithm to reduce the amount of memory usage. The aim is to re-design quantum simulators using at least one of these techniques, or a mix of them, to test quantum algorithms with valuable dimensions.

Even though some quantum computers have come onto the market, they represent prototypes that are not scalable and sufficient to test complex quantum algorithms. The construction of a full-scale quantum computer comprising millions of qubits is a long-term prospect. Quantum computer prototypes are currently tiny and cannot overcome classical computers in terms of exceeding their capacity. This task resembles the early days of programming, in which software was built in machine languages [16]. Then, quantum computing simulators are the only widely available tools to design and test quantum algorithms. Simulating quantum algorithms at this level is essential to learning how a quantum computer will physically operate, how the software can work, and what sort of problems it can solve. However, the simulation of quantum computing models in classical computers requires exponential time and involves highly complex memory management. The problem is that using conventional techniques to simulate an arbitrary quantum process significantly more extensive than any of the existing quantum prototypes would soon require a vast amount of memory on a classical computer. For instance, to simulate a 50 qubits quantum state, the process would take about 16 petabytes [17]. Therefore, researchers try to reduce such challenges by proposing efficient simulators.

This paper presents how to implement quantum computing in simulators supported by HPC architectures as a strategy to run quantum simulations efficiently to reduce classical resource consumption and threaten real problems that need quantum computing solutions. The paper in the Sect. 2 shows important theoretical considerations about Quantum Mechanics and information theory to develop quantum computing models. Section 3 introduces the concept of Quantum Parallelism and Quantum Simulation supported by classical computing. Finally, Sect. 4 shows a proposed discussion and further work.

2 Quantum Computing Modelling

A quantum computing model describes the different scientific approaches to formalizing the transformations over inputs to compute outputs using quantum resources. A model is determined by the essential elements in which the computation is decomposed [18]. The four main models of practical importance are:

- **Quantum Gate Array or Quantum Circuit:** The computation is decomposed into sequence of few qubit quantum gates. This is the best well-known model of quantum computation.
- **One-way quantum computer:** The computation is decomposed into sequence of one-qubit measurements applied to a highly entangled initial state or cluster state.
- **Adiabatic quantum computer:** The computation is decomposed into a slow continuous transformation of an initial Hamiltonian into a final Hamiltonian, whose ground states contain the solution.
- **Topological quantum computer:** The computation is decomposed into the braiding of anyons in a 2D lattice.
- **Quantum Turing Machine:** A quantum Turing machine, also known as universal quantum computer, is an abstract machine used to model a quantum computer proposed by David Deutsch [9].

In this study we are going to work with the quantum circuit model because its popularity. However, due to the strong dependence of Quantum Information Theory of Quantum Mechanics, let us briefly describe the fundamentals of it.

2.1   An Overview of Quantum Mechanics

Quantum mechanics is a theory that describes the world at the scale of the energy level of atoms and other subatomic particles. The early proposed theory about some physical phenomena that could not be explained using classical physics was formulated by Max Planck [19] and Albert Einstein [20]. There are several mathematical formalisms. One of them uses the wave function to provide information about the probability amplitude of position, momentum, and other physical properties of a particle.

Quantum System. A quantum system is a portion of the physical world considered to perform the analysis or study of quantum mechanics related to the wave-particle duality in that system. It involves the wave function and its components, such as the wavelength and the wave's momentum for which the wave function. A physical system consists of a notion of states, properties, and a dynamical law that describes the system's evolution. In the case of quantum mechanics, (pure) states are elements ψ of a Hilbert space $\mathcal{H}$ normalized to 1, which can also consider as rays in a Hilbert space or rank-1 orthogonal projections. Hermitian operators are on this Hilbert space. In this approach, the dynamical law is the Schrödinger equation $i\partial_t\psi(t) = H\psi(t)$ where H is the energy observable in the Hamiltonian. There are equivalent formulations like the Heisenberg approach and generalizations like the notion of mixed states [21].

Two-State Quantum System. A two-state is a quantum system with two independent quantum states (physically distinguishable) or a *superposition*. The Hilbert space that describes such a system is two-dimensional. Therefore, a complete base encompassing the space will consist of two independent states.

Postulate 1 (State Space). In the formalism of quantum mechanics, at each instant, the state of an isolated physical system can be characterized by a **state vector** in a complex, separable Hilbert space of infinite dimension and with an inner product. This space allows expressing any physical state by a countable sequence of vectors, weighted by their **amplitudes** of respective probabilities. These state vectors are written in the standard bracket Dirac's notation [22].

Postulate 2 (Evolution). The temporal evolution of the state of an isolated physical system can be described by an *unitary transformation* that acts on the state vector that describes the system. That is, the state $|\Psi\rangle$ of the system at time t_1 is related to the state $|\Psi'\rangle$ of the system at time t_2 by a unitary operator U which depends only on the times t_1 and t_2 [22]:

$$U : |\Psi\rangle \rightarrow |\Psi'\rangle = U|\Psi\rangle \tag{1}$$

Quantum Mechanics does not specify neither the state space nor the unit operator for a particular quantum system. It just merely assures us that the evolution of any closed quantum system may be described in such a way.

Postulate 3 (Measurement). In classical physics, the disturbance associated with the procedure of measurement of any physical phenomenon, in general, is minimal. In quantum physics, the act of measurement plays an active and disturbing role. Because of this, quantum particles are best described within the context of the possible outcomes of measurements.

Once we have seen the most outstanding aspects of quantum mechanics that influence quantum computing, we will see the contribution of information theory in this area of research.

2.2   Information Theory

Information Theory studies information transmission, processing, extraction, and utilization. It is based on the studies of Claude Shannon (1948) [1], who worked on the ideas of Ralph Hartley (1928) [23] and Harry Nyquist. Hartley tried to define a measure of information. He said that for every symbol of a message, there are s possibilities, and for a message with l symbols, there are s^l different messages. Hartley defined the amount of information as the logarithm of the number of distinguishable messages. In the same way, Shannon demonstrated that all kinds of information could be quantified with absolute precision. Telephone signals, text, radio waves, and pictures, essentially every mode of communication, could be encoded in bits. He raised several critical concepts in the paper "A Mathematical Theory of Communication" [1].

Channel Capacity and the Noisy Channel Coding Theorem. The main idea is that every communication channel has a speed limit, measured in bits per second. It is mathematically impossible to obtain an error-free channel if the speed limit is exceeded. Without losing some information, you cannot make the channel go faster than the limit. On the other hand, if you work under that limit, it is possible to transmit information without errors. The noisy channel coding theorem, or just **Shannon's Theorem**, shows that it is possible to transmit discrete data (digital information) almost without errors on the same noisy channel at a maximum computable rate.

Digital Representation. The message's content is irrelevant to the transmission procedure. The message could be text, image, video, or sound. However, only bits (0's and 1's) are transferred through the channel. The term bit appears for the first time in this work. Shannon also pointed out that once data was represented digitally, it could be regenerated and transmitted without error.

Efficiency of Representation (Source Coding). The main objective of *source coding* is to make the message smaller removing redundancy in the information. Shannon discusses a loss-less method of compressing data at the source, using a variable rate block code (Shannon-Fano code).

Entropy and Information Content. Entropy can be considered as a measure of the uncertainty and information necessary to, in any process, limit, reduce or eliminate the uncertainty. The Shannon entropy equation provides a way to estimate the average minimum number of bits needed to encode a string of symbols based on the frequency of these [24].

It is possible to build the Quantum Information theory from the Information Theory, as shown below.

2.3   Quantum Information Theory

Quantum Information Theory is the study that explores the use of quantum mechanics theory, instead of classical mechanic fundamentals, to model information, process it, and transmit it when it is stored in quantum particles [16]. Quantum Information Theory includes quantum simulation, cryptography, communications, and games [22,25]. The concept of quantum information comes from classical information. Meanwhile, the bit is the information unit in classical information, and the *qubit* is the unit in quantum information.

Logical Qubit. A logical qubit is a unitary vector in a two-dimensional Hilbert space.

$$|\psi\rangle \in H \text{ where } ||\psi|| = 1 \text{ and } dimH = 2 \tag{2}$$

The Boolean states 0 and 1 are represented by a prescribed pair of normalized and mutually orthogonal quantum states denoted using Dirac's notation $|0\rangle$ and $|1\rangle$.

The two states form a *computational basis* and any other (pure) state of the qubit can be written as a superposition $\alpha|0\rangle + \beta|1\rangle$ [26]. The bra/ket notation can be independent of the elements' basis and order. Once this notation becomes familiar, it is easier to read and faster to use. Mathematically, Dirac's notation (*ket*) is a shorthand notation for column vectors:

$$|0\rangle \equiv \begin{pmatrix} 1 \\ 0 \end{pmatrix} : |1\rangle \equiv \begin{pmatrix} 0 \\ 1 \end{pmatrix} \tag{3}$$

In Quantum Information processing, classical bits values of 0 and 1 are represented using distinguished states $|0\rangle$ and $|1\rangle$. With this representation, we can directly compare bits and qubits, where bits can take on only two values, 0 and 1, while qubits can take on those previous values and any superposition.

Quantum State. A quantum state is simply something that encodes the state of a quantum system. Formally, a quantum state is a vector $|v\rangle$ representing a superposition of the elements $\{|\beta_1\rangle, |\beta_2\rangle\}$ if it is a nontrivial linear combination of $|\beta_1\rangle$ and $|\beta_2\rangle$, if $|v\rangle = a_1|\beta_1\rangle + a_2|\beta_2\rangle$ where a_1 and a_2 are non-zero. For the term *superposition* to be meaningful, a basis must be specified [16].

In Classical Information Theory, the amount of information contained by a specific state using n bits is n. There will be only one combination of n 0s and 1s. In Quantum Information Theory, a state composed of n qubits will be a union of all possible combinations of n 0s and 1s. That is to say, the size of information is 2^n. For example, if we use 3 bits, we will have just one of the 2^3 possibilities whose length is 3, for instance, 010. If we use 3 qubits, we will have not only one but all combinations: 001, 010, 011... 111, each multiplied by the corresponding amplitude. If we increase 1 the number of bits, the size will be $n + 1$, but if we increase the number of qubits, we get double the size, that is to say, 2^{n+1}.

Superposition. The unique characteristic of quantum states is that they allow the system to be simultaneously in a few conditions. Quantum bits are not constrained to be wholly 0 or wholly 1 at a given instant. It may also exist in a superposition, or blend of those states simultaneously [21], when a quantum system find to be in one of a discrete set of states, which we'll write as $|0\rangle$ or $|1\rangle$, then, whenever it is not being observed.

Entanglement. It supposes a correlation between different parts of a quantum system that surpasses anything that is classically possible. It happens when the subsystems interact so that the resulting state of the whole system cannot be expressed as the direct product of the states of its parts. When a quantum system is in such a tangled state, the actions performed in one subsystem will have a side effect in another subsystem, even if it does not act directly on that subsystem. It takes $2^n - 1$ complex numbers to describe the states of an n-qubit system. Because 2^n is much bigger than n, most of the n-qubit states cannot be described in terms of the state of n separate single-qubit systems. States that cannot define as the tensor product of n single-qubit states are called **entangled states**. Thus, most quantum states are entangled [16]. If we can write the tensor product of those states, they are said to be **separate states**.

With a quantum computing theory and taking advantage of the opportunities of HPC architectures and parallelism, it is possible to simulate quantum computing in classical computing, as shown in the next section.

3 Quantum Computing Parallelism and Simulation

Quantum superposition, quantum uncertainty, and quantum entanglement are powerful resources that we can use to encode, decode, transmit and process information in a highly efficient way that is impossible in the classical world. In theory, a quantum computer can perform any task that a classical computer can execute, but this does not necessarily mean that a quantum computer exceeds a classical computer for all types of tasks. For a quantum computer to show its superiority, it needs to use new algorithms to exploit the ability to work on all possible states simultaneously. This phenomenon is called quantum parallelism. However, these algorithms are not easy to design and produce spectacular results. One example is the quantum factorization algorithm created by Peter Shor [27].

Quantum Algorithms. Generally, the term is used for those algorithms that incorporate some essential feature of quantum computing, such as superposition or entanglement. David Deutsch is the precursor of the quantum algorithms field. His work went from quantum information to quantum computation [9]. Deutsch asked whether there is a quantum extension of the Church-Turing idea that any computation that runs on a classic computer can be efficiently simulated on a universal Turing machine [28]. Deutsch proposes that to see the Church-Turing hypothesis as a physical principle, not only must computer science be turned into a branch of physics, but also part of experimental physics into a branch of computer science [29]. In consequence, contrary to the popular belief that quantum computers have few applications, the field of quantum algorithms has become a sufficiently large area of study. Then, websites like "Quantum Algorithms Zoo" [30] cite almost 400 articles in this area.

In the computational complexity theory, asymptotic scales of complexity measures such as execution time or problem size are generally considered. In classical and quantum computing, the execution time is measured by the number of elementary operations used by an algorithm. Particularly, quantum computing uses the quantum circuit model, where a quantum circuit is a sequence of quantum operations called quantum gates, each applied to a small number of qubits. Comparing the performance of the algorithms, the notation $O(f(n))$ of the computing style is used, which is interpreted as "asymptotically delimited by $f(n)$". Table 1 contains descriptions of some complexity classes.

Table 1. Computational complexity classes of algorithms

P	A deterministic classical computer can solve it in polynomial time
BPP	A probabilistic classical computer can solve it in polynomial time
BQP	A quantum computer can solve it in polynomial time
NP	A deterministic classical computer can check the solution in polynomial time
QMA	A quantum computer can check the solution in polynomial time

There are three classes of quantum algorithms with clear advantages over known classical algorithms: *Algorithms based upon quantum versions of the Fourier transform*, *Quantum search algorithms*, and *Quantum simulation*[1].

Richard Feynman pointed out that simulating quantum systems on a classical computer is very difficult. Besides, other physicists believe that all aspects of the world around us, including classical logic circuits, can ultimately be explained using quantum mechanics. However, quantum circuits cannot be used to directly simulate classical circuits because unitary quantum logic gates are inherently reversible, whereas many classical logic gates such as the NAND gate are inherently irreversible [22]. To overcome this obstacle, we can replace the original classical circuit by an equivalent circuit containing only reversible gates like *Toffoli* gate [31].

---

[1] A quantum computer simulates a quantum system.

Quantum Parallelism. One of the main features of quantum computing is to take advantage of quantum mechanics effects like superposition and entanglement to speed up the calculations. In 1985, Deutsch [9] found a computational problem solved on a quantum computer in a manner that is impossible classically. In 1992, Deutsch and Jozsa [31] simplified and extended the earlier result.

The modern formulation of the problem is the following. Suppose a classical algorithm that computes some function $f : \pm 1 \rightarrow f : \pm 1$. There are exactly four such functions:

$$
\begin{aligned}
f_1(x) &= x \\
f_2(x) &= -x \\
f_3(x) &= +1 \\
f_4(x) &= -1
\end{aligned}
\tag{4}
$$

Evaluating $f(-1)$ and $f(+1)$ we obtain two bits of classical information and know which of the four functions we have. Obviously this requires two evaluations of the function. All those functions can be categorized as: *Balanced: fore example:* $f(-1) + f(+1) = 0$ or *Unbalanced: or constant.*

It is necessary to acquire a classic bit of information to determine the function's class, which requires two evaluations. Quantum mechanically defines the class with only a single "measurement". The trick is to put x into a superposition of both $+1$ and -1, and a single assessment of the function determines the class. However, it is impossible to decide which position because the measurement returns only one bit of classical information.

Quantum Algorithms Workflow. A typical quantum algorithm workflow on a gate-model quantum computer is depicted in Fig. 1. It begins with a high level definition of the problem, for example, Shor's algorithm. The problem to solve is, given an odd composite number N, we need to find an integer i, strictly between 1 and N, that divides N.

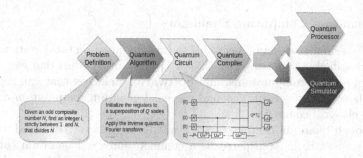

Fig. 1. Quantum algorithm workflow

Hybrid Approach. Current quantum computers cannot execute many main quantum algorithms with asymptotic speedup for practical size problems due to the small number of qubits. Due to decoherence, the limited number of gates run before the accumulation of errors makes the output useless. Several quantum-classical algorithms have been developed to overcome these inconveniences. The general method is to decompose the problem statically or dynamically, solve the subproblems on QPU, and combine them on the CPU to obtain a global solution. One of the most famous hybrid algorithms is the Variational Quantum Eigensolver (QVE). This algorithm combines a small QPU and CPU to find the ground state of a Hamiltonian problem. The trial state (ansatz) is prepared by applying a series of parameterized gates on the QPU and its energy measured. This process is outlined in the Fig. 2. The advantage of this kind of algorithm is that the trial state can be chosen. Therefore, the number of required gates is small enough to run feasibly on a small QPU or noisy intermediate-scale quantum computer (NISQ). Shaydulin et al. [10] describe a hybrid approach for solving practical size problems about local quantum search (QLS) in their work.

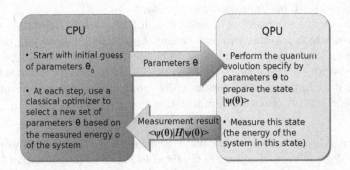

Fig. 2. The general outline of variational hybrid algorithms

3.1   Quantum Computing Simulators

A quantum simulator is an object able to execute quantum computations. They can be classified in two categories [32]: **A Quantum System** that can perform specific quantum computations, and **Software Packages** that can reproduce the fundamental aspects of a general universal quantum computer on a general purpose classical computer.

Although quantum computers are available to use over the cloud, they are still very small to be considered as a complete universal quantum computer. Besides, there has been an explosion of quantum software platforms which can overwhelm to those looking for a platform to use.

3.2   Popular Open Source Quantum Computer Simulators

Many initiatives are working on quantum simulators[2]. LaRose et al. [36] reviewed some important general-purpose projects operating at the quantum gates. Guzik [37] studied the appropriate approach to implementing different quantum computing models. Fingerhuth et al. [38] did an evaluation of a wide range of open-source software for quantum computing, including all stages of the quantum toolchain from quantum hardware interfaces through quantum compilers to implementations of quantum algorithms, as well as several quantum computing models: quantum annealing and discrete and continuous-variable gate-model. Table 2 shows these works with a specific selection of major software quantum simulators developments.

Table 2. Software quantum simulators

Name	Language	Description
Quantum++	C++	General-purpose multi-threaded quantum simulator written in C++ with high performance. It is not restricted to qubit systems or specific quantum information processing tasks; capable of simulating arbitrary quantum processes [39]
Qrack	C++	Quantum simulator in C++, including additional support for GPUs. Emphasis on performance by parallelization over multiple CPU or GPU cores. It supports arbitrary numbers of entangled qubits up to system limitations [40]
Quirk	JavaScript	Quantum simulator less-performance oriented for educational purposes, with a visual user experience that allows beginners and experts to construct quantum circuits via drag-and-drop operations [41]
Cliffords.js	Julia	It only uses quantum gates from the Clifford group. It executes the calculation of Clifford circuits by tracking the evolution of X and Z generators. An exciting feature is that it allows tracking the inverse operations [42]
Qbsolv	C++	It is not a simulator but the closest analog for annealing devices. It finds the minimum value of quadratic unconstrained binary optimization problems (QUBO) [43,44]

Other projects provide a full-stack approach to quantum computing, including a simulator and compilers and the possibility to run the program on real quantum processors. The Table 3 shows some of them.

Beyond popularity, the two tables highlight specific implementations that allow the simulation of quantum algorithms on classical computers. However, these tools create architectural, representation, and performance challenges to discuss in the next section.

---

[2] A list of the recent developments is maintained on several websites [11,12,34,35].

Table 3. Full-stack quantum libraries

Project	Simulator	Language	Description
XACC	TNQVM	C	It is an implementation taking the tensor network theory to simulate quantum circuits [45, 46]
Qiskit	Qiskit Aer		Framework for working with noisy quantum computers at the level of pulses, circuits, and algorithms supported by IBM [47, 48]
ProjectQ	ProjectQ	C++, Python	An open source software framework for quantum computing [49] supported by ETH Zurich
Forest	QVM	Python	Forest full stack library quantum simulator. It is a Python-based simulator for rapid prototyping of quantum circuits [50]

4   Discussion and Further Work

As we study the limit of the non-simulable, it is important to verify that quantum computers behave as intended. Furthermore, it is of fundamental interest to classify the limit beyond which quantum computers do something genuinely unreachable classically (quantum supremacy). Thus, pushing this boundary as far as possible is important to make quantum supremacy meaningful. To fulfill this aim, the interest in general quantum simulation has increased. Already, there are more than 100 classical simulators for various types of quantum systems available [11, 12, 34, 35]. Different results are obtained in various areas of interest within this wide range of simulators. There are two major amplitude-wise approaches to simulate a quantum circuit of N qubits and [13] depth d:

- 1) stores the entire state vector in memory, therefore, here the memory is the principal issue.
- 2) calculates the amplitude α_x for any N-bit string $x \in \{0,1\}^N$.

In 1), memory is the primary concern. Their dimensions have limited the simulation of quantum circuits. One decade ago, the most extensive simulation was a 42-qubit quantum circuit on the Jülich supercomputer [51]. Mikhail Smelyanskiy et al. used an Intel simulator to simulate up to 42 qubits quantum supremacy circuits. A simulation of 45 qubits was carried out on the Cori II supercomputing system using 0.5 petabytes of memory and 8,192 nodes in 2017 [52]. In 2018, a quantum circuit of 7×7 grid of depth 39 was simulated on the Sunway TaihuLight supercomputer [53]. In 2020, on the same supercomputer, a 49 qubits circuit of 55 depth was performed [54].

Several works implement different techniques to make better use of memory. Jianxin Chen et. al. [13] works on a new technique, that implement a single-amplitude simulator that computes $\langle x|\mathcal{C}|0...0\rangle$ for an arbitrary quantum circuit

$\mathcal{C}$. Jianxin tested the simulator for a randomly generated $\mathcal{C}$ from a restricted circuit class that produces a sampling problem classified as intractable [55]. The algorithm uses tensor network contraction [56], where the treewidth is the dominant factor in determining the time and space-complexity.

Aidan Dang et al. [14] studies how the entanglement structure of Shor's algorithm [7] is suitable for a particular matrix product state representation that quantifiably reduces the computational requirements for simulating it in a classical computer. The matrix product states of tensor networks [57] were originally used for simulating one-dimensional quantum many-body systems [58, 59], however, they have been adapted for simulating quantum circuits [60,61].

Thomas Häner et al. introduces a quantum computer emulator making use of the availability of an abstract, high-level quantum code by directly utilizing classical emulation for quantum subroutines. Instead of compiling them into quantum gates before applying them using a series of sparse matrix-vector multiplications enabling an entirely new class of optimizations [33].

The simulation of quantum systems carried out in classical computers has been done for a long time. However, as we present in this paper, the recent boom in real quantum devices has fueled the development of these simulators. It has increased pressure to determine the capabilities of what can be achieved in classical computers, mainly involving highly complex memory management, and our further work goes in this direction.

References

1. Shannon, C.E.: A mathematical theory of communication. Bell Syst. Tech. **27**(3), 379–423 (1948)
2. Born, M., Jordan, P.: Zur quantenmechanik. Z. Angew. Phys. **34**(1), 858–888 (1925)
3. Feynman, R.P.: Feynman and Computation. There's Plenty of Room at the Bottom, pp. 63–76. Perseus Books, Cambridge (1999)
4. Holevo, A.S.: Bounds for the quantity of information transmitted by a quantum communication channel. Probl. Inf. Transm. **9**(3), 177–183 (1973)
5. Poplavski, R.P.: Thermodynamic models of information processes. Sov. Phys. Uspekhi **18**(3), 222–241 (1975)
6. Ingarden, R.S.: Quantum Information Theory. Preprint - Instytut Fizyki Uniwersytetu Mikolaja Kopernika. PWN (1975)
7. Shor, P.W.: Polynomial-time algorithms for prime factorization and discrete logarithms on a quantum computer. SIAM J. Comput. **26**(5), 1484–1509 (1997)
8. Benioff, P.: The computer as a physical system: a microscopic quantum mechanical Hamiltonian model of computers as represented by turing machines. J. Stat. Phys. **22**(5), 563–591 (1980)
9. Deutsch, D.: Quantum theory, the church-turing principle and the universal quantum computer. Proc. R. Soc. Lond. **400**, 97–117 (1985)
10. Shaydulin, R., Ushijima-Mwesigwa, H., Negre, C., Safro, I., Mniszewski, S., Alexeev, Y.: A hybrid approach for solving optimization problems on small quantum computers. Computer **52**, 18–26 (2019)
11. Fingerhuth, M.: Open-source quantum software projects (2019). https://github.com/qosf/os_quantum_software

12. Quantum Computing Report. Qbit count (2019). https:// quantumcomputingreport.com/scorecards/qubit-count/
13. Chen, J., Zhang, F., Huang, C., Newman, M., Shi, Y.: Classical simulation of intermediate-size quantum circuits (2018)
14. Dang, A., Hill, C.D., Hollenberg, L.C.L.: Optimising matrix product state simulations of Shor's algorithm. Quantum **3**, 116 (2019)
15. Wu, X., Di, S., Cappello, F., Finkel, H., Alexeev, Y., Chong, F.T.: Memory-efficient quantum circuit simulation by using lossy data compression (2018)
16. Eleanor, R., Wolfgang, P.: Quantum Computing, A Gentle Introduction. The MIT Press, Cambridge (2011)
17. Haner, T., Steiger, D.S.: 0.5 petabyte simulation of a 45-qubit quantum circuit. In: Proceedings of the International Conference for High Performance Computing, Networking, Storage and Analysis, SC 2017, NY, USA, pp. 33:1–33:10 (2017)
18. Imanuel, A.: What is quantum computing? Top 18 quantum computing companies (2018). https://www.predictiveanalyticstoday.com/what-is-quantum-computing/
19. Planck, M.: Zur Theorie des Gesetzes der Energieverteilung im Normalspektrum. j-VERH- DTSCH-PHYS-GES **2**(17), 237–245 (1900)
20. Einstein, A.: Uber einen die Erzeugung und Verwandlung des Lichtes betreffenden heuristischen Gesichtspunkt. j-ANN-PHYS-1900-4 **322**(6), 132–148 (1905)
21. Lein, M.: Quantum mechanical systems (2016). https://physics.stackexchange. com/questions/278413/what-exactly-is-a-quantum-mechanical-physical-system
22. Nielsen, M.A., Chuang, I.L.: Quantum Computation and Quantum Information: 10th Anniversary Edition. Cambridge University Press, New York (2011)
23. Hartley, R.V.L.: Transmission of information. Bell Syst. Tech. J. **7**(3), 535–563 (1928)
24. Wilde, M.: From Classical to Quantum Shannon Theory. Cambridge University Press, Cambridge (2018)
25. Barnum, H., Wehner, S., Wilce, A.: Introduction: quantum information theory and quantum foundations. Found. Phys. **48**(8), 853–856 (2018)
26. Hayden, P., Ekert, A., Inamori, H.: Basic concepts in quantum computation. In: Kaiser, R., Westbrook, C., David, F. (eds.) Coherent Atomic Matter Waves. Les Houches - Ecole d'Ete de Physique Theorique, vol. 72, pp. 661–701. Springer, Heidelberg (2001). https://doi.org/10.1007/3-540-45338-5_10
27. Shor, P.W.: Algorithms for quantum computation: discrete logarithms and factoring. In: 1994 Proceedings 35th Annual Symposium on Foundations of Computer Science, pp. 124–134 (1994)
28. Humble, T.S., De Benedictis, E.P.: Quantum realism. Computer **52**(6), 13–17 (2019)
29. Jordan, S.: Quantum Algorithm Zoo (2018). https://quantumalgorithmzoo.org
30. Papadimitriou, C.H.: Computational Complexity. Addison-Wesley, Boston (1994)
31. Deutsch, D., Jozsa, R.: Rapid solution of problems by quantum computation. Technical report, University of Bristol, Bristol, UK (1992)
32. Karafyllidis, I., Sirakoulis, G.Ch., Dimitrakis, P.: Representation of qubit states using 3D memristance spaces: a first step towards a memristive quantum simulator. In: Proceedings of the 14th IEEE/ACM International Symposium on Nanoscale Architectures, NANOARCH 2018, New York, USA, pp. 163–168 (2018)
33. Haner, T., Steiger, D., Svore, K., Troyer, M.: A software methodology for compiling quantum programs. Quantum Sci. Technol. **3**(2), 020501 (2018)
34. Quantiki. List of qc simulators (2019). https://www.quantiki.org/wiki/list-qc-simulators

35. Quantum Open Source Foundation Team. Quantum open source foundation (2019). https://qosf.org/
36. La Rose, R.: Overview and comparison of gate level quantum software platforms. Quantum **3**, 130 (2019)
37. Guzik, V., Gushanskiy, S., Polenov, M., Potapov, V.: Models of a quantum computer, their characteristics and analysis. In: 9th International Conference on Application of Information and Communication Technologies (AICT), pp. 583–587 (2015)
38. Fingerhuth, M., Babej, T., Wittek, P.: Open source software in quantum computing. PLOS One **13**(12), 1–28 (2018)
39. Gheorghiu, V.: Quantum++: a modern C++ quantum computing library. PLoS One **13**(12), 1–27 (2018)
40. Strano, D.: Qrack (2019). https://vm6502q.readthedocs.io/en/latest/
41. Strilanc, A drag-and-drop quantum circuit simulator (2019). https://github.com/Strilanc/Quirk
42. Cliffords.jl (2018). https://github.com/BBN-Q/Cliffords.jl
43. D Wave (2019). https://www.dwavesys.com/
44. Qbsolv (2019). https://github.com/dwavesystems/qbsolv
45. McCaskey, A., Dumitrescu, E., Liakh, D., Chen, M., Feng, W., Humble, T.: A language and hardware independent approach to quantum-classical computing (2017)
46. Tensor Network QPU Simulator for Eclipse XACC (2019). https://github.com/ornl-qci/tnqvm
47. Qiskit (2019). https://qiskit.org/
48. Qiskit aer (2019). https://github.com/Qiskit/qiskit-aer
49. Projectq (2019). https://github.com/ProjectQ-Framework/ProjectQ
50. QVM Reference (2019). https://github.com/rigetti/reference-qvm/
51. De Raedt, K., et al.: Massively parallel quantum computer simulator. Comput. Phys. Commun. **176**(2), 121–136 (2007)
52. Smelyanskiy, M., Sawaya, N.P.D., Aspuru-Guzik, A.: qHIPSTER: the quantum high performance software testing environment. CoRR, abs/1601.07195 (2016)
53. Li, R., Wu, B., Ying, M., Sun, X., Yang, G.: Quantum supremacy circuit simulation on Sunway TaihuLight (2018)
54. Li, R., Wu, B., Ying, M., Sun, X., Yang, G.: Quantum supremacy circuit simulation on Sunway TaihuLight. IEEE Trans. Parallel Distrib. Syst. **31**(4), 805–816 (2020)
55. Boixo, S., et al.: Characterizing quantum supremacy in near-term devices. Nat. Phys. **14**(6), 595–600 (2018)
56. Boixo, S., Isakov, S.V., Smelyanskiy, V.N., Neven, H.: Simulation of low-depth quantum circuits as complex undirected graphical models (2017)
57. Orus, R.: A practical introduction to tensor networks: matrix product states and projected entangled pair states. Ann. Phys. **349**, 117–158 (2014)
58. Vidal, G.: Classical simulation of infinite-size quantum lattice systems in one spatial dimension. Phys. Rev. Lett. **98**, 070201 (2007)
59. Schollwock, U.: The density-matrix renormalization group in the age of matrix product states. Ann. Phys. **326**(1), 96–192 (2011). Special Issue
60. Wang, D.S., Hill, C.D., Hollenberg, L.L.C.L.: Simulations of Shor's algorithm using matrix product states (2015)
61. Vidal, G.: Efficient classical simulation of slightly entangled quantum computations. Phys. Rev. Lett. **91**, 147902 (2003)

Functionality Testing in the Automation of Scientific Application Workflows in an HPC Environment

Felipe de Jesús Orozco Luna, Jesús Manuel Alemán González,
and Veronica Lizette Robles Dueñas[✉]

University of Guadalajara (CADS Data Analysis and Supercomputing Center), Zapopan, Jalisco, México
{forozco,lizette}@cads.udg.mx, felipe.orozco@academicos.udg.mx,
jesus.aleman4182@alumnos.udg.mx

Abstract. This paper presents the results obtained in performance tests of task automation in the supercomputing cluster of the University of Guadalajara (CADS Data Analysis and Supercomputing Center).

The main objective was to design an automated workflow process to take advantage of high computational performance in scientific applications, routines in R, Python or shell that by nature consume only one core, and that by the volume of data to be processed could allow the execution of multiple tasks at once in a supercomputing cluster environment, or even in the cloud, for an efficient use of the infrastructure. In addition to using Singularity containers to encapsulate applications or scripts to be used in workflows.

The following tools were tested: Snakemake as a tool for workflow automation and scaling, as well as Singularity container technologies for application encapsulation and SLURM for managing resource usage in the cluster.

The results are presented as well as the experience gained in using these technologies.

Keywords: Automation · Snakemake · Singularity containers · Scaling · Reproducibility · Supercomputing cluster · Parallelization

1 Introduction

We are currently faced with the need to process large amounts of data with tools that use a single processing core, which makes scalability and automation difficult.

This problem is very common in the scientific context, as many scientific applications use a single processing core for a large amount of data. For this reason, and because of the computational resources required, these applications are candidates for use in a processing flow that enables scalability and automation.

To address this issue, tests were conducted to quantify the performance and scaling of the parallelized tools. These tests were performed by creating a container in Singularity with a scientific application.

We test the functionality and performance of the tools required for workflow automation, scaling, and reproducibility. The following themes motivate our study:

P. Navaux et al. (Eds.): CARLA 2022, CCIS 1660, pp. 220–232, 2022.
https://doi.org/10.1007/978-3-031-23821-5_16

- Framing within an automated processing flow with containers. Within containers, scientific applications that require only a processing core or routines in R, Python, or shell.
- Create a suitable environment for executing tasks, many of which cannot inherently be parallelized but require large amounts of data and information processing and storage capacity.
- Create processing workflows that are scalable and automated.
- Design and test workflows with parallelized tasks for optimal use of resources provisioned in the supercomputing cluster.
- Use Python scripts integrated as processing boxes (one core per job) in these processing flows.

The present study helped us to test and design processing flows with different scenarios of tools and cluster capacities, testing since one compute node using partially all available cores (up to 36 cores per node), and performance tests using a maximum of 28 compute nodes.

Parameters to be tested included the scalability and automation capabilities of a workflow to make the best use of the supercomputing cluster resources.

An additional motivation is to gain experience using these processing schemes for CADS and supercomputing users who wish to leverage the use of processing in these work scenarios that inherently lack scalability and parallelization capabilities.

2   Infrastructure Used

The Data Analysis and Supercomputing Center (CADS) is a space created by the University of Guadalajara, located in the facilities of the University Center for Economic and Administrative Sciences, in Zapopan Jalisco, México.

Within the CADS is the University of Guadalajara Supercomputer, associated with large processing, storage and communications capabilities, whose purpose is to enable and accelerate scientific research and technological development of the university community.

Up to 28 compute nodes of the Leo ATROX Supercomputing equipment were used for these tests, each with the following characteristics:

2 Xeon-6154 (SKYLAKE) processors with 18 cores at 3.0 Ghz Between 188 - 392 GB RAM

3   Tools Used

3.1   Slurm

Slurm is an open source tool used in supercomputing environments that handles the management and allocation of resources within the cluster. It is based on a configuration file where you can specify the amount of resources to use along with the routines or commands for processing your work.

Slurm's operation is based on queue management, where each job is assigned an identifier and given a priority for execution. Slurm is in charge of managing the job contention in the cluster, since it has the ability to send jobs in parallel. Due to this operation, Slurm allows to start, stop and monitor the jobs in a very simple way, so that the user knows at all times in which state his job is.

3.2 Singularity

Singularity is an open source platform for the management, creation and execution of containers within local and supercomputing environments. It was created primarily for the encapsulation of computationally demanding projects, therefore, it has become an ideal tool to be installed in an HPC environment.

Compared to other container platforms, Singularity offers greater security, scalability and reproducibility, in addition, it allows transforming Docker images to its format to be used and executed with Singularity. Last but not least, Singularity can communicate perfectly with other tools that allow you to improve the development of your project and optimize aspects of it.

3.3 Snakemake

Snakemake is a workflow management system for creating scalable and reproducible data analysis. It is based on Python because it is so simple and easy for humans to understand.

Snakemake creates a workflow based on rules that contain the input files to be processed to create the final output files, as well as the scripts or commands needed to process the workflow.

Snakemake also lets you adjust the amount of computing resources needed to run the workflow. This allocation depends heavily on the project and the amount of resources the user has on their machine. However, Snakemake is excellent for supercomputing environments, for running projects with high computational requirements.

Automation, reproducibility and scalability are the words that sum up Snakemake. Finally, Snakemake adapts to many tools. For example, you can use Singularity, Kubernetes and Slurm in your workflow, making the extension and combination of technologies even more powerful.

Summary of tools used and their versions. See Table 1.

4   Design of the Processing Flow for Testing

Several processing flows were designed for these performance tests:

- A Singularity container was used by taking a Docker image with a scientific tool used for high-energy particle simulation.
- In addition to Python routines for NumPy data processing.

Additional considerations are:

Table 1. Versioning used for testing.

Tool	Version	Source
SLURM	20.11.3	https://slurm.schedmd.com/
Singularity	3.6	https://docs.sylabs.io/guides/3.6/user-guide/
Snakemake	6.15.5	https://snakemake.readthedocs.io/en/v6.15.5/getting_started/installation.html
Centos OS	8.2	https://www.centos.org/

- A processing box is defined as a routine application, script, or library that can execute inside or outside a container, generally receiving input, performing processing, and returning output.
- The tests consist of two stages of processing. The first stage uses a processing box in a Singularity container with the capacity to execute a large number of tasks simultaneously and without dependencies on each other; and the next stage uses Python processing boxes that depend on the output data from the previous stage to perform the tests, see detail in Fig. 1.
- In both processing boxes mentioned above, only one computational core was consumed per task.
- The tests were performed with 360, 720 and 1,000 files as output data for data processing.
- The maximum number of compute nodes used for the performance test was 28.

5 Analysis of Possible Cases

5.1 Running Python Script

The benefits of using tools like Snakemake to automate and scale work processes in a supercomputing cluster with containers like Singularity can be seen in Table 2, which shows the different tool scenarios.

It is important to note that the grid above the diagonal was not included to avoid repeating the scenarios.

The above leads me to answer the premise with which the tests began: How can I fully exploit the capabilities of a supercomputing cluster in a container environment and/or Python routines? The answer is as follows: Use Snakemake as a tool that supports reproducibility and automation of tasks that result in less time spent running a large number of jobs and using the installed infrastructure.

5.2 Running Python Script with SLURM and Singularity

In the case of using tools such as Snakemake, whether or not using tools such as SLURM or Singularity, we can see the possible processing scenarios. See Table 3.

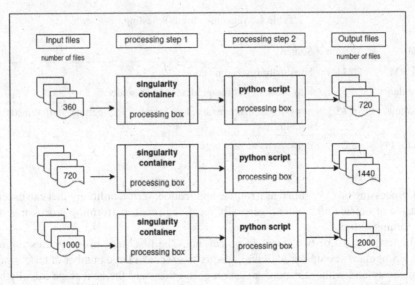

Fig. 1. Details of the designs used in the tests. The number of input files for each test, The number of processing steps executed, At each processing step, a routine may be encapsulated in python, r, shell, or a scientific application that uses only one processing core. The output files, the number of files expected as a result of the processing.

Table 2. Possible capabilities per scenario using Python routine.

Capabilities possible when running Python scripts vs. Tools				
Python Script	**Without SLURM**	**SLURM**	**Snakemake**	**Singularity**
Without SLURM	A single core	-	-	-
SLURM	NA	A single core	-	-
Snakemake	Multiple nodes	Multiple nodes	Multiple nodes	-
Singularity	A single core	A single core	Multiple nodes	A single core

5.3 Running a Singularity Container with Snakemake Using SLURM

This table analyzes the case of using a scientific tool for data processing, running on a single processing core within a Singularity container, and how to make its use more efficient with massive processing and data in the supercomputing cluster. See Table 4.

5.4 Notes for Tables 2, 3 and 4

Single core: Only uses one processing core.

Table 3. Possible capabilities using Python routines inside a container.

Possible Python scripting capabilities inside a container		
Snakemake	**Without SLURM**	**SLURM**
Singularity	A single node	Multiple nodes

Table 4. Capacities using singularity containers.

Send to run APP in container		
Snakemake	**Without SLURM**	**SLURM**
Singularity	A single no-de	Multiple nodes

Single node: It can only run on one node, using from 1 to 36 cores per node.

Multiple nodes: Ability to run on multiple compute nodes, using multiple cores.

6   Results of Executions

6.1   Case 1:

The following data were used for the first test:

- 360 initial input files, using Snakemake.
- Maximum of 10 compute nodes.
- Using two stages of processing using a Singularity container and Python script to process data in NumPy.

The results of the first test can be seen in Fig. 2, where 360 files were processed. The test started with 36 cores and the processing time was 2,222 s; when the 360 cores were used, the time dropped to 322 s.

Figure 2 shows that while the applications and scripts used only consume one processor core. However, with tools to automate the processing flow such as Snakemake and a reasonable amount of data, a large number of tasks can be run simultaneously, making the processing time more efficient. It is worth noting that thanks to the functionalities of Snakemake and SLURM, the use of multiple computing nodes is achieved.

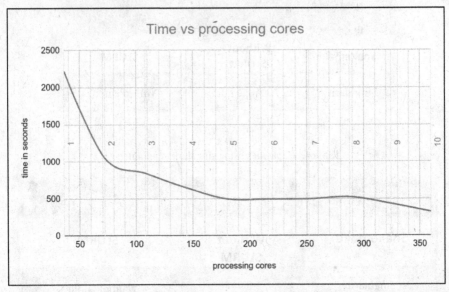

Fig. 2. Processing 360 files. This figure shows that applications scale better from node 1 to node 4, the more cores, the less processing time. From node 5 to node 8, there is no improvement in performance. And from node 9, performance improves again. This behavior is related to the number of processing steps and the routines that are processed in each step.

It is important to note that we want to demonstrate the benefit and advantage of automating applications that do not scale natively and how they can take advantage of the supercomputing cluster infrastructure (Table 5).

6.2   Case 2:

The following data were used for the second test:

- 720 initial input files, using Snakemake.
- Maximum of 20 compute nodes.
- Using two stages of processing using a Singularity container and Python scripts to process data in NumPy.

The results obtained in the second test can be seen in Fig. 3, where 720 files were processed, the test started with 36 cores and the processing time was 5156 s, when using the 720 cores, the time dropped to 447 s.

Table 5. Detail of processing times of 360 files.

Processing time for 360 files	
Number of cores	**Time in seconds**
36	2222
72	1053
108	842
144	648
180	495
216	493
252	496
288	523
324	432
360	322

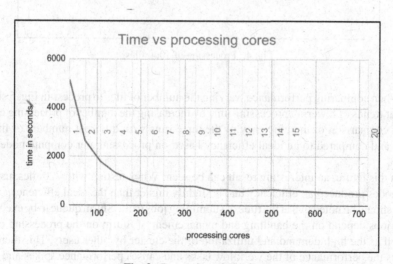

Fig. 3. Processing of 720 files.

6.3   Case 3:

The following data were used for the third test:

- 1000 initial input files, using Snakemake.
- Maximum of 28 computational nodes.
- Use of two processing stages with a Singularity container and Python scripts to process the data in NumPy.

The results of the second test can be seen in Fig. 4. When processing 1,000 files, the test was started with 36 cores and the processing time was 6,567 s; when using the 1,008 cores (28 compute nodes), the time dropped to 567 s.

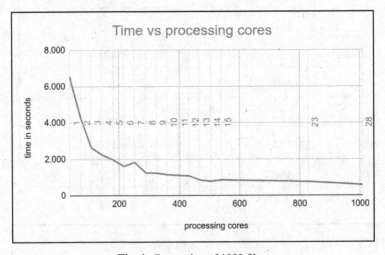

Fig. 4. Processing of 1000 files.

When comparing performance, varying the number of files to process in Fig. 5 shows similar trends of lowering processing time by increasing the number of processing cores.

A comparison of the efficiency of the three runs with different numbers of files is made and compared to an ideal efficiency based on processing per compute node. See Fig. 6.

In this figure, an interesting result can be seen: When testing with 720 files, using 5 to 6 nodes produced an efficiency that is slightly higher than the ideal efficiency.

It should be noted that at the time of submitting jobs to the Slurm queue to be executed, these jobs depend on the handling and management of Slurm on the processing cores, as well as the high demand and utilization of the cluster by other users. This therefore affects the performance of the workflow tasks and causes performance spikes and dips, as can be seen in Fig. 6.

It is assumed that efficiency can be affected by the amount of RAM in each node, although this depends on the applications running in the workflow.

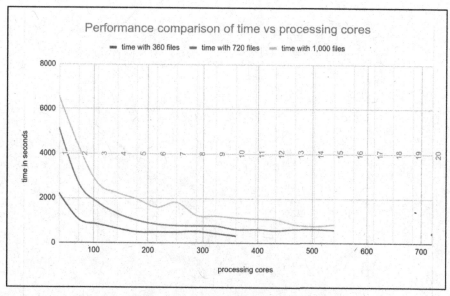

Fig. 5. Performance comparison Scale the processing flow not the application.

7 Discussion of Results and Conclusions

There are important considerations in discussing the results, as these tests and their results compare the improvements in execution times in a framework of parallelizing and automation of a particular use of processing using processing boxes. The first using a tool that consumes only one processing core within a singularity container, and the second processing step using a Python routine that consumes a single processing core. Reviewing the benefits that can be achieved in an automation and parallelization framework in a supercomputing cluster.

Based on the above considerations, it is not intended to serve as a basis for subsequent performance comparisons, but rather to demonstrate the benefits of sharing these applications.

These performance tests should serve as a reference for those who need to build robust automation and parallelization frameworks, even if their tools do not inherently allow parallelization.

Based on the tests carried out with the combination of the 3 technologies used, the following results and observations were obtained:

7.1 Testing Time

For the analysis, the times of Snakemake were used, since it is the tool that manages the entire workflow, from the input files to the generation of the output files, and also the processing times of Slurm. It is worth noting that Slurm manages its own processing times. For this reason, it may happen that Slurm completes a series of files and releases the used resources, but the job queue still appears as a busy node because Snakemake is trying to complete the workflow for that series.

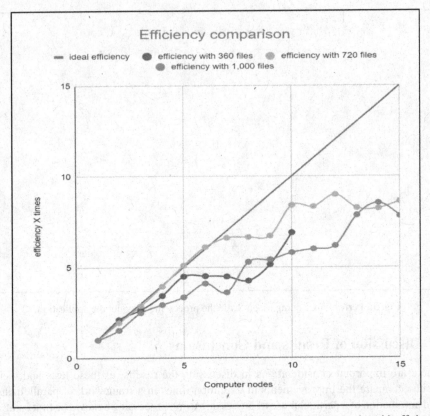

Fig. 6. The ideal efficiency shows the same ratio, in the increase of compute nodes with efficiency gains.

7.2 Duration of Tests

From the design of the processing sequences, the construction of the test container, the design of the automation scripts, as well as the execution of the scripts, up to the analysis of the results, about 3 months were needed.

7.3 What Limitations There Were

Although it is possible to integrate several scientific applications that only consume a processing core, or use R, Python or shell scripts, it will not always be beneficial to integrate them into a processing flow, since there will be the limitation of the volume of data and how they are processed.

One of the observations that had the most impact on the tests and the results of the different scenarios to be run was the management and the amount of cluster resources available, since in some cases resources (compute nodes) have to be shared with other users because the resources that should be used are not provided due to the high demand of users using the cluster.

This resource sharing limitation can occur at any time and is something that we as users cannot control, since Slurm is responsible for resource allocation. For this reason, it is ideal to run the operations in a custom working partition that contains the set N amount of resources to be used, for example not in a general partition where many users use the same resources.

7.4 Learning

In cases where better execution efficiency has been shown, the number of nodes is chosen to match the number of processing cores with the number of jobs to be processed simultaneously, i.e., if 360 files are sent for execution, it would be ideal to take 10 nodes since the infrastructure has 36 cores per node to execute 360 processing cores simultaneously.

This results in greater optimization of the total job duration. Using a large number of nodes is not always the best solution, as this depends on the SLURM queues and the amount of processing in the cluster.

Better performances were shown using the total number of cores per node.

7.5 Conclusions and Benefits

Scaling capabilities were tested with Slurm, Snakemake, and Singularity technologies and found to have parallelization capabilities that can be applied to projects that require large processing capacities and data volumes and are limited by their applications that do not have parallelization capabilities.

Glossary

- NumPy: Python language library used for the creation of vectors and matrices along with the collection of mathematical functions.
- Python: High-level programming language for developing applications of all kinds.
- Container: Technology used for the encapsulation of projects (work environments).
- Docker: Open-source platform for managing and creating containers.
- Kubernetes: Open-source platform for container and microservices management.

References

1. Mölder, F., et al.: Sustainable data analysis with Snakemake. F1000Res. **10**, 33 (2021)
2. How to Manage Workflow with Resource Constraint on HPC. https://www.sichong.site/workflow/2021/11/08/how-to-manage-workflow-with-resource-constraint.html
3. GitHub smk-simple-slurm, smk-simple-slurm. https://github.com/jdblischak/smk-simple-slurm
4. Slurm Workload Manager. https://slurm.schedmd.com/documentation.html
5. Snakemake. https://snakemake.readthedocs.io/en/v6.15.5/
6. Singularity. https://docs.sylabs.io/guides/3.6/user-guide/

7. Sokolov, S., Idiriz, O., Vukadinoff, M., Vlaev, S.: Scaling and automation in cloud deployments of enterprise applications. J. Eng. Sci. Technol. Rev. Special Issue on Telecommunications, Informatics, Energy and Management (2019)
8. Vaquero, L.M., Rodero-Merino, L., Buyya, R.: Association for Computing Machinery. SIGCOMM Comput. Commun. Rev (2011)
9. Caragnano, G., et al.: Scalability of a Parallel Application in Hybrid Cloud. IEEE Computer Society (2014)
10. Sarkar, S., Abdulla, P.P., Ramaswamy, S.: Analysis, evaluation, and assessment for containerizing an industry automation software. In: 2020 IEEE International Conference on Systems, Man, and Cybernetics (SMC), pp. 1972–1979 2020. https://doi.org/10.1109/SMC42975.2020.9282840

Author Index

Printed in the United States
by Baker & Taylor Publisher Services